A HISTORY OF

Poland

By

O. HALECKI

SPECIAL MILLENNIUM EDITION
*Published by the Coordinating Committee of
Poland's Christianity Millennium*

Translated by
MONICA M. GARDNER and
MARY CORBRIDGE-PATKANIOWSKA

PRINTED IN THE U.SA.

Foreword

Pope Leo XIII *wrote that the first law of a genuine history is "that it dare say nothing which is false, nor fear to utter anything that is true." Fidelity to truth is an indispensable requisite of, but not necessarily a guarantee of, historical objectivity. Prevarication in history is possible without any positive misstatement of facts. By emphasizing certain facts and omitting others, and also by interpreting events according to a preconceived outlook on life, false impressions can be created.*

Marxism contends that human activities are prompted and guided by economic factors. This economic interpretation of history constrains Marxism to force all historical events into a preconceived mold of economic determinism. The Marxian theory of history is used by Communists as an instrument of defense and as a means to promote its own ends and purposes.

According to the Marxian theory, the specific form which religion takes is a direct product of the economic basis of the time and place, i.e., man develops a religion which will safeguard and foster the current method of production. Obviously such a theory cannot possibly explain the fact that Catholicism has flourished for centuries throughout the world, and for ten centuries in Poland under the most primitive and under the most highly developed methods of production. Nevertheless, Marxists continue their efforts to interpret and force historical events into the preconceived mold of economic determinism. The Communist regime in Poland is relentless in its efforts to interpret the historical events of Poland's one thousand years of Christianity in terms of the theory of economic determinism.

To insure an accurate account and interpretation of the history of Poland, the Coordinating Committee for the observance of Poland's Millennium of Christianity, comprising the states of Connecicut, New Jersey, New York, and Pennsylvania, has resolved to sponsor an up-to-date edition of Professor Oscar Halecki's HISTORY OF POLAND. Professor Halecki's fame for historical scholarship is universally acknowledged. His one volume HISTORY OF POLAND, in its multiple editions and translations, is without doubt the best single volume history of Poland. It also has the distinction of being on the Warsaw regime's index of forbidden books.

As the Patron of the Coordinating Committee, it is my privilege to present this new edition of Professor Halecki's HISTORY OF POLAND as a lasting contribution of the Committee, and as a true and objective history of the nation and people of Poland.

✠ *JOHN J. KROL*
Archbishop of Philadelphia

July 19, 1966

Unfortunately the great anniversary in the history of the Polish nation has come at a moment when Poland has found itself, contrary to its will, under a government imposed by force by its eastern neighbor. From this sad reality arise consequences which often are contrary to the interests, the past and the future of Poland. That is why, in observing this anniversary, the Polish nation cannot fully express its convictions, nor impartially explain historical facts.

The Millennium of Poland's Christianity is not only the anniversary of its Baptism, but also of the creation of the glorious, original Polish culture based on Christianity, which spread from the Oder and Neisse in the West to the Dnieper and Dzwina rivers in the East. We believe, together with the whole Polish nation, that the present western frontiers of Poland will be maintained, and that historical justice will restore to Poland her eastern boundaries, established in the peace treaty of 1921.

The enemies of the Polish nation are trying to deform, undermine and even abolish the historical facts. In order to counteract this, even in a limited way, the organized Polonia of the four eastern states—Connecticut, New Jersey, New York and Pennsylvania—decided to unite the work of its Millennium Committee in the framework of a Coordinating Committee under the patronage of His Excellency J. J. Krol, D.D., Archbishop of Philadelphia. The Committee set out to prepare by common effort, religious and lay celebrations. But, more that that, it set out to create a permanent record of the attitude of the Polonia toward the Millennium of Poland's Christianity to be left to future generations.

The result of these decisions and the work of the four committees are three books, one of them this work by

Professor O. Halecki, outstanding scholar and world-famous historian.

The History of Poland by Professor Halecki presents Polish history as it really developed during the centuries. It reminds us that Lwow and Wilno were as much Polish as Gdansk and Wroclaw.

The History of Poland by Professor Halecki is not contained between the Oder and the Bug rivers as the present Warsaw regime decrees. This history recalls the civilizing, cultural and religious mission of Poland, which went far beyond the so-called Curzon Line, or, rather, the Ribbentrop-Molotov line.

History should be the report of what "really took place" and not what "should have happened" written to serve this or that political purpose.

The work of Professor Halecki presents the past as it really happened.

Coordinating Committee of Poland's Christianity Millennium
New York, N.Y.

MEMBERS OF THE COORDINATING COMMITTEE:

New York Millennium Committee for Poland's Christianity

The Connecticut Committee for the Millennium of Poland's Christianity

Committee of Poland's Christianity Millennium in Philadelphia, Pa.

Committee of Poland's Christianity Millennium for the State of New Jersey

Contents

CHAPTER   PAGE

Introduction ix

PART I

THE FORMATION OF THE STATE AND
OF THE NATION

1. Early Origins 3
2. The First Kings 11
3. The Disintegration of the Kingdom . . . 21
4. The German Colonization and the Mongol .
    Invasion 31
5. The Reconstruction of the Kingdom . . . 41
6. Casimir the Great 52

PART II

THE CENTURIES OF POLAND'S GREATNESS

7. Jadwiga of Anjou 65
8. Grunwald and Horodlo 75
9. Varna and Danzig 85
10. The Zenith of a Dynasty 95

CHAPTER   PAGE
11. The Epoch of the First Congress of Vienna   .   .   106
12. The Union of Lublin   117

PART III

THE EXPERIMENT OF THE ROYAL REPUBLIC

13. John Zamoyski   131
14. The Last Great Designs   142
15. The Deluge   153
16. John Sobieski   165
17. The Decay   176
18. The Regeneration   189
19. The Partitions   202

PART IV

THE ORDEAL

20. Napoleonic Poland   217
21. Romantic Poland: The Insurrections   .   .   229
22. Romantic Poland: Her Poets   .   .   .   242
23. Organic Work   252
24. Waiting for Freedom   263

PART V

NEW POLAND'S TRAGEDY

25. Resurrection   275
26. Reconstruction   290
27. Destruction   307
28. Ten Years of Trial   326
         Index   347
         Epilogue   361

Introduction

POLAND, who will shortly reach her millennium, is often regarded as one of the new States. This oblivion of the Poland of the past is at the root of all the misunderstandings which stand in the way of a correct comprehension of the Poland of to-day. True, Polish history is not entirely unknown to the foreigner. But his mind usually retains only a few isolated facts of a specially striking nature, such as that of the Partitions. Rarely, on the other hand, does he go back to the origin of our historical evolution. More rarely still does he grasp its continuity, which even the Partitions were not able to break. Above all, he scarcely ever realizes the role that Poland has played in the general history of Europe from early times.

To remedy this state of affairs, regrettable not only from the point of view of contemporary Poland, but also from that of historical science, a simple manual of Polish history, more complete and more widely read than those which already exist in universally accessible languages, is not sufficient. What is needed is a philosophy of our national history conceived as an integral part of European history.

This little book sets out with a more modest object. The philosophy of history, even that of an individual history, has nothing chimerical in its nature, as was at one time believed. But to have a truly scientific character its study should be prepared by attempts at a synthesis which, without losing sight of their final object, will not form definite conclusions in advance.

To make the reader reflect on the essential problems of Polish history, and on their relations with the destinies of other countries, perhaps to induce discussions on this subject, and, in any case, to bring forward the general questions presented by our past—these are our aims in the following pages. Strictly based on positive facts, as established by the progress of science, inspired by concern for impartiality and loyalty in regard to every other nation, these pages will, however, not be false to the national conscience or even to the personal opinions of their author.

The personal, therefore subjective, element is inevitable, not only in critical judgments which in our opinion are the right and the duty of the historian, but even in the choice of the facts mentioned and of the problems to be treated in so short a synthesis. Let us, therefore, indicate in advance the principles which have guided this choice.

The importance of an historical event is the greater in proportion to the durable character of its consequences. This reasoning ought to determine the attention we should pay to all facts, even distant ones, which have retained a character of actuality up to our own days. The foreign reader will, moreover, require the Polish author to show him what the particular features of Polish history have been, and the contribution that his people have brought to the common patrimony of European civilization. But, in addition, he will be interested in Poland as a member of that European community, in the manner by which Poland became a part of it, and in the relations which she maintained with other countries. And we do not hesitate to add that in the course of all those works of ours which have preceded and prepared the way for this one, we have examined, often with a passionate interest, everything which has seemed able to enlighten us on the providential mission that Poland has, as well as might be, fulfilled in the general evolution of humanity.

What in any case seems to us indispensable is the necessity of basing every historical synthesis on a division into periods, corresponding as logically as possible to the march of events and to their leading ideas. As regards Polish history, this chronological division is relatively easy; because the generally accepted and apparently conventional periods in reality prove to be the only ones that can satisfy the requirements which we have just formulated.

The period of our first dynasty, that of the Piasts, shaped our State and our nation. The second, the great centuries of the Jagiellonian dynasty, from its outset enlarged the framework of our history into unforeseen dimensions by joining to the country, as the result of a whole series of unions, territories and populations which, until then, had been strangers to it. It left as its legacy a 'Republican Commonwealth,' which, under kings freely chosen from the most varied families, attempted during the third period a great constitutional experiment which finally collapsed. The unparalleled catastrophe of the Partitions by its very nature inaugurated a new period, the fourth, in which Poland offered to the world the tragic spectacle of a nation without a State, divided territorially, but profiting by the experiences of the past to preserve all her traditions until the moment which should restore her independence.

That moment came with the Great War. The period that

then began for Poland, as well as for the whole world, far
from being closed, cannot yet be the object of any final,
synthetic treatment. But in view of recent and current events,
it would be simply impossible to describe Poland's tragic
destinies without bringing the narrative up to the present
day.

We still owe our readers some words of explanation concerning the proportions we have observed in treating of the
periods of Polish history. In our opinion historians have
often exaggerated in according a privileged place to the times
nearest our own. In the case of Poland this exaggeration
seems particularly inopportune, since it attaches a dispro-
portionate importance to the period when our nation was in
great measure obliged to play a passive part and when its
creative powers had no way of manifesting themselves except
in the sphere of thought.

For Poland, as for every other country, the most vital
historical traditions are those of her great centuries, even if
those centuries should be relatively distant. The fact that
they are the least known abroad is an additional reason for
dwelling upon them. In doing this we have likewise hoped to
avoid the grave mistake, more manifest to-day than ever, of
making the Partitions the centre of the whole past history of
Poland. This central place belongs rather to the epoch of the
Jagiellos, and, even in that of the Piasts—the furthest removed but the longest—we at times find ourselves in the
presence of events whose repercussions may be felt in our
own days. Hence, each of these four great periods occupies
an almost equal place in our story.

*   *   *

The first edition of this book, limited to the first four
parts, until 1914, was written in French in 1932–3, and ap-

peared in a year of peace just before the International Congress of Historical Sciences which was so successfully held in Warsaw. To-day that city is in ruins and, with the whole of Poland, occupied by hostile invaders. Of our original allies the British Empire is continuing, and continued alone for a year, to fight for the freedom of all nations. Therefore I considered it a real honor when in 1941 the publication of an edition in English was kindly suggested by a well-known British publisher. A few months before it appeared in London, the United States of America entered the war and that is one of the reasons why I am particularly glad to see a third, American, edition published in this country whose hospitality I enjoy since more than two years.

Any English edition required not only some minor changes, chiefly in the light of my recent research work, but more than all else a good translation of both the main French part and the supplement, which I could not but write in my own language. I have been extremely fortunate to find an ideal translator in the person of Miss Monica Gardner, who has written so many remarkable books on Polish literature and history, and now has translated this volume with all her talent and devotion. To her I should like to express my deepest thanks. Unfortunately she was killed in an air raid on London early in 1941. She had completed the translation of Parts I to IV (the French edition), and had made a first draft translation from the Polish of the new Part V. The latter has been completed by Miss Gardner's friend, Mary Corbridge-Patkaniowska, and she has corrected Parts I to IV for press. To her, too, I am very obliged.

* * *

The success of the first American edition which had several printings in this country and as early as 1945 appeared in Canada in a French, and in Buenos Aires in a Spanish translation, has encouraged the writer to bring it to date. The present date, 1955, does not yet seem to be a final turning point, but permits a clearer interpretation than was possible in 1942, in the midst of World War II. Chapter twenty-seven, dealing with that war, had to be revised and completed, and an entirely new chapter, the twenty-eighth has been added, covering the last ten years.

O. HALECKI

Part I

THE FORMATION OF THE STATE
AND OF THE NATION

THE KINGS OF POLAND
Drawings by Jan Matejko

MIESZKO I from about 960–992

DOBRAWKA
(Mieszko's wife)

BOLESLAW I CHROBRY
992–1025 (the Brave)

MIESZKO II 1025–1034

KAZIMIERZ I ODNOWICIEL
1038–1058 (the Restorer)

BOLESLAW II SMIALY
1058–1079 (the Bold)

WLADYSLAW I HERMAN
1079–1102

BOLESLAW III KRZYWOUSTY
1102–1138 (Wry Mouth)

WLADYSLAW II
1138–1146

THE KINGS OF POLAND
Drawings by Jan Matejko

BOLESLAW IV KEDZIERZAWY
1146–1173 (the Curly)

MIESZKO III STARY
1173–1177 (the Old)

KAZIMIERZ II SPRAWIEDLIWY
1177–1194 (the Just)

WLADYSLAW LASKONOGI
1202 (Spindleshanks)

LESZEK I BIALY
1202–1227 (the White)

HENRYK BRODATY
1234–1238 (the Bearded)

KONRAD MAZOWIECKI
1241–1243 (of Mazovia)

BOLESLAW V WSTYDLIWY
1243–1279 (the Chaste)

LESZEK II CZARNY
1279–1288 (the Black)

THE KINGS OF POLAND
Drawings by Jan Matejko

PRZEMYSLAW
1295–1296

WACLAW CZESKI 1300–1305
(Vaclav of Bohemia)

WLADYSLAW LOKIETEK
1307–1333(the Short)

KAZIMIERZ WIELKI
1333–1370 (the Great)

LUDWIK WEGIERSKI 1370–1382
(Louis of Hungary)

JADWIGA
1384–1399

WLADYSLAW JAGIELLO
1386–1434

WLADYSLAW WARNENCZYK
1434–1444

KAZIMIERZ JAGIELLONCZYK
1447–1492

THE KINGS OF POLAND
Drawings by Jan Matejko

JAN OLBRACHT
1492–1501

ALEKSANDER
1501–1506

ZYGMUNT STARY
1506–1548 (the Old)

ZYGMUNT AUGUST 1548–1572

HENRYK WALEZY 1573–1574
(Henry of Valois)

STEFAN BATORY
1576–1586

ZYGMUNT III WAZA
1587–1632 (Vasa)

WLADYSLAW IV
1632–1648

JAN KAZIMIERZ 1648–1668

THE KINGS OF POLAND
Drawings by Jan Matejko

MICHAL KORYBUT WISNIOWIECKI
1669–1673

JAN III SOBIESKI
1674–1696

AUGUST II SAS
1697–1733 (of Saxony)

STANISLAW LESZCZYNSKI
1704–1710

AUGUST III SAS
1733–1763 (of Saxony)

STANISLAW AUGUST PONIATOWSKI
1764–1795

THE BATTLE OF GRUNWALD (1410)

by Jan Matejko

by Jan Matejko

STEFAN BATORY AT THE SIEGE OF PSKOV (1581)

SOBIESKI AFTER HIS VICTORY BEFORE VIENNA (1683)

by Jan Matejko

1

Early Origins

I N ORDER to find an adequate approach to Polish history, it is essential to observe in what epoch and under what conditions Poland passed from the prehistoric stage into history: that is to say, from an isolated and legendary existence to a life related to the life of neighbouring peoples, upon which light is thrown by documentary evidence. In the case of the majority of European nations, with the exception of the Greeks and Romans, this transition was effected either at the moment when they entered into contact with the Graeco-Roman world, or in that of their conversion to Christianity. At times these two moments are almost simultaneous: and this is precisely the case with Poland, where their respective dates are as near to each other as 963 and 966.

These dates are in themselves highly eloquent. They lead us into the midst of the tenth century, which was an epoch of profound transformation for the whole of Europe. It was not only Poland who then made her entry into history. Up to this date only the southern and western part of Europe was well known to history. Henceforth the historic community, so long limited to the ancient territories of the Roman Em-

3

pire and to its sphere of influence, was gradually extended
towards the north-east, to the entire Slavonic world, and to
the Scandinavian countries.

On the other hand, this same tenth century, which was for
many countries a century of chaos, saw the consolidation of
the two universal powers which were to preside over the
destinies of Europe during the course of the following centuries: the Papacy and the Empire. It was the latter which,
after the transitory Carlovingian restoration, was first definitely reconstituted and transferred to the King of Germany.
It is worth emphasizing that this important event took place
exactly one year before the first Polish-German conflict which
inaugurated the political history of Poland. The new Empire,
in return for its renovation by the Papacy, assured its protection to the latter, which enabled it to emerge from one of the
gravest crises through which the Holy See has passed, and to
prepare, together with the reform of the Church, the way for
its temporal power. At the same time, the Church of Rome,
being leagued with the Empire of the West, alienated the
Empire of the East, and although the schism was not yet consummated, the rupture with Byzantium was impending. At
the moment, therefore, when Poland accepted the Christian
faith she had to choose between the two centres of Christianity, and at the same time between the two increasingly divergent centres of European civilization.

But what was the reason which had retarded the opening
of Poland's historical role until the moment when she was
faced with such a delicate position? Why had the other western Slavs, indeed, even the eastern Slavs, preceded her in
their relations with the external world? This reason is easily
to be found in her geographical situation.

This situation, which was to influence but not determine
all its historical evolution, soon proved very dangerous to the

Polish State then forming. But, on the other hand, it had been favourable to its first pagan beginning. Dwelling in the centre of the Slav world, removed from the routes of the great migrations and even from the great trade routes, the tribes which were to form the Polish nation only experienced later the grave difficulties and dangers that beset their neighbours. These immediate neighbours, who had sprung from the same race as the Poles, but were separated from them by vast forest frontiers, had to face far earlier the double danger which surrounded the Slavs: on one side, the Germanic danger; on the other, the Asiatic danger.

However, the stubborn resistance that the Slav populations between the Elbe and the Oder offered to the German conquest was nearing its end. Bohemia was gradually entering the orbit of German influence, and Great Moravia had only been an ephemeral power. At the same time the tribes which were to form the different Russias were uniting, thanks to Norse conquerors, in one vast state, extending almost indefinitely its colonization and expansion to the east, but not succeeding in hurling back the Asiatic nomads who were successively occupying the steppes bordering the Black Sea.

Under these conditions the relative security which prehistoric Poland had enjoyed was becoming increasingly precarious. Soon she would no longer be able to keep apart from the struggles which were being waged still outside her frontiers, but which were approaching her own territory in an alarming fashion. Moreover, the limits of that territory were far from being established, and in proportion as the young State consolidated itself it was bound to anticipate numerous territorial disputes even with its Slav neighbours.

We speak of a State in formation, because the beginning of the Polish State goes back to an epoch anterior at the very least by a century and a half to its first contact with the German Empire and to its christianization. Unfortunately, this beginning is lost in prehistoric obscurity out of which the most penetrating archaeological and linguistic researches can disentangle but little of value. Their results compel us to admit that the primitive life of the Polish population in no way differed from that of the other Slav tribes of the same epoch. But this discovery, which was moreover one easily foreseen, tells us nothing that is of particular interest. It is likewise of slight importance from the point of view of general history whether one or another of the Slav chiefs who had chance relations with the Carlovingian Empire can be reasonably held to have been Poles. From this same point of view it is scarcely more important to know whether a small part of the future Poland was really attached, more or less closely, to Great Moravia, because, in any case, even the Christian influences which then seem to have penetrated there under the form of the Slavonic rite had no result.

But, on the other hand, there is another long-disputed problem which is of interest, not only to the erudite specialist and to the Pole curious to learn the condition of his first ancestors. It is the question of ascertaining whether the Polish State was formed by way of conquest, particularly Norse conquest, similar, perhaps, to that which formed Russia.

Now we know as a matter of fact that there was nothing of the sort. No hypothesis put forth to this effect can be maintained. Certainly the union of the different Polish tribes in a single political organism could not have been effected without struggles. But the conquests that these struggles, the details of which are completely unknown, necessarily implied, were only, so to speak, internal conquests, subjecting one tribe to another, and ending in the hegemony of one among them, the Polians, and of its princely dynasty, the

Piasts. These two names hold a place in Polish history which deserves a brief comment.

The Polians, which signifies dwellers in the fields, have left their name, hardly modified, to the whole Polish nation. Their territory, the region of Gniezno, the first capital, and that of Poznan, the seat of the first bishop, became the nucleus of the Polish State. This region was to remain for a long time simply Poland: Poland properly so called, although from a very remote epoch it bore the name of Great Poland, as in our own days.

Among the other tribes that soon became subject to the Polians we must mention at least the Silesians and the Masovians. The region of these latter, neighbours of the Baltic peoples, of the ancient Prussians of Lithuanian race, for centuries kept a special and somewhat archaic character. We know to-day that the region of the Upper Vistula with Cracow was also, in pagan times, joined to that of the Polians; but it was precisely this region, the future Little Poland, the new Poland often opposed to the ancient Poland, which was gradually to take the first place in the common State where regionalism, based on such old traditions, never ceased to be clearly manifested.

It is likewise in the region of Cracow that these traditions, in regard to the local princes who reigned there before the unification of Poland, are the most explicit. The legends consecrated to the prehistoric memories of this region, in part confirmed by scientific research, have retained great popularity to this day. But they are not of equal importance to the traditions which enlighten us on the origin of the Polish princes, the direct ancestors and immediate predecessors of the dukes and kings of historic Poland.

According to the legend this dynasty, which towards the

middle of the ninth century replaced another more ancient, descended from a simple peasant of the name of Piast. This name became that of our only national dynasty, which governed the whole of Poland until 1370, its Masovian branch not being extinguished until 1526, and its Silesian branch only in 1675. In addition, the name of Piast has remained the symbol to the Polish people of their purest ethnical traditions, of the continuity of their race on the soil of their fathers, of their national unity from the king to the labourer.

Was this Piast, whose son was raised to the throne of Gniezno, really a peasant? It is very doubtful. Several hypotheses have been formed around this problem. The most ingenious suggestion is that Piast is not a proper name, but the title of a high functionary, of a master of the palace, whose descendants took the place of their ancient sovereigns. The striking analogy with the almost contemporary origin of the Carlovingians will be observed.

On the other hand, tradition seems trustworthy when it enumerates the three first Polish monarchs of the House of Piast. Their names do not tell us much. What is certain is that one after the other worked at the unification of the Polish tribes, and that they left to the fourth, named Mieszko, an already considerable State.

We are ignorant of the date of his accession, and we know no more of the commencement of his reign than we do of that of his predecessors. This is all the more reason for supposing that their programme of unification was little troubled from outside. It was not until 963 that Mieszko, hitherto scarcely known abroad, saw himself the object of a first attack from the German side.

This was not organized by Germany as such, nor even—at least openly—by the famous margrave Gero, who was using every means to extend his frontiers on the east. It was a simple German count, banished by the Emperor Otto I, who inflicted two defeats on Mieszko of Poland.

The latter realized the danger of seeing his country become, like the other Slav lands, the object of continual invasions which would end in her conquest by Germany. Instead of exhausting himself in fruitless conflicts, he hastened to enter of his own accord into contact with the Emperor himself. It was probably in the same year that he succeeded in concluding a treaty with Otto I which recognized the Duke of Poland as a friend of the Emperor, to whom he promised to pay tribute levied on the western confines of his territory.

Mieszko thereby gave an indisputable proof of his diplomatic talent. At the price of a strictly limited concession to which his agreement was freely given, he made Poland a State officially recognized by the young imperial power and one which could no longer be invaded on any pretext by her German neighbours. But this was not all. If she remained pagan Poland could always be threatened from that direction under the pretext of Christian propaganda, and could not be definitely accepted on a basis of equality among the European nations.

We are ignorant of what were Mieszko's real religious sentiments. In any case, he had understood that it was necessary to adopt immediately and voluntarily the Christian faith, without waiting for pressure on the part of the Germans. It was moreover necessary to avoid accepting it from their hands. The Duke of Poland had no intention of effecting this by addressing himself to distant Byzantium, although the influence of the latter had already made itself felt among its eastern neighbours. He would have thereby escaped all German interference, but at the same time he would have given Poland an orientation that was contrary to his intentions. It was his desire to consolidate his relations with the

Latin West, and fortunately he was able to find another
intermediary than Germany. In 965 he married Dubravka,
a Bohemian princess, thus allying himself with a Slav neighbour which had been Christian for some time; the following
year he was himself baptized, and immediately took in hand
the conversion of all his nation.

In this manner he was able to make his people accept the
new faith with comparative ease and rapidity; in spite of
inevitable reactions of paganism, the new faith soon penetrated into the soul of all Poland, guiding her to a new
future. If the hopes which Mieszko had attached to a political
alliance with Bohemia were soon deceived, its immediate
results, the christianization of Poland, bore all its fruits. Poland took her historic place in Christian Europe.

2

The First Kings

In the dawn of her history Poland experienced an epoch of unquestioned splendour. This splendour was not lasting, but nevertheless that first great century has left an unforgettable memory. Tradition has linked that memory with the personalities of the kings who bore the henceforth illustrious name of Boleslas. But their work was greatly facilitated by the solid foundations which Mieszko I had established. He never wore the royal crown. It is not even known whether he took any sort of steps with the object of obtaining it. Nevertheless, the first Christian Duke of Poland, to whom foreigners sometimes gave the royal title which corresponded to his actual position, deserves a place of honour by the side of her first kings.

Until his death in 992 the policy of Mieszko I was dominated by anxiety to regulate his relations with Germany. In this respect his attitude was extremely well balanced, taking into account the situation in Germany and the policy of the first three Emperors, his contemporaries. Very prudent when faced by Otto I, he was able to repulse the expedition that Otto II led against Poland, but he recognized the suzerainty

of the young Otto III, and even marched with him against
the Slav tribes, still pagan, that then separated Germany from
Poland.

There is no doubt that he hoped thereby to secure for himself a part of their territory; but while avoiding useless conflicts with the Empire he never lost sight of the most important problem, that of Poland's access to the Baltic Sea. In
fact, he succeeded in subjecting to his authority Pomerania,
the inhabitants of which were, moreover, the most nearly
related among all the Slav populations to the Poles. This
success, decisive in the history of Poland, was the more
valuable since Mieszko was obliged to reckon not only with
the rivalry of the Germans on this territory, but also with
that of the Danes, who desired to establish themselves at the
mouth of the Oder, and who had even created a species of
military colony there, a base for the Norse Vikings.

The only charter of Mieszko I which is known to us shows
beyond doubt that Poland then stretched as far as the *longum
mare*. But at the same time it bears witness to another initiative of this prince which proves still more clearly his extraordinary far-sightedness and his anxiety to assure the future of
his State. At an epoch when the Papacy was still far distant
from it future political influence which was to counterbalance
that of the Empire, Mieszko gave all his territory into the
hands of the Holy See, made it part of the patrimony of St
Peter, and thus placed it under pontifical protection.

This act of an only recently converted prince was more
than an act of homage paid to the Church, and the Peter's
pence that Poland was to pay under this understanding more
than a simple symbol. In compensation for his acts of submission to the Empire, Mieszko thus gave his young State the
best possible guarantee for its independence and security.
Centuries later, this close and never-forgotten tie with the

Holy See was to serve Poland as a solid support in the gravest crises through which she passed. Opposed to the imperial pretensions, it was to ensure the integrity of her frontiers, and even her national character. It was to be at the same time the external expression of a principle of the spiritual order which animates the whole of Polish history.

His constant solicitude in regard to German affairs did not lead Mieszko to neglect the development of his relations with other countries, notably with the young Scandinavian kingdoms, always very influential on the Baltic Sea; also with Hungary, who soon herself accepted Christianity, and who was so often to be a valuable ally to Poland. But, his attention being turned essentially to the west, he seems to have neglected the eastern problem, which Poland was never able to escape. Vladimir the Great of Kiev profited by this in 981 to take from the Poles Przemysl on the San, and other strongholds along the Bug.

This fact might seem insignificant in a synthesis like ours. Nevertheless, it calls for our close attention as the starting-point of a long territorial conflict, many times renewed, under the most diverse forms, between the Poles and their Ruthenian neighbours. As, moreover, this same Vladimir, when, like Mieszko, he was converted some years later, turned not to Rome but to Byzantium, this conflict was soon intensified by religious divergence, increased by equally differing cultural influences.

Mieszko's eldest son and successor, Boleslas I, took a keen interest in the eastern problem, despite his preoccupations on the side of the west, which were still more absorbing than those of his father. This, so to speak, parallel interest at once indicates the primary difference between the policy of these two princes, the second of whom far surpassed the example left by the founder of historic Poland. In order to grasp all the new elements that during the thirty-three years of his reign Boleslas introduced into Polish history, it is by no means necessary to describe here the numerous campaigns which led him from the Elbe to the Dnieper, and won for him the surname of the Brave. If tradition has also ascribed to him that of the Great it is for another reason. It is because athwart the epic of his exploits we catch sight of the outlines of a great design which stretched far beyond the ethnical limits of Poland. While following up all the schemes initiated by his father, Boleslas extended them to the scale of a truly European conception.

Two striking events stand out against the background of his immense activity: the Congress of Gniezno in the year 1000, and his coronation in 1025, on the eve of his death. These indicate the first of the objects that Boleslas had proposed to himself, and the one which he fully realized: the complete independence of Poland, recognized by the Empire and perpetuated by the royal crown.

Profiting by a fortuitous circumstance to which we shall have occasion to return, Boleslas, freed from the rivals he had found in the bosom of his family, solemnly received in his capital the Emperor Otto III, the same who, following the example of Otto I, had received Boleslas's father in Germany in the character of a vassal. We know the idealistic and generous conception which, in agreement with Pope Silvester II, young Otto had formed of the imperial power and its universal mission. A free and independent Poland under a king who would collaborate with the Emperor in the restoration of Christian order in the world could easily find her place in this conception, so far removed from the plans of conquest entertained by other German emperors. Otto III, therefore, did not limit himself to sanctioning the independent organization of the Church of Poland with a metropolitan see at

Gniezno and several bishoprics dependent upon it: he did not hesitate to place his own crown on the head of Boleslas and to present him with the lance of St Maurice, a symbol of royalty.

It is difficult to determine the exact significance of this gesture, and in general the political plans adopted in common by the two monarchs. In any case, it was with the consent of the Emperor that Boleslas addressed himself immediately to the Pope, who alone could authorize his consecration. There were, however, several delays in Rome, and during this time Otto III died, to be soon succeeded by Henry II, who, solicitous for the interests of Germany, opposed Boleslas's ambitious projects.

The latter was fully determined not to abandon any one of them. Only, as it had become impossible to realize them in agreement with the Empire, he at first devoted all his energies to the inevitable struggle with the new Emperor. This war lasted, with some interruptions, until 1018. The peace which was at last concluded at Bautzen secured to Poland a great part of the conquests that Boleslas had made since the beginning of his reign in Slav territory between the Oder and the Elbe, advancing one moment as far as the Elster. It is noteworthy that Lusatia then passed to Poland, whose frontiers have never extended further towards the west.

But what is no less significant is the fact that in 1003 Boleslas, profiting by internal troubles in Bohemia, temporarily occupied the throne of Prague, retaining throughout his reign Moravia as well as a good part of Slovakia. On the other hand, closely following Russia's affairs, he immediately made use of the peace of 1018 to make his victorious entry into Kiev. It was from there that he sent his message of triumph and of defiance to the Emperors of the West and the East.

Naturally, Boleslas never intended to annex Bohemia and

Russia to Poland, as he had succeeded in doing with the pagan populations which would otherwise have fallen under the power of Germany. He returned from Kiev, contenting himself with having strengthened Polish influence there and recovered the adjacent territory that had been wrested from his father. His Czech and Ruthenian policy is chiefly explainable as a consequence of his conflict with Henry II, who was anxious to have a docile vassal in Prague and an ally against Poland in Kiev. Poland was thus threatened by a league of her principal neighbours and, above all, as so often was to happen in the future, by a simultaneous attack from the west and the east. To avert this danger Boleslas probably thought of grouping all the Slavs of the north in a large political community which would have taken its independent place in the European system between the two divisions of the Christian world, one of which was subject to the preponderance of Germany, the other to that of Byzantium.

This idea was, without any doubt, premature. The part of Europe which Boleslas would have wished to organize in this manner was certainly not ripe for such a co-operation, and Poland was not ready to take upon herself its direction. Yet this idea, which impresses us by its magnitude, will reappear in another period of Polish history, thus creating a link between Poland of the eleventh and Poland of the fifteenth century.

It was likewise under Boleslas the Great that another idea appeared; one, moreover, connected with the former, and which also was to be fully realized in the Poland of the Jagiellos. What attracted Otto III, that great Christian Emperor, to Gniezno was the desire to visit the tomb of St Adalbert, formerly Bishop of Prague, who, encouraged by Boleslas, had departed to preach the faith to the Prussians, and had recently found a martyr's death among them. St Bruno also, who was a German, but who reproached Henry II for his alliances with pagans against Poland, found at the court of Boleslas a starting-point and support for his missionary activities, which reached even the Petchenegs and finished with his death in the borderlands of Lithuania and Ruthenia. And when Boleslas married his daughter to a grand duke of Kiev he sent his Bishop of Pomerania there on a mission that was at once diplomatic and ecclesiastical. From these facts there emerges the vision of a vast movement of Christian propaganda, a propaganda at the same time of Latin civilization, organized by a Poland who herself had only very recently been converted.

Furthermore, all this bears witness to the efforts that in the midst of all his wars Boleslas the Brave was able to devote to the internal organization of his country and to the raising of her culture. The royal crown, obtained at last with the assent of the Holy See, was his well merited reward, and also became the symbol which, in spite of the premature death of the first king, prevented destruction of his work in the future.

This destruction was never so threatening as it became almost immediately after 1025. Boleslas I had left his heritage to his younger son, Mieszko II, who was at once able to inaugurate his reign by the ceremony of consecration as king for which his father had so long waited. The new king was by no means the puppet that legend has imagined. On the contrary, what destroyed him was his rash attack upon the Emperor Conrad II. The war he thereby provoked was the more inopportune as Mieszko II was threatened by the pretensions of a disinherited elder brother, who was able to find supporters both in the country itself, including the royal family, and among Poland's neighbours. Humiliated by Germany, and only maintaining the unity for his state with great difficulty, Mieszko perished in 1034 in tragic circumstances, like his brothers and shortly afterwards his eldest son. In the chaos which followed these catastrophes the work of the first Piasts seemed as if it must founder. Christianity itself was rudely shaken in Poland by a revolution of the masses of the people who, in certain regions, were still pagans, and who at the same time recalled their primitive particularism. The Czech invasion of 1038 consummated the ruin of the country, including the capital.

That Poland was able to rise from this ruin at the end of only a few years, and to resume a little later the part which she had played under Boleslas I, is undoubtedly the best proof of her vitality. But this is also owing to two princes, one of whom recalls the memory of Mieszko I, the other that of his great successor.

Casimir I, to whom the title of the Restorer has justly been given, the youngest son of Mieszko II, had taken refuge in Germany. He returned to Poland with the support of the Emperor himself, the latter being disquieted by the anarchy on the German frontier and by the unexpected success of his Bohemian vassal. With equal moderation and patience the new Duke of Poland—he prudently abstained from aspiring to the royal crown—resumed his great-grandfather's work of organization. Recognizing the suzerainty of Conrad II and of Henry III, his successor, he likewise profited by the Ruthenian alliance to crush the centre of revolt which was maintained in Masovia. Passing over irreparable losses beyond the ethnical boundaries of Poland, such as those of Lusatia and Moravia, he obtained the return of Silesia, which the Czechs had temporarily occupied. Finally, he reorganized the religious life of his country, from that time making a return to paganism impossible.

It was thus a well consolidated state that Casimir left in 1058 to his eldest son, Boleslas II, called the Bold, with the result that the latter was at once able to resume the great policy of the first King of Poland. There are very pronounced analogies between the activities of the two Boleslases. Like his glorious ancestor, Boleslas the Bold made Poland completely independent of the Empire. Following his example, he made an adventurous expedition to Kiev to intervene in favour of princes who were his allies. Like Boleslas the Brave he had himself crowned King of Poland at the Christmas of 1076.

Let us, however, note certain differences between the policies of the two kings. The capital of restored Poland being now at Cracow, Boleslas II made less effort to extend her western frontiers. On the other hand, he exercised a considerable influence on the affairs of Hungary. Together with that country, where he supported the party that was hostile to the Empire, he took a lively interest in the quarrel over investitures which then divided the Christian world. Closely bound to the Holy See, Boleslas, like his Hungarian ally, adhered to the side of Gregory VII, and the support that he found from the great Pope enabled him to give his policy a genuinely European expansion. The opposition of Poland to the pretensions of Henry IV, an opposition which, moreover, was not unconnected with that of the Saxons in the interior of Germany, was greatly facilitated by her close understanding with Rome, which was strengthened on the actual eve of Canossa. The policy of the King and that of the Pope were closely bound together even in Russia, since the pretender to the throne of Kiev, supported by Poland, was at the same time protected by Gregory VII as a partisan of union with the Roman Church. It goes without saying that the definite regulation of the ecclesiastical questions which concerned Poland herself was carried out in full accord with the Pope and his legates, in the spirit of the Gregorian reforms.

We might have supposed that under these conditions the kingdom of the Piasts would have advanced towards a stable and prosperous future as an increasingly important and active member of the Christian community. It was not the case. This great impulse was abruptly interrupted in 1079 by a catastrophe far more difficult to explain than that which had so closely followed the death of Boleslas I. On his return from Kiev, Boleslas II, whose character seems to have been passionate and vindictive, put the Bishop of Cracow, Stanislas, to death.

The motive of this act of violence was an accusation of high treason. But none of the numerous hypotheses built up around this perplexing enigma have been able to show why and with whom the bishop would have betrayed his king. The martyrdom of the man who later became the patron saint of Poland and the symbol of her national unity provoked an immediate reaction against Boleslas the Bold. Supported by some of the powerful families of the land, his younger brother, Ladislas Herman, took the opportunity of seizing the royal power. Boleslas II died in exile, and his legendary tomb is shown in an old monastery in distant Carinthia, where he is said to have expiated his crime.

3

The Disintegration of the Kingdom

THE epoch of the dismemberment of the kingdom of the first Piasts has generally been held to have only begun at a date posterior by nearly sixty years to the fall of Boleslas II. The disintegration of his heritage did not, in fact, take place at once, and before it became final Poland once more recovered herself under a monarch of worth, a third Boleslas, glorified by his chronicler—most probably a Frenchman by birth— and resembling in certain respects the great kings whose name he bore.

But neither he nor the immediate successor of Boleslas II dared to claim the royal crown, and we shall see that the dynastic troubles, in spite of an attempt made to allay them by dividing the national territory, began in the reign of Ladislas Herman, to the detriment of Poland's external situation.

The details of this troubled epoch are of little concern to general history, but its essential character is worthy of attention inasmuch as it corresponds in a certain measure to the feudal parcelling out of the western kingdoms. Feudalism proper was never known in the social evolution of Poland. The formation of a privileged class which, moreover, always ignored the feudal hierarchy, as well as the recrudescence of regional particularisms, were more a consequence than a cause of the internal crisis from which Poland suffered for more than two centuries, and which retarded her national development. The true cause of this crisis was of a dynastic character.

In the epoch of the first Piasts the want of a regulating principle that would have legally fixed the order of succession, as well as, on the other hand, the right each member of the dynasty possessed to a territorial apanage, had at different intervals created great difficulties. If we have not dwelt upon this, it is because these difficulties had then been surmounted by the energy or the prudence of the inheritor of the throne. Ladislas Herman, who occupied, thanks to favourable circumstances, the throne of Boleslas II, and who succeeded in keeping it from the son of the vanquished king, unfortunately possessed neither of these qualities.

His reign of twenty-three years, signalized by its weakness, was indisputably a period of decadence. In her external relations we witness a surprising change of Poland's policy, in turning from the Pope to the Emperor: a policy contrary to her traditions and to her interests, and one which soon condemned her to an increasingly insignificant and passive role. As regards her internal policy, the duke became the instrument of one of the great lords to whom he owed his accession to power, the Palatine Sieciech, with whom the prototype appears in Polish history of the magnate with inordinate ambitions, solicitous beyond all else for his private interests, and leader of a faction combated by a no less violent opposition.

The opposition against the Palatine was directed by the duke's two sons: Zbigniew, the elder, whose legitimacy was disputed, and Boleslas, the younger, who aspired to occupy

the first place. Ladislas Herman was obliged during his lifetime to grant vast territories to each, thus inaugurating the
disintegration of the ancient kingdom. After the fall of Sieciech and the death of Ladislas in 1102 a fratricidal struggle
soon began. Zbigniew, driven into exile, took refuge in Germany, and committed the imprudence of asking Henry V for
help. The Emperor profited by this to march against Poland.
The year 1109 is memorable for the heroic defence of Silesia
organized by Boleslas. The imperial army suffered such
severe defeats under the walls of Glogow and before Breslau
that it was forced to retreat, leaving Boleslas III, called the
Crooked-mouthed, master of the whole of Poland. He even
recalled his brother, but suspecting him of treason had his
eyes put out, which brought about Zbigniew's death.

Was this crime, of which Boleslas afterwards repented bitterly, counterbalanced by the merits of his foreign policy?
His principal anxiety was to recover Pomerania, which in
spite of its ethnical ties with Poland had emancipated itself
under local dynasts and remained stubbornly opposed to
Christianity. By a series of obstinate campaigns that extended
over more than twenty years Boleslas III did, in fact, re-
establish Polish supremacy there. He likewise encouraged
the definite conversion of the Pomeranians by pacific missions. But coming into collision with German influences in
the political domain as well as in that of ecclesiastical organization, the Duke of Poland had to resign himself in 1135 to
accept Pomerania with the island of Rugen in fief to the
Empire. Thus he became the vassal of Lothair II. Under these
conditions Poland's domination in Pomerania, which was
only strongly established in the south and east of the country, was precarious, and Polish independence, so energetically defended in 1109, was again compromised.

However, Boleslas III's most pressing anxiety towards the

end of his life was to prevent internal troubles, the easier
to foresee from the fact that he had several sons. A new division of the former kingdom seemed to him inevitable, but
he endeavoured to regulate it systematically and once for all.
In his will—a real organic statute of the Polish monarchy,
the unity of which he maintained in principle—Boleslas ap-
portioned four territories as hereditary duchies. His eldest
son, Ladislas, received Silesia; the second, Boleslas, Masovia;
the third, Mieszko, the principal part of Great Poland; the
fourth, Henry, the region of Sandomierz, to the east of
Cracow. We must add that after Henry's premature death in
1166 the fifth brother, Casimir, probably a posthumous child,
for whom no portion had been provided, inherited this latter
duchy. But what is more important is that the throne of
Cracow, with all the central part of Polish territory and the
suzerainty over Pomerania, was henceforth always to belong
to the eldest of all the dynasty, thus passing in rotation to
the representatives of the different branches.

This system might have seemed ingenious. In practice it
gave rise to endless disputes. Each prince installed in Cracow
inevitably ended by wishing to transmit the supreme power
to his direct descendants. Inevitably also this tendency was
bound to disturb the other dukes, dissatisfied at the prerogatives reserved to the elder and impatient to see their turn
arrive. On the other hand the different hereditary duchies,
corresponding approximately to the territories of the prehistoric tribes and situated at the boundaries of Poland, soon
became accustomed to entrench themselves in their individual interests, and to pursue their own policy, which was often
incompatible with the common good. Moreover, this by no
means prevented further divisions in the interior of each
duchy, and it was in this manner that in proportion to the
ramifications of the dynasty certain parts of Poland split, lit-

tle by little, into minute principalities. Finally, a powerful aristocracy which was in process of formation, headed by the high clergy and the chief functionaries, and which became accustomed to play a decisive role in the struggles between the princes, profited by all these dynastic rivalries.

These struggles that Boleslas III had intended to avert began almost immediately after his death in 1138. In 1146 his eldest son, against whom all his younger brothers had combined, was driven not only from the throne of Cracow, but even from his own duchy of Silesia. Married to a German princess, sister-in-law to Conrad III, he was led to seek the most dangerous of supporters, the Emperor, who immediately undertook an expedition against Poland. Terminated by a compromise and followed by pontifical intervention, the German attack was repeated in 1157 under Frederick Barbarossa. The second son of Boleslas III, who bore his father's name, could not defend himself as well as his predecessors in similar circumstances, and was obliged to humiliate himself as no other Polish prince had done before the Emperor. It is true that he was able to keep the supreme power in Poland, but on conditions which clearly demonstrated the imperial suzerainty. After a second campaign by Frederick II, he was obliged, in 1163, to consent definitely to the establishment of the sons of Ladislas in Silesia, which thus remained the apanage of the elder branch of the Piasts.

When he died in 1173 Boleslas IV left his only son under the tutelage of the young Casimir, who was the most gifted of Boleslas the Crooked-mouthed's sons. The latter, for his part, was awaiting in his duchy of Sandomierz the moment for mounting his father's throne. This moment arrived far sooner than the dynastic law had foreseen, because Mieszko, Duke of Great Poland, who as third heir should have reigned at Cracow until his death in 1202, soon lost the sympathies of

the barons of Little Poland on account of his hard and im-
perious character. In 1177 Mieszko the Old—as he was called
later, when he was making attempts which only ended with
his life to take the position which had legally fallen to him—
was driven from Cracow, where Casimir immediately installed himself. After having inherited, as he had hoped, the
duchy of Masovia, this prince united in his hands all the
centre and east of Poland.

Surnamed the Just and, like his father, glorified in a contemporary chronicle, written this time by a Pole, Casimir
really governed in a manner which distinguished him among
the Polish princes of his generation. From a general point of
view his reign of seventeen years claims our attention for two
different reasons.

Let us first observe that, thanks to his spirit of initiative,
Poland at last resumed a more active foreign policy. Given
the geographical situation of the provinces directly subject to
Casimir the Just, the orientation of this policy could only be
towards the east. It was, moreover, dictated by two exterior
circumstances. One was the result of the powerful movement in favour of the Crusades, which for a hundred years
had been sweeping through Europe. Before Casimir II's
reign the Polish princes, unable to embark for the Holy Land,
had already been desirous of at least combating the infidels
in their immediate vicinity, but they did it without a precise
plan or positive success. Contrary to their own interests, they
at times helped the Germans to subjugate the last of the Slav
tribes remaining on the west of the Oder. More frequently
they marched against the Prussians, who were not threatening them seriously, but who, when attacked, offered a decided resistance, and at times inflicted on them severe defeats.
Casimir turned upon the Baltic tribe which had advanced
the furthest towards the south, namely the Yatvegians, who,

in the region of the Bug, constituted a real danger to Poland. He succeeded in subjugating at least a part of the country, which later was called Podlasia, and was to be colonized by the Masovians.

This crusade was not without its connection with his Ruthenian policy. The Russia of the first Ruriks had disintegrated still more rapidly and irremediably than the Poland of the first Piasts. Kiev, passing from hand to hand, and cruelly devastated, had kept nothing more than the faint reflection of its ancient power. Two new political centres had appeared: one in the north-east, where the Slavonic colonization of the basin of the Volga was preparing the future role of Moscow, the other in the south-east, in the principalities of Volhynia and Halicz, in the borderlands of Poland. It was precisely here that Casimir the Just desired to reestablish the Polish influence that had been obtained at the time of the first kings. His interventions were not always fortunate, but they accustomed the Ruthenian princes who were disputing for power there to reckon with Poland, and paved the way for Casimir's successors.

They had likewise their repercussion in the internal life of Poland, where different political parties had come into existence. Casimir the Just, desiring to consolidate his position and that of his descendants, could not neglect these. A younger son, raised to the throne in violation of the statute laid down by his father, in 1180 Casimir convoked at Lenczyca the lords of his territories, as well as the bishops of the whole of Poland, and made them recognize that Cracow and the supreme power were to be henceforth hereditary in his house. This reform, sanctioned by the Pope and the Emperor, was naturally always contested by the other branches of the Piasts. Therefore Casimir endeavoured to gain the permanent support of the clergy, to whom, as well as to the great aristocratic families, he forthwith granted a first charter of privileges.

These families constituted, as it were, clans, powerful on account of their landed property and their political solidarity. They were descended either from old tribal chiefs or from foreign knights who had settled in Poland, or, finally, from the most influential members of that numerous military class which had been formed as a result of the wars of the first Piasts, and which at times gathered round the great lords like the *ministeriales* of the western countries. These clans, which subsequently formed the Polish nobility, were in process of adopting war cries which were to furnish them with names, as well as the coats-of-arms that symbolized their unity. Their role proved decisive for the first time during the course of the dynastic struggles which followed the sudden death of Casimir the Just in 1194.

The lords of Little Poland, headed by the Palatine of Cracow, Nicholas, who disposed of the throne as he pleased, for the most part favoured the eldest son of the dead ruler, the young Prince Leszek, whose younger brother Conrad received the Duchy of Masovia. It was not, however, until after eight years of struggle with Mieszko the Old and his son that Leszek, surnamed the White, was able to install himself at Cracow, where he reigned, not without a temporary interruption, for a quarter of a century.

A contemporary of Innocent III, he placed Poland in 1207 under the protection of the Holy See. This act had a more immediate result than the somewhat analogous one of Mieszko I, because this time Poland entered wholly into the system of the vassal kingdoms of the Church which the great Pope opposed to the imperial power. In adopting this attitude, which redeemed the acts of submission to the Empire imposed upon his predecessors, Leszek was led to collaborate closely with the clergy, and notably with the archbishop Henry Kietlicz, who then introduced into Poland the reforms elaborated by Innocent III.

This collaboration of Leszek with the Holy See made itself felt also in his Ruthenian policy, which continued that of his father, but with far more ambitious designs. After the death of Roman of Volhynia and Halicz, a powerful prince who, first supported by Poland, perished in 1205 in a somewhat mysterious conflict with Leszek, the latter allied himself with Hungary to create in these Ruthenian regions a Catholic kingdom under a Hungarian prince, married to a daughter of the Polish duke. This plan which, towards 1214, appeared to be on the point of being realized, soon completely collapsed. Roman's eldest son, Daniel, finally secured his succession to his father, and Leszek, who had hoped to keep for Poland at least the boundaries that had been disputed since 981, was obliged to abandon all his plans of eastern expansion.

He was no happier in his Pomeranian policy. In this direction the Duke of Cracow once again acted as sovereign of all Poland in the interest of all the duchies of which it was composed. Western Pomerania with the mouth of the Oder having been definitely lost, to the gain of the Empire, it was now necessary to obtain at least the submission of that Pomeranian prince who possessed the eastern part of the country with the mouth of the Vistula. But this prince, of the name of Swientopelk, profited by the disputes among the Piasts, and it was with the complicity of one of them that he killed Leszek, when the latter in 1227 attempted to force him to render the homage he refused.

The throne of Cracow again became the object of dynastic struggles, which this time were so prolonged that the downfall of the ancient kingdom might have seemed a certainty.

But it is precisely in the course of these sterile struggles that the idea of returning to the royal traditions of the first Piasts reappeared in the eminent personality of one of the competitors. We must examine more closely the conditions under which this project came to birth, soon to founder in a new crisis. The two essential problems which are about to present themselves will retain their capital importance for the whole future of Poland.

4

The German Colonization and
the Mongol Invasion

At the moment when Leszek the White succumbed to his enemies his only son Boleslas was scarcely two years old. It was an excellent opportunity to dispute his inheritance and, above all, the throne of Cracow, if only under the pretext of tutelage. The conflicts which followed, with the participation, more or less direct, of all the Piasts and principal families of the Polish knighthood, lasted in successive stages for nearly sixteen years. It was not till after a decisive victory had been gained in 1243 that Boleslas V, surnamed the Chaste, became for a long period the uncontested master of Little Poland. But, in spite of the long duration and extension of these struggles, their details are of no greater interest to us than those of other dynastic conflicts of that epoch. On the other hand, it is the personalities of the two principal competitors that throw most light upon their real significance: Conrad of Masovia, uncle of the young prince, and Henry of Silesia, surnamed the Bearded, representing the elder line of the Piasts.

Before, however, placing them in their opposite camps, a preliminary question must be determined. Why did Germany, who formerly had profited by every similar opportunity to reduce Poland to the role of a vassal state, not interfere in this crisis, the most serious of all? The answer is easily found. At the end of Frederick Barbarossa's reign and that of Henry VI, the Empire was absorbed in the question of Italy and in the Crusades, as well as in fresh conflicts with the Papacy. It was the same during the long reign of Frederick II, which followed the internal troubles in Germany at the opening of the thirteenth century, and which ended in a permanent weakening of the imperial power.

But during this time German influence did not cease to penetrate into Poland under another form. Although Poland, anxious to strengthen her links with Latin culture, had from the outset entertained relations with all the west, including the Latin nations, France and Italy, these links were naturally particularly close with Germany, her immediate neighbour. The Polish clergy counted among its members many foreigners, of whom a great part were Germans, especially in the principal monasteries. We know, moreover, that German colonization had begun in certain parts of Poland at the end of the twelfth century, and had developed increasingly during all the thirteenth. It is true that the villages which were founded in such great numbers by the dukes, the bishops, and the lords, often obtained only the franchises of German law, although the majority of the settlers were Polish. It is equally true that the origin of urban life, which was then organized in a definite manner in Poland, was not so exclusively German as has been supposed. Nevertheless, we do not attempt to deny the very great importance of the role that the German elements then played in these different spheres.

It would be equally absurd to deny its advantages. These advantages, tangible even in the intellectual life of a country which was relatively a young one in the Christian community and removed from the regions where western civilization had its first roots, were valuable, especially in the sphere of material culture, of economic and commercial life, and of the social organization of the municipal and rural community. In this respect German law was of itself a powerful factor of progress. Nevertheless, this German influence, although seemingly of a purely pacific order, represented a danger scarcely less grave for Poland than the military expeditions of the Emperors. It was, in fact, a case of foreign infiltration, doubly menacing in a divided State and in a population whose national consciousness was scarcely in process of formation. The towns with their essentially German inhabitants, and the monasteries, which sometimes did not even admit Poles among their religious, while being important focuses of culture, were at the same time so many foreign islands in the very heart of Poland. And the country districts, too readily abandoned to German settlers, and to institutions of Germanic character, could only too easily detach themselves, little by little, from Poland, especially those which were situated in the neighbourhood of her frontiers.

This danger continued to increase in proportion as the drive of Germany's political expansion to the east took a new impulse. From the first half of the thirteenth century it gave rise to anxiety. Therefore this grave problem must not be overlooked when we compare the methods and results of the policy of the two princes who were disputing for the first place in Poland.

The Duchy of Masovia, which served as a base for Conrad's conquests, somewhat isolated to the north-east of the state of the Piasts, was scarcely touched by German influences. Conrad, therefore, might have seemed the representative of the purely Polish element. And we likewise know that this prince was by no means an adventurer, extending his dominion through pure greed, as has been long imagined. It was he, however, who, while labouring to reunite a large part of Polish territory, committed in his relations with Germany the most disastrous mistake to be found in Polish history, a mistake the consequences of which are influencing general history even to our own day. At the very moment when he was attempting to assume the sovereignty in Cracow, Conrad of Masovia introduced the first members of the Teutonic Order into Poland.

The war with the Prussians was continuing without intermission along the northern frontiers of Conrad's duchy. In spite of interesting attempts at co-operation with the other Polish princes he did not succeed in extending these frontiers, nor even in protecting them against Prussian incursions. Also the Christian mission in Prussia, although organized with the concurrence of the Polish bishops at the Lateran Council, made but slow progress. In despair of the situation, Conrad then appealed in the beginning of 1226 to one of the great orders of chivalry, which were founded in the Holy Land to fight the infidels. Hermann von Salza, Grand Master of the Teutonic Order, accepted his offers the more readily because the project of establishing that Order on the borders of Hungary had just fallen through, the real intentions of the German Knights having been discovered in time. Conrad was less prudent and less discerning. In 1230 members of the Order planted themselves in considerable numbers on the bank of the Vistula, and soon founded the stronghold of Thorn, or, in Polish, Torun.

The question, so much debated, of the authenticity of the first charters which regulated the legal situation of the Teutonic Order in its new field of action matters little here. What is certain is that the intentions of the two contracting parties differed completely. Conrad, while offering the territory of

Chelmno to the new arrivals, fully intended to keep entire sovereignty over it. The future conquests of the Order in Prussian territory were likewise to be subject to the ducal authority. The Grand Master's conception was wholly different. According to him, the base of operations provided by Conrad, as well as the whole of Prussia, was destined to form a new State of ecclesiastical character, governed by the Teutonic Order: a State completely independent of Poland, and recognizing only the authority of the Holy See and that of the Empire. Frederick II hastened to confer upon the Order an imperial charter, in which this point of view found its first confirmation.

The conquest of Prussia took the Teutonic Knights more than fifty years. They had to break the resistance of each tribe one after the other, and subsequently organize a completely new life. A vast German colony was thereby created from the mouth of the Vistula to that of the Niemen, where a German population, crowding in from all parts of the Empire, superimposed themselves upon the natives, and even replaced the latter, who were either enslaved or exterminated. They finished by usurping the very name of the former Prussians.

However, this 'new Germany,' as it was called later, remained geographically separated from the Empire by Danzig Pomerania, which was still independent. The duke of this Pomerania, the fiery Swientopelk, whom we saw resisting the Piasts, speedily understood that a far greater danger was beginning to threaten him. But the war that he carried on for ten years against his new German neighbours changed nothing in the situation. When he began it in 1242 it was already too late. In 1233 the Order had inflicted a decisive defeat upon the Prussians so that their insurrection, encouraged by the Duke of Pomerania, had no chance of suc-

cess. Moreover, in 1237 the Teutonic Knights had federated
with another German Order, that of the Sword Bearers, who
had founded a somewhat similar colony at the mouth of the
Dvina in Livonia. Lithuania and Samogitia, situated in the
centre of the Baltic populations, thus found themselves, like
Pomerania, surrounded on two sides by Germanic conquests.

All these events seem to have aroused no anxiety whatever
in Conrad of Masovia, to whom this German colony of a
political character owed its striking success. One can still
understand that he helped the Order at the outset of the
campaign in Prussia, as other Polish princes and Swientopelk
himself had also done. But, misunderstanding Poland's real
interests, Conrad, with his sons, also supported the Teutonic
Knights against the Duke of Pomerania.

We can feel no surprise that a prince who showed so little
political foresight did not succeed in removing from the
throne of Cracow a rival as energetic and as prudent as Henry
the Bearded. The Duke of Breslau, the grandson, son, and
husband of German princesses, also encouraged the German
colonization. But he did it in a very different fashion. He
profited by it to raise the general level of culture in his
duchy, which included the greater part of Silesia, and to give
his authority a solid economic basis.

This authority rapidly extended beyond the Silesian frontier. Henry, before securing in 1229 the sovereignty in Cracow, had made no less persevering efforts to bring Great
Poland also under his dominion. From the beginning of the
thirteenth century he had not ceased to intervene in the disputes which were carried on between the descendants of
Mieszko the Old. At last, in 1234, a good half of that province
was formally ceded to him. But he aimed higher. This Silesian prince not only intended, like Conrad of Masovia, to

enlarge his possessions: he proposed to make them the nucleus of a restored kingdom of Poland.

The royal crown, almost forgotten since the fall of Boleslas II, was destined by him for his eldest son, whom he associated in his rule towards the end of his life. This Henry II, who succeeded his father in 1238, was, in fact, entirely worthy of the heritage of the first Piasts. Pursuing the very.able policy of Henry the Bearded, his son, surnamed the Pious, was, moreover, able to obtain the support of the clergy, with whom his father had had frequent disagreements. Following the old tradition of his race, he placed himself under the protection of the Holy See, with which he also allied himself against Frederick II. In spite of all his German connections, Henry the Pious would, therefore, assuredly have maintained the independence and the prestige of the kingdom if all his plans had not been annihilated by an unforeseen catastrophe. In 1241 he died as a Christian hero in the battle of Lignica, in which he was attempting to arrest the Mongolian invasion. In his little army Poles and Germans fought bravely side by side against the barbarians who were invading Europe.

Poland, so often during three centuries threatened from the west, had never yet suffered so directly and so brutally an assault from the east. For the first time she had to fill the splendid, if ungrateful, part of the front bastion of Christendom. All the Russias, first the new Russia, established in Finnish territory, then the old Russia, with her glorious metropolis Kiev, had been devastated and conquered by the Tartars between 1237 and 1240. The following year Batu Khan hurled himself upon Poland, and after crushing the knights of Little Poland in the battle of Chmielnik, triumphed equally at Lignica. But this victory was to be the last, at least in those regions. Together with rumoured events in Asia the desperate resistance of Poland contributed to make the Mongolian hordes retreat. Europe was saved.

For Poland also the sacrifice of Henry the Pious was not in vain. She escaped for ever from the Tartar yoke. Her frontier became that of free Europe and of triumphant Christianity. But she had suffered cruelly from the passage of the enemy; and for long centuries she remained exposed to the perpetual danger of a new Tartar invasion, of which the next was perpetrated in 1259, and to the terrible neighbourhood of the Khans of Kipchak, the masters of the whole European east.

It is true that they were not immediate neighbours. The power of the Khans, residing at Sarai on the lower Volga, weighed heavily on eastern Russia, where the historic role of Moscow was then beginning, but was less felt in the Ruthenian principalities bordering on Poland. Daniel, the son of Roman, the former adversary of Leszek the White, was still reigning in Halicz and Volhynia. Wishing to liberate himself from the Tartars, he turned spontaneously to the side of the Catholic west. Ready for religious union with Rome, he entered into negotiations with Innocent IV, who was deeply interested in all aspects of the eastern question. In 1253 he received the royal crown from the hands of a papal legate. The Pope had just conferred the same dignity on a Lithuanian prince, Mendog, who had accepted Catholicism in order to escape from the political aggression of the Teutonic Order. He, too, put up an energetic resistance to the Tartars and, by attaching the Ruthenian lands which surrounded her on the south-east to Lithuania, he put a limit to the Mongolian conquests.

The consolidation of these two new Catholic kingdoms was to the interest of all Europe, and more especially Poland. But for the moment both needed to be supported by efficacious help. Unfortunately, the west was too absorbed in the conflict between the Papacy and the Empire to be able to intervene in these distant regions. The Teutonic Order's only concern was to wrest territorial concessions from Mendog, and as regards Poland, she was too divided and too enfeebled to undertake common action with the two kings.

The Polish clergy alone endeavoured to make use of a situation so favourable to Catholic propaganda in the Lithuanian and Ruthenian lands. The princes of the House of Piast played the part of intermediaries between the Holy See and Daniel. It fell to their lot to collaborate with the latter against the Yatvegians who separated them from Mendog's Lithuanian kingdom. But that was all. Under these conditions Daniel, obtaining no help from the west, was obliged to humble himself again before the Tartars, and even to provide them with reinforcements against Poland. Mendog, carried away by a violent pagan reaction, not only recommenced his struggles with the Germans, but also his incursions into Poland.

The latter did not at that time possess a monarch who understood the needs of the hour, and who had at his disposal the necessary authority to place himself at the head of all the Piasts. Henry the Pious, who alone could have played that part, was no more. His sons, who were disputing his heritage, proved themselves completely unequal to it. Their influence no longer extended beyond Silesia. Conrad of Masovia took this opportunity to occupy Cracow for the last time, from 1241 to 1243, but he could not hold out there and died shortly after, dividing his duchy between his sons. Boleslas the Chaste, at last established on his father's throne, was not lacking in good qualities, but possessing only Cracow and Sandomierz, and dependent on the great noble families, he was incapable of imposing the supremacy that had reverted to him upon the other Polish princes.

He allowed himself to be led with them to take part in a war which was entirely foreign to the interests of Poland.

Hungary, where Boleslas had found a remarkable wife, and Bohemia, which under Ottakar II had attained to great power, were disputing with each other for the Austrian heritage of the Babenbergs, and we see the princes of Poland fighting for twenty years to no purpose in the two opposite camps. Ottakar II, who gained a great hearing, above all in Silesia, made an appeal to Slav solidarity so as to associate all the Piasts with himself on the eve of his decisive campaign against Rudolf of Hapsburg in 1278. But, in point of fact, only the Germans, notably the margraves of Brandenburg, made any profit out of this long disorientation of Polish policy. All along the Oder and the Warta they wrested important territories from the Piasts of Silesia and Great .Poland, extending their influence into Pomerania. With this new German advance, a new danger had, therefore, come to menace Poland, who seemed condemned to an increasingly passive role both in the west and in the east.

Her princes of the next generation, however, succeeded in finding the remedy.

5

The Reconstruction of the Kingdom

THE thirteenth century, which in the west was the century of St Louis and of a brilliant efflorescence of medieval culture, was an epoch of trouble and undeniable weakness in Polish history. After the new successes of the German colonization, which was assuming an increasingly political aspect, and after the glorious but disastrous day of Lignica, the dissolution of the ancient kingdom of the Piasts seemed final.

Nevertheless, the first of our modern historians to have drawn a synthetic picture of this confused epoch has been led to maintain that the general impression is not so discouraging as might have been expected, and that in the midst of an apparent decadence an early regeneration was preparing. Moreover, the great historian of Polish law and Polish institutions, who has studied this regeneration of the kingdom of Poland in the fourteenth century with particular care, has found strong elements of unity in the preceding century which ensured the continuity of our historical evolution.

Taking these elements of unity, let us begin by considering that one among them which, in spite of everything, the old national dynasty represented. True, it was this dynasty

itself which had made Polish history a veritable mosaic of
duchies whose number increased unceasingly. But this divided Poland of the thirteenth century still remained the
common patrimony of only one family, whose members, even
while fighting each other, were still conscious of their ties of
close relationship. In spite of their individual titles, they all,
including the Silesian princes, who were the most numerous,
remained dukes 'of Poland.'

If that subdivided Poland did not at that time disappear
from the map of Europe, as she did after the partitions between foreign powers at the end of the eighteenth century,
this is also due to another circumstance. Medieval Poland was
not only a political conception: she was also an ecclesiastical
province. Being at different periods the subject of the Holy
See, she kept for that reason a unity in the whole extent of
her territory that was recognized by the highest authority of
the Christian world. In Rome even the provinces lost by the
Piasts were always regarded as forming part of the Poland
which belonged, in all its entirety, to the patrimony of the
Church and which paid Peter's pence. At the same time the
clergy of the whole of Poland, headed by the archbishops of
Gniezno and the bishops of Cracow, several of whom particularly distinguished themselves in the thirteenth century,
remained closely united by the links of ecclesiastical organization, and this of itself formed a further link between the
different duchies.

We can say almost the same of the great families of the future Polish nobility, despite the heavy responsibility which
they incurred by the part they took in the struggles between
the princes. They often helped to prolong, indeed to embit-
ter, these fratricidal struggles, and to weaken the authority of
the dukes whom they changed so easily. But, on the other
hand, as nearly all of them had residences in several duchies

at the same time, and some—the most powerful—were scattered over every part of Poland, these strongly united families created a whole network of permanent connections between the different regions that were separated politically.

To these positive facts another and more intangible one was added: the national consciousness which, little by little, became more pronounced. Born of the ancient community of language and of customs, that consciousness was asserted in the reaction against Germanism. In the second half of the thirteenth century, the clergy, the great majority of whom were now recruited from among the Poles, protested against the German exclusiveness of certain religious orders, and constituted themselves the defenders of the rights of the national language in the churches and in the schools dependent upon them. At the same epoch the Polish knighthood showed its indignation against those princes who were too much disposed to surround themselves with foreigners. And if the antagonism between knights and citizens had also social causes, yet it was inspired in the first place by displeasure at seeing the German element dominating the towns.

Yet a real and deep national feeling cannot be developed in a negative sense alone, by opposition to another nation. The Polish nation has been formed, above all, by the cult of a common past, by that sense of tradition—let us even say by that historic sense—which she manifested from a very ancient epoch. The glory of the first century of Polish history seemed to gain in splendour by its contrast with an increasingly painful present. And precisely in the midst of her greatest straits, in 1253, an act which had doubtless been considered for a long time played its part in recalling the glories of the past, in explaining their eclipse, in symbolizing a mystic faith in their return. Stanislas, Bishop of Cracow, the victim of Boleslas the Bold, was canonized. The following year the ceremony

of the exposition of his remains on the altar of the Vavel
Cathedral at Cracow gathered together the princes of the
whole of Poland. On the part of the dynasty this was an act of
expiation. As for the nation, she saw in it the guarantee that
the reparation of the crime would soon efface its consequences, and that the divisions of their torn country would.be
reunited. Thus the religious element which we find at the base
of Polish patriotism in every epoch fostered its early growth.

The canonization of St Stanislas recalled at the same time
the traditional role of Cracow. Hence the new attempts to
reconstruct the unity of Poland sprang from the intention of
giving the ancient capital the strongest possible monarch, who
would reunite to Little Poland other important parts of the
old kingdom. From this standpoint, the nomination of the
successor of Boleslas V, who had no children and who died in
1279, was by no means a happy one. Leszek the Black, the
eldest of Conrad of Masovia's grandsons, belonged to the
branch which had divided between them the central provinces of Poland, Kujavia and the territories of Lenczyca and
Sieradz; he joined only this last and unimportant duchy to
Little Poland. The new duke was looked upon coldly by a
powerful party who favoured the candidature of a prince of
the younger branch that had remained in Masovia proper,
and it actually revolted on two different occasions against
Leszek. The latter, who died in 1288, likewise childless, was
more ingenious in the choice of his successor. Passing over his
brother of Kujavia and his cousins of Masovia, he nominated
Henry IV of Breslau, grandson of the hero of Lignica.

It is true that Silesia was submitting more and more to the
influence of German culture and to the political influence of
the kingdom of Bohemia. But did not this constitute all the
greater reason for renewing its ties with Cracow? It is true
that Henry IV himself, famed as a poet in the German lan-

guage, had committed the imprudence of submitting the duchy of Breslau to the suzerainty of Rudolf of Hapsburg and promising the succession to Venceslas II of Bohemia. But after he was raised to the throne of Cracow he not only proved his excellence as an administrator: he resumed the Polish policy of his ancestors, a policy that aimed at the reconstruction of the kingdom of the Piasts. He immediately began to take steps in Rome towards obtaining the royal crown. His premature death in 1290 prevented the realization of this plan, but the Duke ot Cracow and Breslau was still able to communicate his last desire to the prelates and lords who surrounded him.

Henry IV left Little Poland to Przemysl II, Duke of Great Poland, and the duchy of Breslau, not to Bohemia, but to his cousin, Henry of Glogow. It was probably understood that the latter would subsequently also inherit the possessions of Przemysl, who had no son. Three-fourths of the kingdom would have then been united in his hand. But the fact. alone of an immediate reunion of Little and Great Poland under a monarch of great promise stood for progress of the first order. Great Poland, so rich in national traditions, long torn by internal strife, had for thirty years again been playing an often decisive role, mainly owing to Przemysl's uncle, Boleslas the Pious, the indefatigable defender of the Polish frontiers on the side of Brandenburg and Pomerania. After the death of Boleslas in 1279, his nephew had not only reunited Gniezno and Poznan, but in 1282 he had been nominated as heir by the Duke of Danzig Pomerania, son of the famous Swientopelk. We cannot sufficiently insist on the significance of this success, which restored Poland's access to the sea, arrested German expansion, and allowed Przemysl to resume the traditions of the first Piasts.

He was installed at Cracow immediately after Henry IV's

death; but he found himself faced by two equally dangerous rivals. On one side, the nearest kindred of Leszek the Black had never renounced his heritage; even in Henry of Breslau's lifetime one of them, Ladislas the Short of Kujavia, Leszek's younger brother, forestalling all the others, had made attempts which, pursued with unparalleled tenacity, ended by making him the real renovator of the kingdom of Poland. On the other side, Venceslas of Bohemia, availing himself of the Duke of Breslau's former promises and of Rudolf of Hapsburg's support, also put forward his own pretensions to the throne of Cracow. Several Polish princes of Upper Silesia having become vassals of the King of Bohemia, the latter was enabled to march straight on Cracow with such considerable forces that Przemysl and soon Ladislas were compelled to yield the town to him.

However, neither of them was discouraged. Moreover, all those who, constantly increasing in numbers, desired to hasten at all costs the restoration of the Polish royalty, considered that even the occupation of Cracow by a foreign monarch should not prevent their design from being effected. The first plan had been to begin by uniting the greater part of the Polish territories round the capital and then to obtain the crown for the prince who was to reign there. But could they not proceed in the reverse order: crown the Polish prince who seemed the most worthy and use the prestige of royalty to draw the other regions of Poland to this monarch? This seems to have been the idea of the Archbishop of Gniezno, James Swinka, the principal promoter of the restoration of the kingdom. With the approbation of the Holy See he crowned Przemysl King of Poland on 26th June 1295. The Vavel being still inaccessible, this long delayed ceremony took place in the cathedral of Gniezno.

the religious capital of the whole of Poland. The opinion has been expressed that Przemysl's kingdom was only the kingdom of Great Poland, and essentially differed from that of of the first Piasts. This hypothesis seems to us untenable, but what it contains of truth is the fact that from this moment Great Poland, proud and jealous of the first place, once more acquired after so many centuries, was often to oppose the preponderance of Little Poland, although the latter soon resumed her central role in Polish history.

On the eve of his consecration, Przemysl also had the great satisfaction of entering into actual possession of Pomerania after the death of the duke who had bequeathed it to him. But the following year he was assassinated, the victim of a plot hatched between the margraves of Brandenburg and some discontented lords of the young king, who, therefore, was never able to rise to his full capacity. The crisis which followed this catastrophe took a fatal course. While Ladislas the Short and Henry of Glogow mutually disputed the succession to Przemysl, it was Venceslas of Bohemia who profited. Master of Little Poland, he occupied Great Poland in 1300, and the same archbishop, who five years earlier had been instrumental in the triumph of the national idea, was compelled to place the crown of the Piasts on the head of a foreigner.

The renovation of the kingdom of Poland had thus become pure fiction, because the kingdom appeared to be nothing more than an annexe to that of Bohemia, together with which it would have been easily incorporated in the German Empire. Fortunately this situation did not last. Ladislas the Short, exile as he was, did not waste his time. He succeeded in gaining, on one hand, the moral support of the Pope, Boniface VIII; on the other, the help of the Hungarians. In

1305 he reappeared in Little Poland. The following year he occupied Cracow. In 1314 he became the master also of Great Poland.

This success of the national candidate, obtained in spite of the opposition of the German burghers, who went so far as to revolt against him, was due, in great measure, to the indefatigable perseverance with which he worked for his aim, to the experience acquired in the course of so many years of desperate efforts, and to the sympathy of the population which he at last succeeded in gaining. It is also true that Ladislas was aided by circumstances. Venceslas III, who had succeeded his father in 1305, and who at once marched against his rival, was assassinated the following year. The dynasty of the Premyslides expiring with him, Bohemia herself became the object of a prolonged rivalry between the candidates for the throne. In 1309 Henry of Glogow also died, and his sons proved incapable of maintaining themselves in Great Poland against the partisans of Ladislas the Short. Finally, taking advantage of the dynastic quarrels in Germany, and of the goodwill that he still found at the Curia, in Avignon as formerly in Rome, Ladislas had himself crowned King of Poland in 1320 at Cracow itself.

This time the restoration of the kingdom of the Piasts was definite. But it was not their integral inheritance that passed into the hands of the new king. In the course of his contests, of which we have only been able to trace the chief stages, he had lost one province of the greatest value, Pomerania. In 1307 the treachery of the powerful Swienca family had almost let it fall into the power of the margraves of Brandenburg. It was then that the Poles made an appeal to the Teutonic Order, installed at the frontiers of Pomerania by the king's grandfather. The Knights did, in fact, check the advance of the Brandenburgs, but only to seize the disputed province for themselves, beginning with Danzig, where, in 1308, they massacred the royal garrison and a great part of the population. In 1309 the whole country was subjugated by them and, determined never to loose their hold, they transferred the seat of their Grand Master to the recently constructed castle of Marienburg.

Ladislas never resigned himself to abandoning this ancient Polish province to them, indispensable to the kingdom as its only access to the sea. He only waited for his coronation to direct all his efforts towards the scarcely less important object of regaining Pomerania, without even waiting for the reunion of all the other duchies of the Piasts. In 1320 he requested the Holy See to nominate a tribunal which, as the result of a canonical process, recognized the rights of Poland over Pomerania. In the same year he confirmed his alliance with Hungary by marrying his daughter Elizabeth to the successor of the Arpads, Charles Robert of Anjou. Five years later he allied himself with Lithuania, whose power had considerably increased, thanks to the Grand Duke Gedymin, the inflexible defender of his country against the Teutonic Order. But the collaboration with a still pagan Lithuania ceased in 1331, not without having, at times, compromised the King of Poland in the eyes of the Catholic west; and in the midst of such complicated conflicts as were then agitating that west, Ladislas did not always succeed in choosing the most efficacious diplomatic course.

He was to be found, generally speaking, among the partisans of John XXII in the struggle of that Pope with the Emperor Louis the Bavarian. He was the more justified in taking this side inasmuch as the House of Bavaria, having succeeded the former margraves of Brandenburg, was carrying on their policy, which was a very dangerous one for Poland. But Ladislas even approached the Wittelsbachs when it was a case of finding support against another neighbour, a particularly menacing one since he energetically abetted the Teutonic Order. This was John of Luxemburg, the new King of Bohemia, who by reason of this title put forward claims to the crown of Poland. These claims were not particularly serious in themselves, and John preferred to employ another means of extending the influence of Bohemia to the detriment of the 'King of Cracow.' He was well aware that among the princes of the House of Piast only those of Kujavia, the nearest relations of Ladislas, recognized the latter's authority and collaborated with him. The King of Bohemia, on the other hand, succeeded in exacting homage in 1327 and 1329 from nearly all the Silesian princes, and even from one of the dukes of Masovia who, like himself, had ranged themselves on the side of the Teutonic Order.

Taking advantage of this diversion in the quarter of Bohemia, the Order no longer hesitated to enter into open war against Ladislas. The Teutonic invasions of 1331 and 1332 were most disastrous. It is true that during the first the Poles gained a victory, albeit incomplete, over the Teutonic Knights at Plowce. But on two occasions all the north-west of the kingdom was terribly devastated and, what was still more serious, Kujavia, including Ladislas's own patrimony, remained, together with the territory of Dobrzyn, in the hands of the enemy.

At his death in the following year the king therefore left to his only son a Poland that was mutilated and menaced, enfeebled and impoverished, the more so because, absorbed by his innumerable campaigns, Ladislas had been obliged to neglect the needs of the country's internal life. This prince, short of stature, as his untranslatable surname *Lokietek* witnesses, seemed in no wise predestined to the amazing role which he played, and the opening of his career had been signalized by many checks and sterile adventures; nevertheless, this prince, heroic in his defeats, had accomplished the task which, during more than two centuries, Poland had in vain awaited from her dynasty. The vast territories that he had definitely united, at the same time restoring to them the henceforth undisputed rank of an independent kingdom, offered a solid basis for the remarkable work which his successor was to undertake, completing in every respect that of his father.

6

Casimir the Great

It was more than six hundred years ago that the son of Ladislas the Short, succeeding his father without difficulty, was crowned King of Poland. But to this day Casimir the Great has remained for the Polish nation the ideal of a sovereign; and whenever the historian would grasp the origin of any problem concerning the subsequent development of Poland he must return to that epoch. Let us point out in advance King Casimir's two chief titles to greatness. On the one hand, it is the universal nature of his genius, which, in his external policy, recalls Boleslas the Great, and which remains without an equal in all that concerns the regulation of internal questions. On the other hand, it is the excellent method, one of skilled wisdom and patient moderation, which he applied to the solution of the numerous problems that awaited him.

As only the chief of these can be considered here, let us begin with his settlement of a political situation which was seriously compromising the security of Poland. Seeing that he could not remedy it by a new war which offered no chance of success, as it would have to be carried on simultaneously against both the Teutonic Order and Bohemia, Casimir decided to negotiate a compromise. The terms were fixed in 1335 at the Congress of Visegrad in Hungary, where he went to meet his father's implacable adversary, John of Luxemburg, at the court of his brother-in-law, Charles Robert. Taking into account the actual situation created before his accession, young Casimir recognized the suzerainty of the King of Bohemia over the Silesian Piasts who had rendered him homage. It was at this price that John at last renounced his pretensions to the throne of Poland.

Having thus isolated the Teutonic Order, the king could realize, on that side at least, the minimum of his programme: the securing of Kujavia with Dobrzyn at the price of a temporary renunciation of Pomerania and Chelmno. This was obtained in 1343 by the Treaty of Kalisz. We have said 'temporary renunciation,' because Casimir enveloped this surrender with ingenious reservations, and lost no subsequent occasion of preparing for the return of these regions to Poland. He had clearly indicated this ultimate intention in the course of the preliminary negotiations. In 1339 he organized a new canonical process in Warsaw against the Order, which recalls that organized in the time of Ladislas the Short. But this time it was no longer the Polish bishops who were nominated as judges. Desiring to give the tribunal an impartial character, he summoned to Poland, as representatives of the Holy See, two eminent French prelates, one of whom was the Nuncio, Gailhard de Carces. And this time it was no longer some twenty persons, but a hundred and twenty-six representatives of all classes of the population, who were cited as witnesses to answer a long interrogation investigating the whole relations between Poland and the Teutonic Knights.

The judgment which accorded to Poland all the disputed territories, including Danzig Pomerania, as well as large reparations for the losses she had suffered, was unconditionally rejected by the Order. But all the same the judgment retained all its moral force, and thanks to this initiative the whole Polish nation—princes and knights, clergy and functionaries, citizens and peasants—emerges for the first time as conscious of her unity and rights.

Silesia likewise had not been abandoned without reservations, and Casimir seized every occasion of formulating all the claims that could prevent the rupture of the traditional ties between the kingdom of Poland and that province, where he supported the last independent Piasts. Moreover, if the great king had not been able to regain all the territories that his country had lost on the western side, he immediately found large compensations on the eastern side, where he opened almost unlimited vistas to Poland. This constitutes the second problem which dominated his foreign policy.

Let us first state the facts. Ten years before Casimir's accession the last Ruthenian princes of Halicz and Volhynia, descendants of King Daniel, had perished in their struggles against the Tartars, and it was a Piast of Masovia who as their nephew had succeeded them. This Polish prince died by poison in 1340, and Casimir, whom he had probably appointed his heir, at once claimed the succession. In his first campaigns he came into collision with the hostility of the Tartars, and with the rivalry of a Lithuanian prince, the son of Gedymin, who based his claims on ties of relationship with the ancient Ruthenian dynasty. After a victorious advance by the King of Poland in 1349 the Lithuanians recaptured Volhynia from him, and the truce of 1352 left him only the region of Halicz with the increasingly flourishing town of Lwow. It was not until after new Polish victories in 1366 that a treaty with the Lithuanian princes ensured western Volhynia also to Casimir and extended his influence over the descendants of Gedymin, established in the east of that province, as well as in Podolia.

All these important acquisitions were subject to the royal crown of Poland. This was not, however, an annexation pure and simple. Although part of these regions had been Polish in the time of the first Piasts, the boundaries of the kingdom now exceeded the territory of ethnographical Poland. Casimir scrupulously respected the traditions, institutions, and customs of his new Ruthenian subjects, and even while preparing the organization of a Catholic hierarchy in their country he appealed to the Greek patriarch of Constantinople to reestablish the ancient Orthodox metropolis at Halicz. The king even secured the collaboration of some of the princes of Lithuanian origin by attaching them as vassals to his crown. He thus inaugurated that supple and liberal method which enabled vast new territories, inhabited by the most diverse populations, to be united to the kingdom of Poland under different constitutional forms.

At the same time, in spite of repeated conflicts, he inaugurated a policy of closer intercourse with Lithuania. For, in addition to a common antagonism against the Teutonic Order, there was now the urgent necessity of regulating by a common agreement the political situation of the Ruthenian territories, from which the Poles and Lithuanians were successively thrusting back the Tartars. Therefore Casimir also encouraged every project of at last winning Lithuania over to the Christian faith, not by the sword of the German Knights, but by pacific means with the active participation of Polish missionaries and clergy.

It was thus that the extension of the frontiers, and of Polish influence in eastern Europe, became one of general importance for the Christian world. Louis of Hungary, who had succeeded his father, Charles Robert, in 1342, assisted his Pol-

ish uncle in several of his campaigns, not, however, forgetting
the old Hungarian pretensions to the 'kingdom of Galicia.'
Charles of Luxemburg, King of Bohemia since his father's
death at Crecy, and at the same time Emperor of the Romans,
took a lively interest in the plan of converting pagan Lithuania, and associated himself with Casimir's efforts.

For Casimir, while basing his external policy on an increasingly close alliance with Hungary, succeeded, as soon as
circumstances permitted, in establishing relations with the
House of Luxemburg. He thus placed his relations with both
Bohemia and the Empire on a peaceful footing, while at the
same time he fixed the western frontiers of Poland, which
were to undergo no modification until the epoch of the Partitions, except from the side of the Teutonic Order. He also
made Poland participate in the policy of the whole of central
Europe, displaying a diplomatic talent of the first order, and
gradually gaining an undisputed authority among all the
great contemporary monarchs.

To illustrate the extent of his political relations, it is
enough to emphasize that Polish embassies succeeded each
other at Avignon without intermission; that Casimir sent
reinforcements to the Pope in the Italian wars; that he allied
himself with Valdemar Atterdag of Denmark; that together
with the Scandinavian kings he had himself named protector
of the archbishops of Riga; that finally he intervened in the
affairs of the young principality of Moldavia. But nothing is
a better proof of the change that had been effected in Poland's
international position during the reign of Casimir the Great
than the political congress which assembled at Cracow towards the end of his reign in September 1364, that 'moult
grand parlement,' which a French poet of the epoch, Guillaume de Machault, describes with magniloquence.

This congress had been convoked to facilitate the propa-

ganda of the King of Cyprus, Pierre de Lusignan, in favour of
a new Crusade. In the capital of Poland he found, as guests of
her king, renowned for his campaigns against the infidels, the
Emperor Charles IV, who had just married a granddaughter
of Casimir, the Kings of Hungary and Denmark, as well as
many other princes, naturally including those of the House of
Piast. The receptions were sumptuous and, in addition to the
discussions devoted to the eastern question, which was considered no longer possible to treat without the co-operation
of Poland, Casimir, in the character of arbitrator, decided the
differences between Louis of Anjou and Charles of Luxemburg. What a difference when we remember the Congress of
Visegrad at the outset of his reign!

But what a difference also between the Poland which his
father had left to him, and that which he had succeeded in
creating during thirty years! Among the Piasts who surrounded the head of the dynasty, even the duke of that
Masovia which had nearly become a Czech fief, and which,
thanks to Casimir's patient efforts, had again become an integral part of the kingdom of Poland, was not absent. But we
have said enough of political questions. The congress of 1364
coincided with the foundation of the University of Cracow.
The creation of this first Polish university—following that of
Prague, the second to be opened in the whole of central Europe—bears witness both to the high level of culture which
Poland had reached, and to Casimir's desire to raise it higher
still.

It was in his mind that the new school, organized on the
model of the Italian universities, should primarily cultivate
the study of law; for the king, who severely repressed all
disorders and who condemned to death a Palatine guilty of
fomenting troubles in Great Poland, was, above all, distinguished as a legislator. We are indebted to him for a remark-

able work of codification, his celebrated statutes at which he laboured for over twenty years.

Glancing over their numerous articles, chiefly devoted to penal law, we are struck by the merciful spirit they disclose. In vain do we search this very humane code for the atrocious penalties enjoined by other legislations of that epoch. These statutes were, moreover, dictated by respect for national traditions, being not only largely based on common law, but also drawn up originally in two different versions, one for Great, and the other for Little, Poland. The king said justly that he aimed at establishing a uniform law for all the kingdom; but this great unifier, who had nothing of the brutal centralist in him, took into account the individualities of the different parts of his state.

Finally, let us emphasize that Casimir's statutes, as well as his other legislative acts, show a great care for equity for all the social classes. Certainly, the nobility which, grouping together the descendants of the old clans of Polish chivalry, had definitely taken shape, appears in the foreground in the full possession of its rights that were already guaranteed by many individual charters. The king even began to associate the nobles with himself in the most important political decisions for the country's future. But he likewise extended his protection to the Polish towns, for which he created a special tribunal and whose commercial interests he carefully safeguarded. He was also deservedly given the name of 'the King of the Peasants,' whom he protected against all ill treatment and succoured during famines. And the Jews, persecuted in other countries, took refuge in Poland to a greater extent than they had ever done before his reign, certain of finding there favourable conditions of existence.

These characteristic features of his government are in strict accord with his desire to develop economic life. Casimir was as interested in the salt mines of Wieliczka as he was in the commercial routes to the Black Sea which he had opened to his country. He covered this country, even in the forests of the Carpathians, with new villages to which he granted extensive liberties. And, a great constructor, he built, besides numerous churches, solid fortresses designed to protect the frontiers.

When we contemplate this very varied activity we ask ourselves who were this powerful personality's collaborators. It was among the higher clergy that Casimir seems to have found the most faithful servants, the best interpreters of his ideas, such as the archbishop Jaroslaw Bogorja, or his nephew John Suchywilk. This is not surprising, considering the profound piety of the king, who lived in constant and confidential relations with the Holy See. But it is also explainable by the fact that Casimir, himself highly cultured, rivalling the brilliant courts of Prague and Buda, chose to surround himself by these prelates of fine intelligence, graduates of foreign universities. Naturally, he also utilized the talents which he found among the knighthood, choosing by preference the less powerful families upon whom he bestowed the highest offices. He was careful to perfect these talents, with the result that many of the politicians who were to distinguish themselves after his death had been trained in his school.

Unfortunately, providence withheld from him that collaborator whom he most ardently desired to continue his work. Although he married three times, Casimir had no son. He was haunted for a long time before his death by his anxiety to find a successor. No one among the Piasts of the collateral lines seemed to him worthy of the crown. He therefore destined it for his nephew, Louis of Hungary, and this promise of the succession, often formally stated, was, at the same time, the price of the Hungarian alliance. But Casimir was counting very reasonably upon the eventuality of Louis also leaving no son. He therefore considered in advance what would happen after the Polish-Hungarian union, which he foresaw would be temporary. He had a favourite grandson who bore his name, born of the marriage of one of his daughters to a prince of western Pomerania. This part of Pomerania round Stettin, subject to the Empire, still kept its Slav character under a local dynasty. By a slight, but important, modi fication of the frontier, Casimir established an immediate contact between this duchy and his kingdom, at the same time separating the New March, an annexe of Brandenburg, from eastern Pomerania, occupied by the Teutonic Order. A glance at the map is enough to enable us to grasp what the elevation of a prince of western Pomerania to the throne of Poland would have brought about. Casimir the Great intended to pave the way for it by adopting Casimir of Stettin and by bequeathing to him in his will the Polish provinces adjacent to the two Pomeranias, as well as vast territories in the very centre of the kingdom.

Immediately after the death of the king, who in 1370 succumbed prematurely to a hunting accident, Louis of Hungary took care to frustrate these plans. Thus the ingenious project of Casimir the Great concerning his succession was not realized. He left, however, a far more important legacy to Poland. We see it in the positive results of his reign and still more in the course that he marked out for the future development of Poland. He had made her a state as powerful and influential as that of the first Piasts, but infinitely more solid, thanks to the relations established with nearly all the countries of Europe, thanks to her excellent internal organization, and, above all, thanks to the fact that the fate of this state no longer depended exclusively upon the personality of her king.

For the real successor of Casimir the Great, that last king of the national dynasty, was the whole Polish nation, which after the ordeal of so many dynastic crises had been prepared by Casimir's clear-sighted guidance to shape its future lot by itself. The last Piast likewise prepared the Polish nation to collaborate with other nations in the framework of a common state, even were it under a king of foreign origin. This explains how the end of the epoch of the Piasts was, at the same time, the starting-point of the epoch of the Jagiellos.

Part II

THE CENTURIES OF POLAND'S GREATNESS

7

Jadwiga of Anjou

POLAND'S great centuries are inaugurated by the remarkable history of a princess of the fleur-de-lis, who was raised to the throne of the Piasts when scarcely eleven years of age, and died fifteen years later in the odour of sanctity. This life, so short, but entirely devoted to a great cause, marks, like the life of Joan of Arc in the history of France and the west, the most decisive turning-point in the destiny of Poland and eastern Europe.

Fourteen years passed between the death of Casimir the Great and the arrival of Jadwiga of Anjou. They have been described to us with a number of picturesque details by a former vice-chancellor of the dead king, who was filled with admiration for his master's glorious reign, which he contrasts with the decadence that set in under his successor. This tendency, expressive of the author's personal rancour, is so evident that the historian cannot utilize without reserve these first memoirs to be written by a Pole. It is none the less true that under Louis of Anjou, who in Hungary was Louis the Great, the general situation of Poland underwent a very marked retrogression, as the whole policy of these last years of his life was dictated by only one concern, that of ensuring to his daughters the succession to his kingdoms, including, if possible, that of Naples.

As regards Poland, the agreements concluded in the time of Casimir the Great only recognized this right of succession as accruing to the eventual sons of Louis, sons for whom, like his uncle, he waited in vain. It was necessary, therefore, to make the Polish nobility accept a modification of these contracts. Assisted by his mother, Casimir's sister, as well as by the faithful partisans he possessed in Little Poland, Louis at last triumphed over opposition.

In 1374, the Polish representatives, summoned to Koszyce in Hungary, found themselves obliged to guarantee the crown of the Piasts to whichever daughter of Louis should be named by the king. In return, the latter granted them a charter of great importance which, for the first time, guaranteed all the rights of the Polish nobility, while considerably extending them. Among other privileges it was freed from all imposts with the exception of an infinitesimal tax, more of a symbolic nature, levied upon its landed property.

Louis's first idea was to leave Poland to his eldest daughter Catherine, and as she was betrothed to a son of Charles V of France, the future Louis of Orleans, the latter seemed destined at one moment to become the presumptive successor of the Piasts. But Catherine died before her father, who then destined Poland for his second daughter, Maria, betrothed to Sigismund of Luxemburg, son of the Emperor Charles IV. However, this project also was not realized. Immediately after the death of Louis the Great in 1382, Maria was raised to the throne of Hungary, and as the Poles would have no further personal union between the two kingdoms and had no liking whatever for Sigismund, then Margrave of Brandenburg, the queen mother, Elizabeth of Bosnia, proposed to them her youngest daughter, Jadwiga.

It was, therefore, against every expectation that this princess, who was to have reigned in Hungary, gathered round her all the Poles who desired to respect the promises made to her father. The great majority of the Polish nobility was in full agreement upon this point, and even desired to hasten Jadwiga's arrival so as to put an end to the troubles of the interregnum. But this same majority was wholly opposed to the fiancé whom Louis had given to his third daughter, William of Hapsburg, son of Leopold III of Austria. There was no wish to see a German prince reign in Poland; and, moreover, this candidate was apparently not powerful enough to bring any advantage to the kingdom. It was equally in vain that a Piast, Ziemovit of Masovia, who was supported for some time by a party of the nobility, especially in Great Poland, aspired to Jadwiga's hand in order to gain with it the throne of his ancestors. Even before the arrival of the little princess in October 1384 a far more influential party had decided her fate. The chief aristocratic families of Little Poland, such as the lords of Tenczyn of the House of Starza, the lords of Tarnow and Melsztyn of the House of Leliwa, and with them a whole group of politicians, who succeeded in sparing the kingdom the grave dangers of a prolonged chaotic situation, also succeeded in finding a candidate to the throne who represented a whole programme for the future, worthy of the traditions of Casimir the Great. This candidate was Jagiello, Grand Duke of Lithuania.

Since Gedymin's reign Lithuania had again enjoyed years of power under his son Olgierd, who had closely associated with himself his brother Kiejstut. Dividing the rule between them, they succeeded in defending themselves against the invasions of the Teutonic Order, and at the same time in extending their state in Ruthenian territory, where it reached Kiev and approached the Black Sea. But the frail nature of their work appeared after Olgierd's death in 1377. His son Jagiello, to whom he left the supreme power, soon became embroiled with Kiejstut. The latter, vanquished after the long vicissitudes of a civil war of which the Germans made skilful use, perished in 1382 in the prison where Jagiello had thrown this last hero of pagan Lithuania. But the position of the conqueror became still more precarious. A son of Kiejstut, Vitold, having taken refuge in Prussia and been converted to Catholicism, provided the Order with an excellent instrument with which to conquer Lithuania, under the pretext of restoring his patrimony to the exile. Possibly Jagiello could have resisted had he been able to dispose of all the forces of a consolidated state. But that state, one of the vastest in Europe, still remained the patrimony of the very numerous descendants of Gedymin, each of whom, master of an autonomous principality, followed his individual policy. Those who governed the vast Ruthenian lands that were grouped round the Lithuanian nucleus had joined the Orthodox Church on their own account, and were gravitating towards the new Great Russian and Orthodox state of Moscow, the inflexible rival of Lithuania, which Olgierd had fought against in vain. Moscow was, on the one hand, shaking off the yoke of the Tartars, and, on the other hand, was still itself deeply penetrated by Mongolian influence. And on the horizon there was already appearing the new menace of the Asiatic orient incarnated in the terrible Tamerlane.

It was not only in his personal interest, but to save the existence of Lithuania, to give her at last an integral part in the Christian world, that Jagiello, if he did not instigate them, readily accepted the Polish proposals. In the beginning of 1385 his ambassadors appeared at Cracow and Buda to ask the hand of Jadwiga, meeting, at her mother's court, the French ambassadors who were asking the hand of Maria of Hungary for Louis of Orleans. This latter project failed, and the civil war in Hungary ended two years later with the triumph of Sigismund of Luxemburg, who married his fiancée. William of Austria was less fortunate. It was in vain that he betook himself to Cracow without even waiting for Jadwiga to reach marriageable age. The Polish lords would not allow him to establish himself in the Vavel, and at the same time, on 14th August 1385, their envoys concluded, at Krewo in Lithuania, the most important treaty in the whole of Polish history.

Jadwiga at first rebelled. It was her wish to rejoin her childhood's companion, who, a veritable Prince Charming, had reappeared to save her from the 'barbarian' whom stern reasons of state destined for her husband. But this generous child of the race of St Louis soon understood that the project, whose realization now depended on her alone, was far more than a mere political combination like so many others. At Krewo, Jagiello had promised that he would unite his Lithuanian and Ruthenian lands to the crown of Poland forever.

A great state was thereby formed, capable of resisting both Germanism and the East, those two perils which since the dawn of history had threatened the nations that were henceforth to be federated. Sinking, once for all, their mutual differences, these nations could ensure for themselves a common access to two seas—the Baltic and the Black Sea. They thus resumed the designs of the great Piasts, the realization of which was beyond the strength of Poland alone, as well as the designs of Mendog and Daniel, who separately had each in vain attempted to make the Lithuanians and Ruthenians enter into the system of western civilization. Jagiello also promised, more sincerely than the first King of Lithuania, to convert his dynasty and all his nation, the last pagan people in Europe, to Catholicism, and this was the article of the treaty which was bound to make the deepest impression upon

Queen Jadwiga. The cross, at the foot of which she accepted her own cross, is still shown in the cathedral of Cracow.

As soon as Jadwiga had reached the age of twelve Jagiello came to Poland with several of his brothers and his cousin Vitold, with whom he had been reconciled. Immediately after his baptism, at which he received the name of Ladislas, on 18th February 1386, he married Jadwiga, and a fortnight later his coronation was celebrated. William, who had returned to Vienna, could take no action, as his father was at war with the Swiss and soon fell at Sempach. It was the Teutonic Order which took upon itself the task of opposing the events which, if once Lithuania were converted, would have deprived it of its own reason for existence. In agreement with a brother of Jagiello, hostile to the king, and with the Grand Duke of Smolensk, who oscillated between Moscow and Lithuania, the German Knights invaded the latter at the moment when her princes were being baptized in Cracow. But Jagiello's other brothers, returning in haste, repulsed the aggressors, and at Christmas time he went back himself to his native country to carry out his promises.

In the month of February 1387 Catholicism was officially introduced into Lithuania; a first bishopric, founded at Wilno, at once received privileges analogous to those of the Church of Poland, and a first charter of privileges was simultaneously granted to the Lithuanian boyars. It proclaimed the principle by which the latter were to obtain all the rights enjoyed by the Polish nobility; this grant was the best means of introducing into Lithuania the essential elements of the new social order that was to replace the arbitrary absolutism of the pagan epoch in that country. The Ruthenian provinces of the Grand Duchy with their Orthodox population kept their traditional autonomy; the princes of the House of Gedymin, who governed these territories, were only asked to swear fidelity to the King and Queen of Poland.

Jadwiga was never set aside, and, young as she was, she inaugurated from that moment her political role at the side of a husband who submitted to the ascendancy of her character and intelligence and that of her high culture. Jagiello, who, on his side, was remarkably gifted and who seems to have undergone a profound moral transformation after his baptism and marriage, was certainly not a simple prince consort; but Jadwiga, who herself, in 1384, had been crowned 'king,' became, after 1386, a co-ruler whose influence increased with her years.

At the moment when King Ladislas was drawing up the new statute of Lithuania, Jadwiga, at the head of an expedition which scarcely required to have recourse to arms, restored to Poland the regions of Lwow and Halicz that Louis of Anjou had detached from his Polish kingdom and where he had left Hungarian governors. The influence of the new state was so considerable that the Voivode of Moldavia soon paid homage to the crown of Poland, while at the other extremity of the territory subject to Ladislas Jagiello, the rich republic of Novgorod showed itself willing to receive one of his brothers, who was to become its 'governor.' The whole of ancient Russia, whose links with the west had never been entirely broken, would thus have been withdrawn from the influence of the new Muscovite Russia, as well as from that of the Tartars, and on the side of Livonia the German expansion in the basin of the Baltic would have been arrested.

But in the midst of all these almost dazzling successes Jagiello committed one mistake that had serious consequences. Even after his accession to the throne of Cracow, he had hesitated to give his cousin Vitold the privileged position in Lithuania to which the latter always aspired. His political talent of the highest order distinguished him among all the members of the dynasty, and yet he only received a modest apanage, while one of Jagiello's brothers replaced the king at

Wilno as well as at Troki, the patrimony of the line of
Kiejstut. After having attempted in vain to modify this state
of affairs, in the beginning of 1390 Vitold took refuge a second time in Prussia, compromising in the gravest manner the
interests of his country.

For again the Teutonic Order seized the opportunity to
organize with him 'crusades' against Lithuania, calling her
conversion in question and imposing upon the good faith of
many western knights who came, even from France and England, to fight beneath its banners. For two years the situation
remained extremely critical. Only the reinforcements sent
from Poland saved Lithuania, and notably Wilno, which was
twice besieged. At last Jagiello decided to seek the only possible solution. Through the intermediation of the Piasts of
Masovia, whom he had rapidly conciliated, he offered such
important concessions to Vitold that the latter once more
abandoned his German protectors. In 1392 he was reconciled
with the king and queen at Ostrow, and the administration of
Lithuania was conferred upon him, including the Ruthenian
provinces of the former Grand Duchy. Authorized by
Jagiello, he soon even rid himself of all the local dynasts,
without excepting the brothers of the king, whose provinces
were mediatized, one after the other. The close collaboration
of the two cousins, full of promise for the future, had begun.

This beginning of their common work was frequently benefited by intervention on the part of Queen Jadwiga, inspired
by her anxiety for peace and her spirit of moderation. We see
her, for example, appear as mediator when Vitold's policy of
unification came into collision with the interests of the other
Lithuanian princes. But the authority that the young queen
wielded in every sphere, her prudence and moderation, were
still more indispensable in the nation's relations with the
Teutonic Order. The latter was aware that the agreement between Jagiello and Vitold put an end to all possibility of con-

quering a Lithuania supported by Poland. It could only take
its revenge by acting directly against the latter. To effect this
the Grand Master entered into negotiations with Sigismund
of Hungary, who had in the past been humiliated by the failure of his candidature to the Polish throne, as well as with a
Silesian Piast, Ladislas of Opole, who was afraid of losing under the new regime the fiefs that he had obtained in Poland
in the time of Louis of Anjou. They went so far as to speak of
a partition of Poland, which was a chimera. But Ladislas of
Opole did, in fact, pawn his most important fief to the Order,
that same territory of Dobrzyn which the Teutonic Knights
had so long coveted. In order to prove that this transaction
was illegal, Jadwiga, in 1397, went in person to a meeting
with the Grand Master. She did not gain the case, but she
averted an armed conflict which was abhorrent to her and for
which Poland was not prepared.

In the meanwhile, Polish diplomacy, which, thanks again
to the queen, Sigismund's sister-in-law, was successful enough
in regard to Luxemburg, in vain attempted to bring about a
coalition of all the other Baltic Powers against the Order. On
the other side, the Teutonic Knights, while branding Vitold's
'treacheries,' succeeded in again approaching that prince, and
even in imposing upon him a separate peace in 1398. For Vitold was then dreaming of the vast conquests that he was pursuing on the side of the east, where he had occupied Smolensk
and, while fighting the Tartars, had established his domination over the shore of the Black Sea. These were undeniable
successes. But Jadwiga very wisely dissuaded him against enterprises of too ambitious a nature designed to make all eastern Europe subject to him, but which, in fact, led him in 1399
to a disastrous defeat at the battle of the Worskla, impru-
dently launched against the Tartars under Tamerlane's protection.

Moreover, the queen, anxious for the interests of Poland,

while her husband's thoughts were frequently given in preference to those of his dynasty, was uneasy at seeing Vitold arbitrarily exceeding his functions as administrator of the Grand
Duchy. He had certainly no intention of breaking the union
with Poland, the advantages of which were too evident; but
he aspired to the royal crown and, in any case, to a complete
liberty of action. Jadwiga assisted in finding an equitable
compromise in a very delicate situation, which served as the
basis of the acts of union signed shortly after her death.

Before her death she again impressed upon those around
her that the Polish-Lithuanian union must be built up not
merely on constitutional charters, but, above all, on a true
spiritual fellowship. The university of Casimir the Great having fallen into a state of decay, she prepared its renovation;
the Sorbonne, with its brilliant theological department, was
this time taken as its model, because the University of Cracow
was to serve as a centre of faith and civilization for Lithuania,
from which country the queen also sent students as far as
Prague, as well as for the Ruthenian provinces, where new
projects of religious union with the Roman Church were in
preparation.

Dying in 1399, immediately after the death of her only and
new-born child, Jadwiga of Anjou did not see the opening of
the university, which was restored the following year. Nor
did she behold the increasingly fruitful results of all her personal sacrifices. But her contemporaries knew what they owed
to this queen, whose work in history had been a more
astounding miracle than those which soon glorified her tomb.
These brought about the inception of the process of her
canonization in the beginning of the fifteenth century, and to
bring it to a successful conclusion would be an honour to the
Poland of to-day.

8

Grunwald and Horodlo

ALTHOUGH he married again three times, Ladislas Jagiello never forgot his first wife, and during all the rest of his reign, which lasted until 1434, he loyally strove to develop the work he had undertaken with her. Moreover, his cousin Vitold remained his valuable and faithful collaborator for nearly thirty years. It was only on the eve of the latter's death, which preceded by four years that of the king, that an unfortunate misunderstanding came near to embroiling the two cousins, whose good relations had for so long been well known throughout Europe. The consequences of this crisis troubled Jagiello's last years, but they could not compromise the essential results that had been attained in common.

We may best judge what these very important results were if we group them round two events which symbolize, even to this day, a whole epoch of Polish history. Evoking the memory of Grunwald and Horodlo, we see, on one side, a great military success which terminated in serious political disappointments, but which kept throughout the ages all its moral value. And we see, on the other side, a purely pacific work which im-

mediately bore full fruit, and in which, at the same time, the
purest spirit of immortal Poland is incarnate.

The great war between Poland and the Teutonic Order,
crowned by the victory of 1410, narrowly missed breaking out
immediately after the death of Queen Jadwiga. The question
of Samogitia, a Lithuanian province which touched the Baltic
Sea and separated the two German colonies of Prussia and
Livonia, had been added to that of Dobrzyn. Unable to subject the whole of Lithuania, the Order was determined to
wrest from her at least this province, and thus to unite the two
parts of the Teutonic territory. It was evident that here was a
question as vital for Lithuania as that of Pomerania for Poland. Unfortunately, the Lithuanian princes had not always
understood this, and in 1398 Vitold had even believed he was
definitely conciliating his dangerous neighbours by yielding
the whole of Samogitia to them. He soon saw his mistake. The
Order again began to insinuate itself into the internal affairs
of Lithuania by supporting a pretender to the throne who was
hostile to Vitold, and it established so harsh a rule in
Samogitia that the enslaved population turned in desperation
to the prince who had abandoned them.

However, the situation which, on the threshold of the fifteenth century, was extremely strained, appeared to calm
down in 1404 as the result of a treaty by the terms of which
Jagiello and Vitold once more renounced Samogitia. On the
other hand, the Order restored the territory of Dobrzyn to
Poland, insisting on payment of the great sum for which
Ladislas of Opole had pledged it. To collect this sum the King
of Poland was obliged to convoke, for the first time, assem-
blies of the nobility in all his provinces, the regional Diets
which voted extraordinary taxes. But it was only putting off
the evil day. Too many disputed questions remained unset-
tled, including that never-forgotten one of Pomerania; too

many fresh disputes arose along the frontiers; finally, the whole policy of the Order remained too clearly directed against that Polish-Lithuanian union with which its projects of expansion clashed.

The rupture was provoked in 1409 by a general revolt in Samogitia, where the yoke of the Order had become intolerable. The warlike Grand Master, Ulric von Jungingen, was not mistaken when he accused Vitold of complicity with the insurgents. For the Grand Duke had at last realized that he could not sacrifice an essential part of his country and his people. All depended now on the attitude of Poland. She declared her entire solidarity with Lithuania and refused to abandon her. Under these conditions the Grand Master preferred a direct attack upon the kingdom, and soon the territory of Dobrzyn, only just redeemed, saw itself again invaded.

The campaign of 1410, which was foreseen to be a decisive one, was carefully prepared on both sides. Jagiello and Vitold, convinced that the very existence of the federated state was at stake, had assembled all their forces, Polish, Lithuanian, and Ruthenian. They had also Czech and Tartar reinforcements, but the importance of the latter was greatly exaggerated by the enemy in order to scandalize European opinion. The Order, on its side, had proceeded to a general mobilization, and for the last time many knights from all the western countries believed it their duty to fight with the Order against the 'infidels' and their allies. Its army, somewhat inferior in numbers, had the advantage of an indisputable technical superiority.

We know all the vicissitudes of the battle fought on 15th July 1410 between Grunwald and Tannenberg. The strategic talent of the King of Poland, as well as the gallantry of his cousin, were worthy of admiration. Nevertheless, at the outset, the Lithuanian wing of their army was routed by the German Knights. But in the second phase of the battle the latter were crushed in their turn by the Polish nobility, who on that day achieved its most brilliant victory.

The Order, whose Grand Master and chief dignitaries fell on the field of honour, seemed lost. In Pomerania, as in Prussia proper, one town after another and entire districts surrendered to the victors. A partition of the whole state between Poland, who hoped to recover the mouth of the Vistula, and Lithaania, who would have secured the mouth of the Niemen, was regarded as certain. Nothing of the kind took place. On their side also their forces were exhausted, and, in addition, serious strategical mistakes had been committed. They were obliged to raise the siege of Marienburg, valiantly defended by Henry von Plauen, under whose command the Order rallied and regained possession of all its territory. Therefore, the peace concluded at Torun in 1411 in no way corresponded with the hopes of Grunwald. Poland contented herself with insignificant concessions, and the question of Samogitia was regulated in an absurd manner. Jagiello and Vitold were to be its masters until their death, but then it was to return to the Order. After the treaty was signed each party began to accuse the other of not respecting its stipulations. The struggle was resumed three times. These by no means glorious wars offer little that is of interest. They ended in 1422 in a new treaty of peace which obliged the Order definitely to renounce Samogitia.

But the essential point was that after Grunwald all the prestige of the Order had disappeared. Its proceedings could still disquiet Poland and Lithuania, but it had ceased to be a danger to them. It still kept the whole of Prussia, with Danzig Pomerania and the district of Chelmno; but opposition to its rule was daily increasing in the very heart of its state. It still

posed as the defender of the faith against the barbarians; but
the keen interest that so violent and prolonged a conflict had
evoked in all Europe finished by enlightening impartial opinion on the true state of affairs. On the eve and the morrow of
Grunwald the two sides had carried out an intense propaganda to justify their cause. This propaganda was resumed at
the Council of Constance, before which the whole problem
was officially laid. The Polish contention was expounded in
an exceedingly eloquent manner in the treatises of Paul, the
son of Vladimir, rector and delegate of the University of Cracow. He affirmed the right of all nations, even should they be
pagans, to their territorial independence; he openly proclaimed that the doctrine of Christ should be spread by methods compatible with charity; he showed that the Teutonic
Order in the pursuit of its conquests had taken no account of
the conditions of a just war, established by Christian traditions. The Order, on its side, replied by an infamous pam-
phlet, the conclusions of which were inspired by the theme of
tyrannicide, which was defended at the same time by the famous Jean Petit in the interests of the Duke of Burgundy.
This coincidence gained for the Poles the support of the representatives of the King of France and of the University of
Paris.

What, however, most deeply impressed the whole of the
Council was what it saw before its eyes of the positive results
of the Polish-Lithuanian union. A delegation from distant
Samogitia came there to prove that even that only recently
regained province, following the example of the whole of
Lithuania which the Order had never been able to christian-
ize by force of arms, was in process of being converted spontaneously. And a Ruthenian delegation, with the Metropolitan of Kiev at its head, assured Pope Martin V, whose

election had just put an end to the schism of the west, that the schism of the east could on its side be liquidated, thanks to the efforts of Jagiello and Vitold.

These pacific efforts met with the warm approbation of the Pope and the Council, even though it was impossible for them to settle the political side of the conflict with the Order. Parallel with this armed conflict the development of closer relations between the nations united since 1386, and called upon to extend in common the boundaries of Christian civilization, was carried on without a pause. To gain this end it was necessary, in the first place, to regulate the union from the constitutional standpoint. The compromise to which the way had been opened by Queen Jadwiga avoided the primitive idea of an incorporation, pure and simple, of the Lithuanian and Ruthenian territories with the kingdom of Poland. In 1401 Jagiello delegated his grand-ducal power to Vitold, and a statute of autonomy was granted to all Lithuania with her Ruthenian provinces, while at the same time she remained bound to Poland by feudal ties.

This principle was enforced in 1413, when Poles and Lithuanians met at Horodlo on the Bug to sign new articles of union. These articles, dated the 2nd of October, guaranteed to Lithuania that she should have her own Grand Duke, even after Vitold's death, it being understood that this Grand Duke would be nominated by the King of Poland in agreement with the qualified representatives of the two countries. Similarly the throne of Poland could not be filled in the future without the agreement of the Grand Duke and the Lithuanians. Invoking the common interests of the two parties, the principle of absolute solidarity in foreign policy was once more stressed. But what distinguishes the Union of Horodlo from all the other Polish-Lithuanian agreements is the idea of perpetuating it by a tie higher and more intimate than that of legal settlements: the *élite* of the two nations were to form one single, united family, thanks to that 'mystery of charity' which the document drawn up by the Polish nobility extols as the fundamental element of public life.

With this object the representatives of forty-seven houses of that nobility adopted at Horodlo the same number of Lithuanian boyars, granting them, as well as their kindred, the right of bearing the coats of arms of the families into whose bosoms they were thus admitted. These coats of arms symbolized the close solidarity which for centuries had united the clans of the Polish knighthood, and which was now to extend to the newly adopted fraternity of Lithuanian origin. Under the inspiration of this principle it was at once decided that delegates of the two countries, such as had assembled in 1401 and in 1413, should henceforth regularly hold 'conventions and parliaments,' so that the parliamentary institutions which were in course of being developed in Poland could soon be formed in Lithuania likewise. Other articles inserted in the Act of Union granted new liberties and privileges on the Polish model to the inhabitants of the Grand Duchy, completing those which they had obtained in 1387.

The initiative taken at Horodlo proved exceedingly fruitful in results. The Polish-Lithuanian union definitely ceased to be an affair negotiated between the dynasty of Gedymin and a few lords of Cracow: the two nations were thereby associated, assimilated into one another, and growing accustomed to treat together all the questions that concerned them. Increasing numbers of Lithuanians came to Poland, either in the entourage of the king or to go through their university studies there, while Poles crowded into Lithuania to take their part in the Grand Duke's military campaigns and to serve in his court or his chancellery.

For Vitold, solicitous as he was for the prestige of his

Grand Duchy, and for the extension of its administrative
limits in the federated State, favoured, none the less, the entrance of Polish civilization into all the territories subject to
him and into every domain of life. He exercised at the same
time considerable personal influence even in purely Polish
affairs. It is true that he followed more particularly the eastern questions by maintaining the ancient Lithuanian pretensions to the republic of Novgorod in rivalry with Moscow, where, moreover, a grandson of Vitold, subject to his
tutelage, had been reigning since 1425, and by intervening
as arbitrator in the interminable conflicts between the Tartar khans. But he also appeared at the side of the King of
Poland in their relations with Hungary and Bohemia, with
Brandenburg and Denmark, even with France and England.
It was then, in the course of the fifteen years that followed
Grunwald and Horodlo, that the collaboration of the two
princes, who each complemented the other in an extraordinary manner, gave all the hoped-for results.

The authority which they enjoyed in Europe and even with
the emperors of the Greeks and the Turks, an authority
which increased, above all, after the Council of Constance,
seemed to be manifested with the greatest splendour at the
congress which assembled at Luck in Volhynia in the beginning of 1429. There, surrounded by their eastern vassals,
Jagiello and Vitold solemnly received, together with a papal
legate, the Emperor Sigismund of Luxemburg, who some
years since had added the crowns of Germany and Bohemia
to that of Hungary. Despite treaties of alliance renewed on
several occasions, Sigismund's attitude in respect to Poland
had always remained equivocal. An ally of the Order at the
time of Grunwald, he had subsequently attempted to arbi-
trate in its conflict with Jagiello and Vitold. But these two
soon had occasion to learn the Emperor's partiality. In re-

turn they profited by the embarrassments that the Hussite movement caused him, to intervene in the affairs of Bohemia. The sympathy which they found in the Czech opposition, which had even offered them the crown, naturally disquieted Sigismund. A strong reaction against the doctrines of Huss, condemned by the Church, had certainly arisen in Poland, but the two Slav nations remained in close contact, and the Pope even considered entrusting to the King of Poland that pacification of Bohemia which was not succeeding under Sigismund. This was precisely what the latter wished to prevent at all costs; and this explains why he profited by the Congress of Luck to create a serious internal embarrassment for Poland herself by attempting to break the solidarity of that country with Lithuania and her Grand Duke.

Clearly perceiving that Vitold's official position did not correspond either to the role that he was actually playing or to his ambition, he suggested raising him to the dignity of King of Lithuania. It was easy to foresee that the Poles would oppose this by invoking the articles of the Union which considered the Grand Duchy as an integral part of the kingdom of Poland. In fact, they entered immediately into irritating discussions on the interpretation of these articles, and a want of tact on the part of the Polish chancellery exasperated Vitold, who, at the outset, had himself hesitated before so delicate a proposition. Jagiello's attitude complicated the situation. As the sons who were at last borne to him by his fourth wife, a Lithuanian princess, had no hereditary right to the crown of Poland and were obliged to be elected to it by the nobility, the old king was, in principle, favourable to the creation of a Lithuanian kingdom which his sons should inherit after the death of Vitold, who had no sons. In this case, their election by the Poles, who had no intention of breaking the union of the two countries, would be a pure formality. Consequently, while trying to avoid an imperial intervention dangerous for the Polish-Lithuanian union, Jagiello was quite ready to authorize the coronation of Vitold, but the latter died on 27th October 1430.

The conflict which then broke out seems to us the best proof of the merits of that Grand Duke, who, in spite of inevitable collisions, had so well known how to reconcile the individual interests of Lithuania with the principle of her highly advantageous union with Poland. As his successor, Jagiello appointed one of his own brothers, the only one still living—the turbulent Swidrygiello. The latter was immediately possessed by the idea of modifying the legal conditions of the Polish-Lithuanian union; the Poles on their part claimed the cession of Podolia and Volhynia, holding that these provinces had only been administered by Vitold in virtue of a personal right. In the civil war that ensued grave mistakes were committed on both sides. Swidrygiello allied himself with the Teutonic Order, which broke the peace treaty of 1422 and invaded Poland: the latter opposed another Grand Duke to him in the person of Sigismund, Vitold's brother, so that Lithuania found herself divided into two hostile camps. Despite a final victory that was compared, very erroneously, to that of Grunwald, and despite the renewal of the Union of Horodlo by the Grand Duke Sigismund, these fratricidal struggles were prolonged in a deplorable fashion and were still going on when Jagiello died on 1st June 1434. He had not succeeded in checking them, but this failure on the part of the old king did not prevent the following generations from rendering homage to a reign of nearly half a century which, in spite of a violent final shock, had definitely created a new Poland, the great Jagiellonian Poland.

9

Varna and Danzig

THE founder of the Jagiello dynasty, a king of alien origin desirous of gaining the confidence of the Polish nobility, had granted to it new privileges, in a whole series of charters, including the famous guarantee that no one should be imprisoned without a trial. The nobility, however, had only accepted these charters with the explicit reservation that it was free to choose the successors of the king. Legally, therefore, the Polish throne was henceforth elective. In point of fact, there had never been any doubt that Jagiello's eldest son, who, like his father, was called Ladislas, would become king after him.

In 1434 the future hero of Varna was only ten years old. It was, therefore, necessary to institute a regency. There was hardly room for doubt that the real power would fall to the eminent Zbigniew Olesnicki, the Bishop of Cracow, who had succeeded in counterbalancing even the influence of a Vitold. To this day we see nearly the whole of the Polish history of this epoch through the eyes of this great statesman, because the illustrious contemporary historian, John Dlugosz, was his disciple and passionate admirer. And he was not wrong. We may even add that the imposing figure of the first Polish cardinal belongs indisputably to general history. In the first place, Olesnicki was a distinguished humanist, admired by the future Pius II. This in no wise prevented him from being an exemplary prelate, of perfect integrity and piety. And this European of the Renaissance epoch, this prince of the Church, possessed of a universal outlook, was at the same time a great Polish patriot who embodied the national consciousness of all his generation. But he had one great defect, more serious than that of a restless ambition which only became disquieting towards the end of his career: he was a doctrinaire. He proved it in the vital question of Poland's relations with Lithuania, desiring as he did to observe to the letter clauses which no longer corresponded to the actual situation. He proved it in the conflict between the Pope and the Council, a conflict which had such a strong repercussion on Polish affairs, when, together with the great majority of the Polish clergy, whose representatives had played a considerable role at Constance and Basle, he remained attached to the extreme limits of the conciliar doctrine in spite of his country's official neutrality.

This twofold attitude was later to create serious difficulties for Jagiello's two sons. During their minority, Olesnicki and his collaborators, among whom were several members of his family, had, in any case, the merit of putting an end to the civil war which had been raging since the death of Vitold, and which was, at the same time, a new war with the Teutonic Order. At the end of 1435 the latter was obliged to sign a 'perpetual' peace, guaranteed by its own subjects in Prussia, who thus began to play a part, soon to be a decisive one, in the Order's relations with Poland. At the same time, the Order abandoned Swidrygiello, who had suffered an irreparable defeat, but who still held out in the Ruthenian territories. At one moment it could even seem as if the Jagiellonian State would become a tripartite federation, which would not have been without certain advantages. However, the Ruthenian question was settled otherwise, following the principle recognized on the eve of Jagiello's death. The Ruthenian provinces, whose autonomy, in fact, deprived them of the privileges which both Poland and Lithuania proper successively obtained, were granted, some of them the Polish law which they had long demanded, others an equal standing in the provinces of the Grand Duchy. The Grand Duchy then obtained a first charter which was no longer limited to Lithuania proper, and no longer drew any distinction between Catholics and Orthodox.

Having seen the different parts of the Grand Duchy gradually united and pacified, at least to outward appearance, under the rule of Vitold's brother, Olesnicki turned to the grave problems by which Poland was then faced. Sigismund of Luxemburg having died in 1437, his son-in-law, Albrecht of Austria, was to have succeeded him not only in Germany but also in Bohemia and Hungary. The Poles, however, knew very well that the accession of the Hapsburgs was not looked upon with favourable eyes by the national parties in these two kingdoms. They therefore aimed at gaining at least one of these crowns for their own dynasty. A Jagiellonian candidature to the throne of Bohemia, already considered in the time of Jagiello and Vitold, seemed particularly opportune, the more so as ties with Silesia could thus be renewed. This project suited, above all, a fairly considerable group of the Polish nobility which had allowed itself to be gained over by Hussite influences. For Olesnicki, on the contrary, this was precisely a reason for opposing it, and although the younger brother of King Ladislas, young Casimir, had been sent to Bohemia to join his partisans there, his candidature was not seriously advanced, and completely failed.

Soon, however, in 1439, Albrecht of Austria died in his

turn without leaving a direct heir, and this time Olesnicki, who had triumphed over his adversaries within the State, decided to place Ladislas himself on the throne of Hungary. It was not only a case of re-establishing the union with that purely Catholic country in conditions more favourable to Poland than in the time of Louis of Anjou; the Bishop of Cracow intended to go farther. Neither Sigismund nor Albrecht had succeeded in repulsing the Turkish danger, which, after the conquest of the Balkans, was looming ever more menacingly on the frontiers of Hungary to the apprehension of the Christian world. What glory for Poland should her king place himself at the head of a new Crusade, save Hungary, deliver the southern Slavs, and go to the help of Constantinople! The Greeks themselves could then be won over to the Roman Church in a more efficacious manner than by the Union of Florence, which won little sympathy from Olesnicki, because it was concluded by Eugenius IV in opposition to the Council of Basle.

No one could reproach the Polish statesman for his large vision, and for having dreamt of so great a mission for his country and his king. But, on the one hand, he had no conception of the difficulties that awaited Ladislas in Hungary itself, and, on the other hand, he had failed to understand that it was not the Council of Basle with its antipope, but the legitimate Pontiff alone, possessing a true comprehension of the eastern question, who could efficaciously encourage the projected Crusade. In Hungary the King of Poland had first of all been elected without dispute; but the Queen Dowager Elizabeth of Luxemburg, after having given birth to a posthumous son of Albrecht of Austria, like his rival named Ladislas, showed herself firmly resolved to secure for him the whole of his paternal heritage. From 1440 to 1442 Hungary was therefore torn by a civil war between the two

Ladislases, both crowned and each supported by his own party. And when at last an agreement, at least provisional, ensured the sovereignty to the Jagiello and allowed him to turn against the Turks, Poland, after so much time and money wasted, had lost patience, and Olesnicki was ill pleased at the compromise with the Hapsburgs having been concluded under the auspices of a legate of Eugenius IV who formed the league against the infidels.

Instead, then, of fresh reinforcements from Poland, the king only received reiterated appeals demanding his return. But he himself remained faithful to the idea that had led him to Hungary. Having come to an understanding with the Pope, and pronounced in favour of the Union of Florence which he considered useful for his Ruthenian provinces, he counted on the support of the Catholic Powers of the west. During his first Balkan campaign in 1443, this support was entirely lacking. Nevertheless, with his Hungarian army led by John Hunyadi, as well as with the group of Polish knights who had remained attached to his cause, he achieved extraordinary successes, such as the Christian world, assailed by the Ottomans, had never known, and was for centuries not to know again. As a victor he crossed Serbia, penetrated into Bulgaria, and only the advanced season forced him to a return which was marked by new exploits. The following year the Turks offered him a ten years' truce. But at Szeged Ladislas refused to ratify the treaty and proclaimed that he would take up the struggle again until the Turks were driven out of Europe. For the king and the legate, Julian Cesarini, had just been informed that the Christian fleet, provided by Eugenius IV, his Venetian fellow citizens, and Philip of Burgundy, had set out to occupy the Straits and to prevent Murad II from transporting the bulk of his troops from Asia to Europe. Unfortunately, this fleet failed in its task, and it was near Varna on the shores of the Black Sea that Ladislas flung himself into a hopeless battle. In a heroic charge recalling that of the French at Nikopoli, this twenty-year-old king died with the greater part of his Polish comrades, as well as the papal legate. Hungary was saved from destruction by Hunyadi, but the fate of the Balkans, including Constantinople, whose emperor had sent despairing appeals to the Jagiello king, was sealed for hundreds of years.

For long, men refused to believe in the death of the hero of Varna. In Poland, however, where the absence of the king had been severely felt, there was the wish to replace him as quickly as possible. Yet it was not until three years later, in 1447, that his younger brother, Casimir, was crowned in the Vavel cathedral of Cracow. From the beginning he had been the only serious candidate, though there had been talk of Frederick of Brandenburg and Boleslas of Masovia in order to hasten the decision of the Grand Duke of Lithuania. For Casimir had governed the country of his ancestors since 1440, the Grand Duke Sigismund having been assassinated by the leaders of an aristocracy which he had oppressed. This Lithuanian aristocracy, whose influence had increased during the civil war and Casimir's minority, was not willing that he should accept the throne of Poland without having received a guarantee that the Grand Duchy should no longer be subordinate to the kingdom, and that the disputed provinces of Volhynia and Podolia should belong to Lithuania.

When Casimir at last reached Poland he had made the two parties accept a provisional compromise which he succeeded, after six years of persevering efforts, in making final. The new king had none of his brother's mystic and confident enthusiasm. Destined, like his father, to reign for half a century, like him he distinguished himself by his long patience, while at the same time surpassing him by his energy and the clearness of his political conceptions. Resolved to avoid, at all costs, a new internal conflict, he saw clearly that the consequences of that which had followed the death of Vitold could only be effaced by an essential change in the conditions of the Polish-Lithuanian union. He attached little importance to the process of signing new documents as his predecessor Sigismund had done, dissembling a doubtful loyalty. He simply gave the Poles to understand that Lithuania, christianized and organized on the basis of western civilization, was now fit to be placed on a completely equal footing. He made the Lithuanians renounce the institution of a Grand Duke of their own, whose personal ambitions could provoke new dissensions between the two countries. To which of these countries certain disputed territories should belong was, in reality, a question regarded with great indifference by their common monarch, as long as arms were not taken up to contest it. Finally, he admitted the established *status quo,* which, in fact, stood for an equitable division, the chief part of Volhynia remaining with the Lithuanians, and Podolia, with the exception of her eastern borders, with the Poles.

In order to reach this satisfactory result Casimir had been obliged to isolate the irreconcilables on both sides, who were displeased at seeing the king restrain their inordinate influence. In Poland, the oligarchy of Little Poland in general, including Olesnicki, despite the Roman purple which he had obtained not without difficulties, were gradually put aside for the benefit of the gentry and the representatives of Great Poland. In Lithuania the Palatine of Wilno, John Gasztold, who had abused his power during Casimir's minority, now in vain stood forward as the chief of an opposition of which one member after another rallied to the partisans of the king.

But the latter was well aware that nothing could better

cement the Polish-Lithuanian union than a great task undertaken in common and responding to the hopes of Krewo.
The realization of these could not be effected without the
redintegration of the territories lost in the past by the two
nations, and the extension of the federated State to its natural limits: the Baltic and the Black Sea. As regards the latter,
the disaster of Varna, the consequences of which were soon
to be manifest in the political situation of Poland and Lithuania, did not encourage the resumption of any projects of so
risky a nature. Moreover, for the moment, the seaboard between the mouths of the Dniester and the Dnieper remained
beyond dispute subject to Casimir, as formerly to Vitold.
On the other hand, the Baltic was only accessible by a small
corner of Samogitia, as long as the Teutonic Order still kept
the mouths of the Vistula and the Niemen.

Casimir, therefore, closely followed the internal crisis
through which the State of that Order was then passing. The
discontent that was increasing among its subjects had led
them to create a Prussian League, which began by defending
the rights of the nobility and the towns and which finished
by open revolt. Having seized nearly all the strongholds of
the country, the insurgents had recourse, in the beginning of
1454, to the King of Poland, spontaneously placing the whole
of Prussia, naturally including what had once been Polish
Pomerania, under his sovereignty. Casimir, who had just
regulated Polish-Lithuanian relations, did not hesitate to
accept so tempting an offer. True, this time it was Poland
who was breaking the latest treaty of peace, but she did it at
the request of the populations concerned, who turned to her,
attracted by liberties unknown under the rule of the Order.
And no one foresaw that the resistance of the latter was to
impose upon Poland a war of thirteen years, the result of
which was to fall far short of its initial hopes.

Neither the Prussian League nor the Poles had sufficiently

reckoned with the international relations and the material resources which were still at the disposal of the Teutonic Knights. A victory that was almost unexpected, gained over the Polish nobility at Chojnice at the outset of hostilities, enabled the Order to gain time and organize its defence. On the other hand, King Casimir at once experienced a severe disappointment in the discovery that the Lithuanians, misjudging their own interests, did not intend to bring in all their forces. The Samogitians alone attacked Memel and cut the communications between Prussia and Livonia from which the Order was trying in vain to draw reinforcements. The army of the Order was composed chiefly of mercenaries, better disciplined and more accustomed to prolonged operations than the mass of the Polish gentry whom, following tradition, the king had chosen to use. However, Casimir was soon obliged to have recourse, on his side, to mercenary troops or to gain over those whom the Order could no longer pay regularly and who, in 1457, sold the capital, Marienburg, to Poland. Even then the war was far from being decided. Dreary and ruinous, it no longer had the character of a conflict between two nations as at the time of Grunwald. The German element predominated in the Prussian League which was particularly enraged against the Order, and the town of Danzig, in which the majority of the population was at this epoch already German, rendered the most signal services to the king by providing him with large sums of money, and by successfully undertaking the naval war against Denmark, the ally of the Order.

At last, from about 1462, Poland redoubled her efforts, both military and diplomatic. Her troops, better commanded, gained successes which effaced the deplorable impression of the battle of Chojnice, and thrust back the troops of the Order towards East Prussia. Laborious negotiations, in the course of which one European Power after another attempted to play the part of mediator, prepared the compromise which served as the basis of the treaty of 1466. This second Peace of Torun was infinitely more advantageous for Poland than the first in 1411. This time Danzig Pomerania, with the territory of Chelmno, was after a century and a half of alienation restored to her, together with a part of Prussia proper, including the port of Elbing, Marienburg, and the bishopric of Varmia or Ermeland. All this territory, which secured the kingdom extensive access to the sea, and was called henceforth Western or Royal Prussia, remained in the possession of Poland until the first partition.

But the rest of Prussia, with Königsberg as its new capital, remained under the rule of the Order, which Casimir vainly endeavoured to tranfer to the Turkish or Tartar borderlands where it could have resumed its original vocation. However, this East Prussia was no longer to be an independent state but a fief of Poland. According to the treaty each Grand Master was to pay homage to the king and provide him with reinforcements in case of necessity. In addition, the Order was to renounce its exclusively Teutonic character. It undertook to receive Polish knights to the number of half of its members.

The whole question now was whether this treaty would be strictly respected in the future. And in the last resort this again depended on the extent of authority and power at the disposal of the Jagiellonian State. In any case, and in spite of the disquieting concessions which he had been obliged to make, Casimir could be proud of the results obtained. One of the essential objects of the Polish-Lithuanian union, foreseen, perhaps, in part, by Casimir the Great, pursued in vain by Ladislas Jagiello, was attained by one of his sons, whose kingdom now stretched literally from one sea to the other.

10

The Zenith of a Dynasty

HISTORIANS are unanimous in paying homage to all that
Casimir Jagiello effected during the first half of his long
reign. They are far less so as regards the second part of that
reign. It has, in fact, been observed that the policy of the
king, at the outset dictated only by the vital interests of his
people, subsequently became an essential dynastic policy.
But this is no matter for surprise. The Jagiello king only
followed the example of the other monarchs of his time. All
the great states which were then being created in Europe
owe their foundation in a large measure to dynastic interests.
As regards Casimir, they were the more natural inasmuch as
he had thirteen children, six of whom were growing sons,
all born of his marriage with Elizabeth of Austria, a marriage that was concluded on the eve of the Prussian war.

This 'mother of the Jagiellos' was the sister of the hero of
Varna's former rival, Ladislas the Posthumous, who, since
1444, had been the undisputed sovereign of Hungary as well
as of Bohemia. After his premature death in 1457 his Austrian possessions naturally returned to the younger line of
the Hapsburgs, whose head was then the Emperor Frederick

III. But the two kingdoms which Ladislas had inherited through his mother could now be considered as the heritage of his sister, the Queen of Poland, and her children. Such was the principle invoked at the outset by Casimir, who only awaited the opportune moment to avail himself of it, and thus to resume, with a new legal basis, former projects which consisted in establishing the Polish-Lithuanian dynasty either in Bohemia or in Hungary, or even in both countries at once.

Before taking any steps in this direction Casimir was naturally obliged to wait for the end of the thirteen years' war against the Order. He therefore did not oppose the elections which, carried out in Hungary and Bohemia after the death of his father-in-law, summoned native kings to the throne: Matthias Corvinus, son of John Hunyadi, and George of Podiebrad.

The King of Poland even allied himself with the latter in 1462, and he also interested himself in the vast design of perpetual peace and European organization that the King of Bohemia propagated with his French collaborator, Antoine Marini. George of Podiebrad's religious attitude, which favoured the moderate Hussitism of the Utraquists, despite his project of a league against the infidel, greatly disquieted the Holy See. Urged by Casimir to confirm the Peace of Torun, Paul II demanded of him in return that he should advance against the Hussite king. But it was not by force of arms directed against the national King of Bohemia that the Jagiello sovereign aimed at obtaining his throne. It was through Podiebrad himself, whom he supported by overtures of conciliation, that he won the promise that the King of Poland's eldest son Ladislas should succeed him at Prague. This prince was, in fact, elected King of Bohemia when George died in 1471. But there was also another candidate

in the person of Matthias of Hungary, who, in contradistinction to Casimir, had become the instrument of the pontifical
policy directed against George, and now claimed the price
of his efforts.

The King of Poland attempted to prevent his intervention
in Bohemia by sending into Hungary another of his sons,
young Casimir, whom a party hostile to Matthias promised
to raise to the throne. But the Hungarian expedition of the
future saint was a complete failure, and only exasperated
Corvinus against the Jagiellos. In the dispute for the crown
of Bohemia he carried out a war against them which ended
in 1478 with a very precarious compromise: Casimir's eldest
son kept Bohemia proper, but Silesia and Moravia remained
in the hands of Matthias of Hungary, who, on his part,
claimed the title of King of Bohemia. This equivocal situation lasted until the death of Corvinus in 1490. The King of
Poland then profited by the disappearance of his adversary
to claim again the throne of Hungary for one of his sons.
This time he obtained his object, but after a prolonged
struggle between two Jagiello brothers: John Albert, originally supported by his father, and Ladislas of Bohemia, who
won and thus united the two kingdoms, also restoring to
Bohemia the provinces which had been detached from her.

This brief account of the essential facts will suffice to show
both the advantages and disadvantages of Casimir's dynastic
plan, completely realized on the eve of his death in 1492.
The triumph of his house was manifest. It had united under
its rule so extensive a territory—from the gates of Moscow
to the waters of the Adriatic—as to surpass by far that of any
other European Power. This immense Jagiellonian federation seemed a valuable element of equilibrium and peace in
Europe, as none of the Jagiellos dreamt of war, unless it were
to oppose the advance of the infidel, against whom an appar-

ently insurmountable barrier was now raised. This federal
system, heightening the prestige of each of the states that
composed it, did not suppress the independence of any of
them: because the Jagiellos respected their national traditions and the liberties they had acquired, while their strict
solidarity removed any possibility of conflict among these
states.

Naturally, Poland, together with the other federated states,
profited on her side by the advantages of this situation; as
it was her king who had created it she became, in conformity, moreover, with geographical conditions, the centre of
what might be called the Jagiellonian system. But also it was
Poland who had been the first to suffer from the complications that the dynastic policy of Casimir had brought in its
train. Thus, during the Bohemian war, Matthias Corvinus
allied himself with the Teutonic Order, which considered
that the opportunity of breaking the Peace of Torun had
now arrived. The agreement of 1478 forced the Grand Master to pay that homage to the King of Poland which had been
for long withheld; but once the conditions of 1466 were
called into question, the Prussian problem again became the
source of troubles liable to open again at any moment.

This was all the more disquieting inasmuch as the Order
was now regaining the support of the Empire. The House of
Hapsburg, which had held the imperial power since 1437,
had never regarded the success of the Jagiellos in Bohemia
and Hungary with favour, and Maximilian I, far more energetic than his father, Frederick III, had also presented himself as a candidate for the succession to Corvinus. Unwilling
definitely to renounce it, he entered into relations with the
adversaries of the Jagiellos and, like Matthias, he did not
limit himself to the greatly enfeebled Teutonic Order, but
also took into consideration a more formidable enemy who
was threatening Casimir from the east.

We have, in fact, reached the moment to emphasize that it is precisely on that side, indisputably neglected for years together, that the great king, absorbed in the affairs of central Europe, had allowed the growth of a twofold danger, soon to become overwhelming.

Let us begin with that one of the two which was presented by the ally whom Matthias Corvinus and after him the Hapsburgs believed they had found in the borderlands, hitherto almost unknown, between Europe and Asia. We know that since the fourteenth century Lithuania had met with a rival in the rapidly growing power of Moscow. A certain equilibrium of their opposing forces was gradually established. In 1449 a treaty concluded between Casimir Jagiello and the Grand Duke Basil II fixed the spheres of their respective influence. But Basil, who had exhausted himself in long internal struggles from which a strongly centralized state at last emerged, was in 1462 succeeded by his son Ivan the Severe, who soon married the heiress of the Palaeologi, and who was determined to extend the domination of Moscow— a third Rome—over all the Russias. A few years, the same that Casimir had devoted to the Bohemian war, were sufficient for Ivan III to put an end to the independence of the Republic of Novgorod, which, after having counted in vain on Lithuanian help, was crushed and annexed by Moscow. This was a first warning to Casimir which drove him to seek the most varied alliances against so inconvenient a neighbour. But he was not able to prevent fresh successes on the part of Ivan, who, towards the end of Casimir's reign, when the latter was preoccupied with the Hungarian question, began in time of peace to appropriate one after another of the Lithuanian Grand Duchy's frontier districts.

However, these losses, humiliating, but, so far, not very appreciable, disquieted the king far less than a complete change of the political situation which was taking place in the direction of the Black Sea. Here also warnings had not been wanting. Following in his youth Vitold's example, Casimir had established good relations with the Tartar khanate that was the nearest to his frontiers, that of the Crimea where the Gherai family reigned, benefiting by the support of the Jagiellos and, in general, remaining faithful and devoted to them. Moreover, the rich commercial city of Kaffa, an old Genoese colony in the Crimea, had placed itself under the protection of the King of Poland. This protection did not prevent the Turks from taking possession of that town in 1475, and the Khan Mengli Gherai, whom they had made prisoner, soon returned to the Crimea as vassal of the Sultan. Neither was Moldavia, which had many times recognized the suzerainty of Poland, supported in the desperate struggles that she waged against the Ottoman power, especially since the accession of Stephen the Great. In 1484 the Turks tore from her two ports of great importance: Kilia, at the mouth of the Danube, and Akkerman, at the mouth of the Dniester. Thus they had reached as far as the frontiers of the Polish-Lithuanian State which was almost imperceptibly losing its access to the Black Sea, the steppes between the Dniester and the Dnieper having become the field of action for the Tartars of the Crimea, in subjection to Turkey. Their invasions were becoming, at the same time, a perpetual scourge to the Ruthenian lands of Poland and of Lithuania; the latter even entered the risky path of an entente with the Tartars of the Volga, the old Golden Horde, rendered discontented by the emancipation of the Horde of the Crimea.

Without neglecting this method, which could serve equally against Moscow, Casimir was too far-sighted not to be aware that other means were needed to deal with a situation which was seriously compromising the security of all the Jagiellonian states. He knew also that nothing could more effectively heighten their prestige in Europe than victories over the infidels, victories which would avenge the memory of his brother. But while organizing the defence of the Polish-Lithuanian frontiers, the king, now grown old, bequeathed the great task which confronted his dynasty to his sons and successors. He envisaged this task as common to Ladislas, in respect of his title as King of Hungary, to John Albert, whose election he recommended to the Poles, and to Alexander, who was to inherit Lithuania. Lithuania, the most directly threatened by Moscow, was to have her own Grand Duke again; but the latter, while occupying himself more especially with his relations with Ivan III, naturally was also to collaborate in the solution of the Turco-Tartar problem.

Moreover, Casimir had prepared for his sons an excellent team of collaborators in Poland and Lithuania, chosen from the flower of the two nations whom he left closely united with each other. The generation of the Olesnickis and the Gasztolds had long since disappeared. In the kingdom new aristocratic families were grouped around the throne, but it was, above all, the gentry favoured by the king that were coming into power. At the side of the Senate formed by the ancient royal council, the deputies elected by the provincial dietines assembled in a second Chamber, which, together with the Senate, constituted the Polish Diet. Its composition was fixed before its functioning powers, but the determination of these could not be long delayed, since the dietines, of which the Diet was the emanation and the central organ, had to be consulted by the king according to the statutes of 1454 on all important questions of public life. In the Grand Duchy, on the contrary, the general Diets had so far only a very restricted role, and the dietines were non-existent. The Council of the Grand Duke alone limited his power, which fact Alexander officially recognized at his accession, and which left the door open to the rival influences of a few powerful ducal and aristocratic families. We may name at least one, the Radziwills, who were henceforth always to occupy one of the first places—if not the first—in Lithuania.

This constitutional development, fertile in consequences for all the future, enables us to understand better the critical years which followed the death of Casimir in 1492. Not only Ladislas, whose excessive weakness in regard to the States of Bohemia and Hungary has become proverbial, but also his brothers were not entirely free to make their own decisions. Even John Albert, arbitrary though he was, perhaps the only one of the Jagiellos who dreamt of absolute rule, had to begin his reign by conciliating the Diets of 1493 and 1496—the first Diets we know much about—by means of new concessions to the nobility and gentry which were to the detriment of the other social classes. Alexander, who succeeded him in Poland in 1501, thus re-establishing the personal union with Lithuania, hesitated, up to his death in 1506, between the interests of his dynasty and the pressure that was exercised upon him either by the Senate of the kingdom, or by the parties who were fighting each other in the bosom of the Grand Ducal Council, or, finally, by the Polish gentry who, in 1505, compelled him to recognize the legislative power of the Diet.

All this did not prevent the members of the dynasty from at times preparing their common political action in secret meetings—such as a family congress held in Hungary in 1494. This is why the definite result of that action, the expedition to the Black Sea undertaken in 1497, remains enveloped in a mystery which historical research attempts in vain to pierce. After having proclaimed that he was marching against the Turks to recapture Akkerman, Kilia, and perhaps even Kaffa, John Albert suddenly turned upon Stephen the Great of Moldavia. We are ignorant how far this fatal decision was justified by the voivode's action. Be that as it may, the latter inflicted a. sanguinary defeat on the Polish nobility in the forests of Bukovina. His success was aided by the Turks, who in the following year penetrated far into Polish territory, and by the connivance of the Hungarians, who, in spite of dynastic ties and a friendship that elsewhere was traditional, were always Poland's rivals on the soil of Moldavia. It was only Alexander of Lithuania, advancing at the same time towards the Black Sea, who achieved some successes over the Tartars and prevented a complete collapse of John Albert's army. Ladislas of Hungary had to confine himself to subsequently reconciling Stephen the Great with the Jagiellos.

The latter had, in any case, suffered a defeat which put an end to their active policy in the eastern question. This defeat was, in addition, followed immediately by another which most directly affected Lithuania. Alexander, attacked by Ivan on the morrow of his father's death, had hoped to appease his neighbour by marrying the latter's daughter. But this marriage only provided the Grand Duke of Moscow with fresh pretexts to recommence a war, the aim of which was to wrest from Lithuania all her Ruthenian provinces. His victorious campaign in 1500 enabled Ivan to conquer by one blow a substantial third part of these. The frontier of the two states which formerly approached Moscow was thrust back to the gates of Kiev. With the intention of repairing these losses, Alexander allied himself on one side with Livonia, and on the other with the last khan of the Golden Horde; but he was not able to support at the opportune moment the efforts of his allies, the second of whom was crushed by Mengli Gherai of the Crimea, the ally of Ivan of Moscow.

A truce concluded in 1503 ratified, at least provisionally, the situation created by the aggressor.

Even after the death of Ivan, Alexander did not succeed in his retaliation, and before he himself died in the following year he had to content himself with seeing one of the most dangerous invasions by the Khan of the Crimea repulsed. It goes without saying that this decline of the power of the Jagiellos on the eastern side encouraged at the same time their western adversaries. In order the more efficaciously to react against the Peace of Torun, the Teutonic Order had elected a prince of the Empire, Frederick of Saxony, as Grand Master; and neither John Albert nor Alexander succeeded in making him pay the vassal's homage which was due to them. But, in spite of all these sinister facts, the crisis which had followed so close upon the zenith of the Jagiellonian dynasty was not irreparable. In 1500 the three brothers had concluded an alliance with France which crowned the diplomatic relations that had been already knit in the course of the fifteenth century with their first tangible result, and which could become a very valuable instrument in their rivalry with the House of Hapsburg. The King of England himself did not fail to appeal to them when projecting a new league against the Turks.

Moreover, we must not forget that John Albert, who died shortly after the disaster of Bukovina, Alexander, the least gifted of all the Jagiellos, and the indolent Ladislas, the eldest who survived them, were not the only representatives of the family. It is true that their brother Casimir had died young, giving his glorious family a saint, for he was soon canonized by the Church. It is also true that another brother, Frederick, archbishop and cardinal, had passed away in 1503 without having rendered the services that were expected of him. But the youngest of the six princes, Sigismund, who had long waited for a position equal to that of his brothers, had matured in the course of these years; and his high qualities, which showed themselves on several occasions, made him, with good reason, the hope of his dynasty and of Poland.

11

The Epoch of the First Congress of Vienna

DESPITE all the splendour of the fifteenth century, it is the following century that national tradition considers Poland's 'golden century.' It is, therefore, peculiarly instructive to study its essential elements in order to penetrate into the significance of our history, and to realize the manner in which its spirit has been interpreted by succeeding generations.

Nearly half of this sixteenth century, to the memorials of which Poland attaches so much value, was filled by the reign of Sigismund I—from 1506 to 1548. No chronicle comparable with that of Dlugosz has drawn an adequate picture of it. Fortunately, a discerning and well documented contemporary has left us an immense collection of diplomatic papers and even confidential letters, whose texts, written in the beautiful Latin of the Renaissance, evoke before our eyes all the incidents of this epoch. Above all, they show us the fundamental principle of the whole of Sigismund I's policy and of that of his collaborators, which was the constant desire of ensuring to Poland the peace and security indispensable to her internal development. Such was, in fact, the perma-

nent anxiety of the king, to whom, more by way of character-
izing his wisdom, prudence, and noble moderation than to
record his age, the surname of Old was given. Such was, in
equal measure, the preoccupation of the remarkable states-
men who surrounded him. Among these two groups are dis-
tinguishable which at times appeared to be hostile parties.
The one, which had the Archbishop John Laski and his family at its head, certainly held bolder ideas than the other, led
by the Chancellor Christopher Szydlowiecki and his friend,
the Vice-Chancellor Peter Tomicki. But if these groups differed in temperament, and often, also, in the orientation of
their foreign relations, it would be an exaggeration to look
for an opposition of principle between them at the outset. It
was, however, the second, which always inclined to the most
nicely balanced solutions, indeed, to compromises and to
half measures, which finally came uppermost and to which
the king rallied.

The best method of comprehending the diverse and complex problems of the king's foreign policy is to group them
in their mutual relations against the background of an international congress which dealt with all of them. This
congress, which closed in Vienna three hundred years before
another better-known congress that aimed at determining the
composition of modern Europe, did not meet until 1515.
But the principal events of the first nine years of Sigismund I's
reign seem to converge to its deliberations. First elected
Grand Duke of Lithuania, then King of Poland, he at once
occupied himself on parallel lines with the two capital questions for each of these countries, the Muscovite danger and
the situation in Prussia.

In the east it was necessary to put a final stop to the conquests of a neighbour who, in Alexander's time, had been
able to advance almost with impunity. A first war, under-

taken by Sigismund in 1507 under sufficiently favourable conditions, was complicated by the rebellion of Prince Michael Glinski, who, complaining, not without reason, of having lost his old influence, ranged himself on Basil of Moscow's side, although this Catholic magnate of Tartar origin cannot be considered as representative of the Orthodox Ruthenians of Lithuania. The peace of 1508 was broken four years later by the Grand Duke Basil with the very definite object of seizing Smolensk. The first attacks directed against that extremely important stronghold were repulsed, but in 1514 it fell into the hands of the enemy, and the brilliant victory achieved by Sigismund's army at the battle of Orsza did not affect this disastrous loss.

The Lithuanians, commanded by Prince Constantine Ostrogski, himself Orthodox and Ruthenian, had enjoyed the benefit of very considerable Polish reinforcements; but, generally speaking, Poland was absorbed in interminable efforts to force the Teutonic Order at last to put into execution the stipulations of the Peace of Torun. After the death of the Grand Master Frederick of Saxony, who had to the end refused to pay homage as a vassal, the Order, in 1511, nominated as his successor another prince of the Empire, Albert of Brandenburg, of the younger line of the Hohenzollern-Ansbachs. Although his mother was the daughter of Casimir Jagiello, the new Grand Master followed in regard to the king, his uncle, the fundamentally hostile policy of his predecessor, bringing to nothing the projects of agreement that were under negotiation at frequent intervals, and, more serious still, entering into relations with Sigismund's other adversary, Basil of Moscow.

But there was yet another political link between these two enemies of Poland and Lithuania. They were both encouraged in their uncompromising attitude by the Emperor Max-

imilian I. In regard to the question of Prussia, he constituted
himself the defender of the long since obsolete rights of the
Empire; but why, in the critical year of 1514, did he send an
ambassador to Moscow who allowed himself to be won over
to an alliance against the Jagiellos? It was because the Hapsburgs never forgot their pretensions to the crowns of Bohemia and Hungary, and if the Emperor now exercised such
a strong pressure upon Sigismund, it was to make him abandon the interests of his dynasty, and to secure to the House
of Austria the right of succeeding his brother Ladislas.

Always closely united, the two Jagiellos in these circumstances decided on a meeting, first with the Emperor's plenipotentiaries who came to Pressburg, then with Maximilian I
himself. The Treaty of Vienna, signed in the summer of
1515, did not recognize any formal right of the Hapsburgs to
the succession in Bohemia and Hungary. But the double
marriage contracted on this occasion between the children of
Ladislas and the grandchildren of Maximilian naturally gave
a new basis to Austrian influence in the two coveted kingdoms, and to the pretensions that Ferdinand I raised eleven
years later. However, the negotiators at Vienna could not
have foreseen that the only son of Ladislas was to die so early,
leaving no children, and in 1515 the reconciliation with the
Emperor brought to the Jagiellos, and, above all, to Sigismund, indisputable advantages. For Maximilian loyally kept
his promise no longer to support the Grand Master in his
opposition to Poland and to undertake nothing with Moscow
against Lithuania.

It is true that the change which resulted held nothing
decisive, the more so as the Emperor died in 1519, and the
Jagiellos did not succeed in exercising a definite influence at
the time of the election of his successor. In the conflict between Sigismund and Basil, Charles V, like Maximilian I,

made attempts at mediation, but the question of Smolensk prevented any lasting peace. The truce, concluded in 1522, and periodically prolonged, was interrupted after the death of Basil in 1533, and during the minority of his son, the future Ivan the Terrible, by a third war which restored only an insignificant part of her lost territories to Lithuania. All that Sigismund the Old could obtain on that side was the organization of a serious resistance against any new aggression, and the establishment of an equilibrium between the two rival powers.

As concerns the Order, the Grand Master Albert had no intention of yielding, even when abandoned by the Emperor; the armed intervention upon which Sigismund, losing patience, decided in 1519, resulted in no solution. The one which was at last found in 1525 was of a nature to evoke the greatest astonishment throughout the whole of Europe: Albert accepted Poland's conditions, but it was no longer the Grand Master of the Teutonic Order who knelt in his person in the great square of Cracow to pay homage to the king. It was the secular and hereditary prince, the first Duke of Prussia. For he had adopted the doctrines of Luther, and the Order, whose religious mission had for long been pure fiction, was secularized. With it an implacable enemy, who, even though weakened, had remained a veritable nightmare to Poland, disappeared from her vicinity. As had been the case at the Congress of Vienna, it was difficult to foresee the distant consequences of the new state of affairs. It is true that East Prussia thereby became the apanage of a German dynasty, but the right of succession was strictly limited to the direct descendants of Albert and of his brothers, so that the elder line of the Hohenzollerns, that of the Electors of Brandenburg, found itself excluded. As for Albert himself, placed under the ban of the Empire, with which he seemed to

have definitely broken, he found the best guarantee of his
power in the suzerainty of Poland, where he soon attempted
to gain friends and to extend his personal influence.

This solution was in reality little liked by Sigismund I,
since it offended the religious feelings of this profoundly
Catholic king, who was, at the moment, repressing the beginning of the Lutheran movement in the territory of
western Polish Prussia, and notably in Danzig. If, notwithstanding, he decided on the agreement made at Cracow, it
was because he was becoming increasingly uneasy in regard
to the situation of his young nephew Louis, who had succeeded Ladislas on the thrones of Bohemia and Hungary.
The latter country was more than ever threatened by the
Ottoman power, and while the King of Poland was coun-
selling it to avoid, at all costs, a new war with Soliman the
Magnificent, the influence of Austria was impelling the
Hungarians to the conflict which ended in the catastrophe of
Mohacs. In 1526, as in 1444, it was a Jagiello prince who
died in vain, abandoned by the Christian Europe which he
was defending, and the Hungarian army, to which Sigismund
had only been able to send very feeble reinforcements, was
annihilated. At the same time, the question of the succession
once more came forward both in Hungary and in Bohemia.
We know that the treaty of 1515 had not prejudged it. But
the King of Poland, who had felt sufficiently strong to ensure for himself the succession to the last Piasts of Masovia
and at length to incorporate this old Polish province in the
kingdom, hesitated before the crushing task of assuming
power in the two great countries which were escaping his
dynasty. Therefore, Ferdinand of Austria met with no opposition on the Polish side when he was elected, first, King
of Bohemia, and then also of Hungary.

In Hungary, however, the Hapsburg was the candidate of

only one party, while another party had previously elected
the national candidate, John Zapolya. The latter, whose
sister had been Sigismund's first wife, counted on the sup
port of Poland, where he had won many sympathies. But, officially, the Polish policy remained strictly neutral, in spite
of the checks with which several attempts at mediation had
met. Not having succeeded before the battle of Mohacs in
allying himself with the King of France against the House of
Austria, Sigismund hesitated still further before now making common cause with the new adversary of the Hapsburgs,
who was openly protected by the Sultan. An extremely delicate situation resulted for Poland, which was prolonged for
many years and was further aggravated towards the end of
the old king's reign. For, although he had given his daughter
in marriage to John Zapolya, he could neither definitely
reconcile the two parties who were contending for Hungary,
nor prevent the Turks from occupying Buda in 1541, shortly
after King John's death, under the pretext of supporting his
son, who was a minor and, at the same time, the grandson of
the King of Poland.

In order to judge fairly the attitude of Sigismund in the
face of these serious complications, we must take into account one circumstance that was almost without intermission paralysing Poland's forces, above all when it was a
question of taking up her position in regard to the Turks.
We must not forget that, side by side with the great political
problems which we have just passed under review, the king
was obliged to ensure the permanent defence of his Ruthenian provinces against the Tartars of the Crimea. It is true
that he had succeeded before the Congress of Vienna in putting an end to their regular co-operation with Moscow, and
even in allying himself with the Khan. But this alliance,
frequently renewed, remained a very precarious one, in spite

of the 'gifts' that he sent each year to the Crimea. It constituted no guarantee against sudden invasions, justified after
the event by some kind of pretext, but more often dictated
by the will of the Sultan, to whom the khanate of the Gherais
was always subject. To this perpetual danger another was
added from the side of Moldavia, who in spite of several
Polish victories, as that carried off in 1531 by the great cap-
tain John Tarnowski, profited by an interminable disagree-
ment over frontiers to disturb the borderlands of Poland,
and fell eventually under the Ottoman suzerainty.

Under these conditions it is indisputably to the credit of
King Sigismund that he organized, in a far more efficacious
manner than his predecessors had done, the defence of those
vast and threatened borderlands. It was not his fault if the
Polish troops who mounted ceaseless guard at the extreme
boundaries of European civilization were not always as numerous as they should have been. Since his accession Sigismund had maintained that the military and financial means
at the disposal of a King of Poland were in obvious dispro-
portion to the size of the state and the place it held in
Europe. From 1510 projects of reform were brought before
successive Diets as well as dietines, to ensure a permanent
army to the kingdom, destined exclusively, however, to the
defence of the south-eastern frontiers, as well as a treasury
sufficient to maintain it. And, if it were necessary to justify
the concessions made at the Congress of Vienna, it is enough
to point out that it was precisely at this epoch that the fate of
these projects was decided. Unfortunately they were met by
the opposition of the nobility and gentry, and had to be ad-
journed, so that the king was obliged to make a fresh demand from each particular Diet for the most indispensable
taxes.

However, new efforts at reform, launched by the court, reappear in the second half of his reign. But then the initiative emanated less from the king himself than from his second wife, the beautiful Milanese princess Bona Sforza, whom he had married in 1518 by the advice of the Emperor. Recent researches have brought to light the truly superior intelligence and prodigious activity of this queen, whose ideas, dictated by the interests of the dynasty, also agreed in great measure with the interests of Poland. Nevertheless, we remain convinced that the methods applied by Bona, doubtless in conformity with the political doctrines of the Renaissance, departed in a deplorable manner from the Jagiellonian traditions. In contradistinction to the king, who always respected the existing laws, his wife, whose influence was always on the increase, cared little for the legality of the means chosen, even stooping to corruption, and when, towards 1531, the tried collaborators of Sigismund began to disappear, she saw to it that her docile but often unworthy protégés were nominated to the highest offices. The grievances which accumulated against the court were, therefore, in great part justified, and in 1537 the king himself had to acknowledge it after violent discussions with the nobility, whom he had inopportunely mobilized. From that time it was evident that any constitutional reform had, for the moment, become impossible.

In this respect, therefore, the reign of Sigismund the Old, whose authority emerged impaired from this internal crisis, marks a decided halt in the historical evolution of Poland. But by a happy compensation this same reign constitutes one of the most brilliant stages in the development of our civilization. At the Congress of Vienna Maximilian I was struck by finding in his rival as distinguished a humanist as himself, and the prelates and lords who surrounded the king, whatever may have been their political leanings, were, without exception, penetrated with that Renaissance culture which was then taking possession of all Poland and appearing even in far-off Lithuania.

Naturally, the Italian queen, by intensifying the relations of Poland with the land of her birth, contributed on her part to this movement. But when she arrived in Cracow the royal castle was already being restored under the direction of eminent Italian architects, and she could admire in the Vavel cathedral the first monuments sculptured in the new style, which was gradually replacing that of the Gothic epoch. An analogous transformation was making itself felt in intellectual life. In Poland, as elsewhere, it was effected more particularly outside the university curriculum; but the University of Cracow still retained its prestige of the preceding century, and soon its most illustrious pupil, Nicolas Copernicus, covered with glory the school where his genius had been formed.

On the other hand, numerous distinguished members of the nation frequented the foreign universities, subsequently to return in diplomatic missions to the western countries, the culture of which always inspired them with a lively and sympathetic interest. The example of John Dantiscus, who spent many years at the court of Charles V, is particularly significant, because that diplomat and humanist has left us not only circumstantial reports but also fine poetry. On their return to Poland these men of refined culture delighted in the role of Maecenas, encouraging artists who adorned even small provincial spots with works of real talent, as well as poets whom they sent at their own expense beyond the Alps.

Side by side with a literature of Polish inspiration but Latin in language, the first small works to be written in the language of the country were also emerging from our first printing presses. But they were still as rare as the Polish texts that we find among the official documents of the epoch of Sigismund I. It is only towards the end of his reign—the date 1543 is usually cited—that we can record, on the one hand, the birth of a political literature, full of new ideas, and on the other, that of a literary production which at last expressed in Polish, whether in verse or prose, the deepest feelings of our race. And it is only under the son and successor of Sigismund the Old, who was the support of his father in the decline of his life and continued his work, that Latin civilization, so rapidly assimilated by Renaissance Poland, became at the same time a national civilization in that country.

12

The Union of Lublin

SIGISMUND AUGUSTUS, the only son of Sigismund I and Bona Sforza, born in 1520, did not succeed his father until 1548; but, theoretically at least, from 1530 Poland had two kings at the same time, the young prince having been elected and crowned during his father's lifetime. Those acts, by which it was the queen's intention to make the right of the nobility to the free election of the King of Poland an empty illusion, had been preceded in 1522 and 1529 by analogous acts, thanks to which Sigismund Augustus had first become Grand Duke of Lithuania. As on the occasion of his father's accession in 1506, the dynasty had been careful to stress his hereditary right to the Grand Duchy, even though the acts of union, signed in 1501, had stipulated that a common election of the sovereign was to guarantee the lasting bond between the two nations. The opposition between the dynastic interests of the Jagiellos, and the necessity of giving a more solid base to the Polish-Lithuanian union, was again accentuated when Sigismund Augustus was entrusted, in 1544, with the administration of Lithuania, who thus had, for four years, her own Grand Duke. He married there, as his second wife, Barbara

Radziwill, widow of the last of the Gasztolds, sister and
cousin of the two Radziwills, Nicholas the Black and Nicholas the Red, princes of the Holy Empire, who directed the
opposition of the high Lithuanian aristocracy against every
tightening of the constitutional link with Poland.

At the first Diet convoked in Poland by the new king after
his father's death, the Polish nobility openly manifested its
hostility against the queen, whom a premature death soon
tore from Sigismund Augustus's side, but who remained the
only love of his sad and solitary life. The Diet of 1548-9 was
succeeded by many others of which the detailed reports enable us to follow, day by day, the dissensions between the
king and the Chamber of Deputies, who desired to impose
upon him their programme of so-called 'execution,' pressed
for in vain since the latter half of Sigismund the Old's reign.
Under these conditions, at the first glance it seems surprising
that Sigismund Augustus should have rallied to this programme from 1562, devoting the following Diets to its realization until that of 1569, held in Lublin, where the final union with Lithuania was concluded. This termination only becomes comprehensible when we take into account that the
great work accomplished at Lublin, scarcely three years before the king's death, was the logical conclusion of the whole
of his foreign policy, and, at the same time, the natural consequence of the internal transformations, at once constitutional
and intellectual, which took place during his reign both in
Poland and in Lithuania.

In his external relations Sigismund Augustus seems in
many respects to have been inspired by the example of his
father. Like him, he only intervened in the conflicts between
the Hapsburgs and the Zapolyas—his sister and his nephew
—as mediator, without, however, losing his concern with

what went on in Hungary and, above all, in Transylvania. Also like Sigismund I, he remained determined to avoid a rupture with Turkey; and this is why he hesitated every time that the troubles of Moldavia seemed as though they would permit influences of the past, even Polish suzerainty, to be re-established there. Finally, like his father, he attached a capital importance to the defence of his Ruthenian provinces against the Tartar invasions, which he effectually succeeded in making of more rare occurrence. But the second Sigismund undoubtedly surpassed the first by his diplomatic talent and his spirit of initiative, and he proved it, above all, in the grave problems of his eastern policy, to which with good reason he attached the greatest importance.

Sigismund Augustus had no love for the family of his first and his third wife, the Hapsburgs, whom he accused of wishing to dominate the whole world. He mistrusted his cousin Albert of Prussia, whose ambitious intrigues he divined. But the real enemy, to whom he indignantly refused his sister's hand, was, in his eyes, Ivan the Terrible of Moscow. It is, in fact, impossible to imagine a more absolute contrast than that between the last Jagiello, thoughtful and refined, who held all violence in horror, and the first tsar, a despot with revolutionary tendencies, who drew up in cold blood the list of the victims of his pathological cruelty. But it was a case of much more than personal antipathies. In spite of a continual exchange of embassies, which wasted their time in discussing official formulas, the threat of a new Muscovite invasion weighed incessantly upon the Ruthenian provinces of Lithuania, which, despite their common Orthodox faith and all their racial affinities, had no desire to exchange the benevolent rule of the Jagiellos for the tyranny of an Ivan.

Sigismund Augustus soon perceived with anxiety that the dreaded attack this time could come not only from the east, but also from the north. On this side, Lithuania had as her neighbour Livonia, where the Order of the Sword Bearers, formerly affiliated to the Teutonic Order, still held out. Fallen into decadence, like the latter, the Livonian Order was no longer capable of resisting the tsar, who was determined to cut a free access for himself through its country to the Baltic Sea. His threats, followed by cruel invasions, forced the unhappy country to seek efficacious help, which only Sigismund Augustus could provide. He began, in 1557, by settling on his own account without striking a blow the differences there had been between himself and the Knights. Two years later he entered into his first agreements in regard to protection against Moscow. Finally, in 1561, the last Master of Livonia, Gothard Kettler, ceded the entire country to the king, contenting himself with the duchy of Courland which he received in fief. The secularization of the Order was followed by that of the archbishopric of Riga, and that town also placed itself under the royal protection, obtaining, moreover, like the whole of Livonia, privileges which guaranteed the autonomy of the new province.

It is superfluous to insist upon the importance of this acquisition, which made the Jagiellonian Federation a great Baltic Power. But this was the very reason why it at once provoked the rivalry of all the other interested Powers. The House of Brandenburg had hoped to profit by the secularization of Livonia, as it had formerly done by that of Prussia, the more so as a brother of Albert had been the last Archbishop of Riga. Sigismund Augustus succeeded in dismissing these pretensions, but at the price of a concession that the future proved to be disastrous: he extended the right of succession in East Prussia to the elder, electoral line of the Hohenzollerns.

This was, however, the only mistake with which his policy

can be reproached amidst all the complications of the first 'war of the north,' which broke out soon after the submission of Livonia and lasted until the Congress of Stettin in 1570. The inopportune intervention of the Scandinavian kingdoms, which wished to divide between them the inheritance of the Order, did not prevent Sigismund II from allying himself, first in 1563 with Denmark, then in 1568 with Sweden, who had taken Estonia from him, but where his brother-in-law John had succeeded Eric XIV, the ally of Ivan the Terrible. It was against the latter that Sigismund Augustus concentrated all his forces, creating the first Polish fleet in the Baltic to cut the tsar's communications with the west, sending reinforcements to the Livonians, and on several occasions mobilizing the Lithuanian army to defend the White Ruthenian borderlands. In spite of it all he could not prevent Ivan from taking the town of Polock in 1563, a loss even more grievous than that of Smolensk, and from occupying a great part of Livonian territory.

The precarious situation that resulted, and which the truce of 1570 only prolonged, is explained by the fact that until then only one of the Jagiellonian States was directly and fully engaged in the struggle. As always in similar cases, Lithuania obtained valuable Polish reinforcements; but so long as the regulation of the Union remained in suspense Poland declined all responsibility in an affair which seemed to have no connection with her own interests. It was not only the common sovereign who then understood the absolute necessity of creating a more intimate communion between the two countries. The great mass of the Lithuanian gentry, which an oligarchy jealous of power kept outside public affairs, but which had to support all the weight of continual military and financial efforts, began to raise its voice, claiming a closer collaboration with its 'Polish brothers.'

This wish, very clearly formulated in 1562, with a complete programme of union which anticipated the settlement
of 1569, was also dictated by the desire of at last enjoying the
same 'good, free, and Christian' rights, of which the Polish
gentry had so long reaped the benefits. The problem of an
integral constitutional assimilation was still awaiting the solution that had been promised at the beginning of the Union. The highest offices were invariably held by a few great
aristocratic families who combined them with judicial power
and imposed their will upon the Lithuanian Diets. The first
Lithuanian statute, a fine work of codification which in 1529
had accompanied the elevation of Sigismund Augustus to the
grand-ducal throne, needed a fundamental revision in this
respect. The last Jagiello long put it off on account of the attitude of the Radziwills, and meanwhile proceeded with a
vast agrarian reform, the utility of which no one could dispute. It was not until 1564–6 that a new drawing up of the
statute satisfied the demands of the Lithuanian gentry, introducing in the Grand Duchy tribunals and dietines, district
by district, on the model of the kingdom. By law the Lithuanians now possessed a parliamentary system as democratic
as that of the Poles. But, in practice, the deputies elected by
the dietines found themselves reduced to a very modest role,
as long as the Lithuanian Diet met separately under the effective direction of the Grand-Ducal Council, always exclusively
aristocratic. The gentry went further and demanded the fusion of the two Diets, Polish and Lithuanian, into one common Parliament, which, together with the common election
of the sovereign, was, in fact, the essential condition of a lasting union.

Such was likewise the desire of the Polish gentry, which
had long made it a capital point of its programme of 'execution of the laws.' This expression of a conservative character

should not mislead us. It is true that there was no question in Poland of such fundamental reforms as in Lithuania. But, nevertheless, inveterate abuses called for a remedy. Among the ancient laws, the execution of which left much to be desired, there was, above all, that of 1504 which forbade the king to mortgage estates without the consent of the Diet. Now, contrary to this provision, a very large part of the crown domains had, little by little, passed into the hands of the aristocratic families who were enriching themselves inordinately, while the king, lacking revenues, was obliged to demand from the Diets extraordinary taxes. On this point also Sigismund Augustus in 1562 rallied to the programme of the party of 'execution.' The revision of the mortgaged estates, carried out with care by the Diet of 1563–4, did not result in their restitution, but, at least, it was decided that a quarter of their revenues should henceforth be devoted to the defence of the south-eastern frontiers. Thus Poland obtained a public treasury especially destined to ensure the maintenance of permanent armed forces, as Sigismund I had desired.

The Diets of his son were never able to concentrate all their attention on this, the most positive, aspect of the 'execution.' Under the pretext of also carrying into execution the laws concerning the relations between ecclesiastics and laity, these Diets at the same time discussed the whole problem of religious reform, the most absorbing of the epoch. The edicts of Sigismund the Old, severe but scarcely ever applied, had not been able to check the progress of Lutheran propaganda. After his death Poland became a veritable 'shelter for heretics.' The Bohemian Brethren, a survival of the Hussites, driven out of Bohemia, established themselves in Great Poland, competing with the Lutherans. Calvin and the other Swiss reformers exercised a predominating influence in Lit-

tle Poland and Lithuania. But the disciples of their adversaries, the anti-Trinitarians of all shades, including the most
radical, together with the Anabaptists, also found here an almost unlimited refuge and field of action. Encouraged by the
sympathy of the great aristocratic families, as well as by the
indolence of the greater part of the clergy, this movement became so powerful that it was feared in Rome that the whole of
Poland would abandon the Catholic faith.

These apprehensions were by no·means justified. It is true
that for some twenty years the Reformation seemed to be
attracting the *élite* of the nation. By the side of those who
made use of it mainly to rid themselves of tithes and ecclesiastical tribunals, there were also in Poland reformers inspired
by very serious religious convictions, such as John Laski the
younger, nephew of the former archbishop, renowned all
over Europe, as well as several promoters of the Polish 'Ari-
anism,' who also preached very advanced social doctrines.
But in reality all these ideas imported from abroad never
took deep root in Poland. Without touching the masses they
acted exclusively on the urban population and on the nobility, which was jealous of every liberty, including, therefore,
the liberty of conscience, and was curious of every novelty, in
which it desired to experiment, passing from one creed to another. The mutitude of these creeds which, profiting by Polish tolerance, competed with one another, was one of the
chief weaknesses of the Protestant party, which only in 1570
succeeded in creating a species of very superficial union between its adherents, excluding, however, the Arians. The
bishops who were the most devoted to Rome, with in the first
rank Cardinal Hosius, who had been very active at the Council of Trent, made use of this to confront their adversaries
with the unity of the Church, defined with precision, and al-

ready defended towards the end of Sigismund Augustus's reign by the first Jesuits.

As regards the king himself, the Protestants hoped in vain to win him to their cause. He was interested in their ideas, and, above all, he was hostile to all religious persecution. The papal nuncios could only count upon him so long as they gave evidence of great moderation and diplomatic tact. But in spite of his desire to divorce his third wife, Catherine of Austria, he remained firmly attached to Catholic tradition, and was perturbed to perceive how greatly vain discussions on matters of faith were retarding the political work of the Diets.

In this respect the movement set on foot by the Reformation unquestionably had regrettable consequences, even though Poland never knew the horrors of religious wars. It is likewise regrettable that minds of the first order, to cite only Andrew Frycz Modrzewski, whose political writings do honour to Poland and abound in happy and generous suggestions from the social point of view, should have subsequently devoted themselves to sterile theological discussions. But on the other hand these discussions, from which, moreover, Polish Catholicism emerged strengthened, had stimulated and enriched the thought of our golden century, and in Poland, as elsewhere, the Reformation spread the use of the national language and contributed to the development of literature.

Polish literature, in fact, experienced under Sigismund Augustus a first efflorescence which produced works of art of enduring value, like those of Nicholas Rey, a Protestant gentleman who has perpetuated his ideal of the 'honest man,' and, above all, those of John Kochanowski, the Catholic humanist, the Polish Ronsard, who for long centuries remained our greatest lyric poet. The growth of Polish culture was reflected in Lithuania and the Ruthenian regions in a still more striking manner than the constitutional evolution of the kingdom. This explains the progress made there by the Polonization, entirely spontaneous and almost instinctive, of the most cultivated classes of the population. And in its turn it is this assimilation in the sphere of thought, language, even the customs of daily life, which, together with the considerations of a political order that we have pointed out, explains the success of the negotiations in the affair of the Polish-Lithuanian union.

These negotiations, broached in preceding Diets, exacted at that of Lublin half a year more of work before the memorable Acts could be signed on 1st July 1569, which created the Republican Commonwealth, and gave it the constitutional basis destined to endure until the Partitions. The principal credit falls to Sigismund Augustus, who, after having transmitted his hereditary rights over Lithuania to the crown of Poland, appeased with as much patience as skill the extremists on both sides—the radical party of the Polish Chamber of Deputies which wished, purely and simply, to incorporate the whole of Lithuania, and the Lithuanian oligarchy which was averse to the project of creating a common Diet.

To put an end to the resistance of this little group of magnates which was exercising so strong a pressure on the other representatives of the Grand Duchy that for a time they left Lublin, the king assigned to Poland the long disputed provinces of Podlasia and Volhynia. The first was only a narrow intermediate territory between Masovia and Lithuania. The second brought with it the vast regions of Kiev and Braclaw, so that all the Little Russian provinces—Ukrainian, following the terminology of to-day—found themselves gathered within the boundaries of the kingdom of Poland, immediately obtaining a large autonomy. By this action the kingdom assumed the whole charge of defence against the Tartars, and henceforth shared with the Grand Duchy the still heavier responsibility of facing the territory of Moscow; the more so as Livonia became, from that time, a common province of the two component parts of the federated State.

In this State, called the Republican Commonwealth, one and indivisible, Lithuania proper, together with the White Ruthenian provinces, retained all the prerogatives of a grand duchy placed on an equal footing with the kingdom. She therefore kept her own administration, army, treasury, and law. The power of legislation alone was to be shared in common, which guaranteed the unity of the general policy, in the same way as the common election of the sovereign was to guarantee the perpetual duration of the Union.

This solution, which responded to the desire of the great majority of the Lithuanians, was the more urgent, inasmuch as, like the last Piast, Sigismund Augustus waited in vain for an heir. Conscious of having accomplished all his task and of having crowned the work of his dynasty, but full of apprehension in the face of the intrigues of his neighbours, who were aiming at securing the throne after his death for themselves, the last Jagiello could only recommend in his will that the two nations he had united should remain faithful 'to that reciprocal charity and concord which their ancestors had called by the Latin name of union.'

Part III

THE EXPERIMENT OF THE
ROYAL REPUBLIC

13

John Zamoyski

The last Jagiello died on 7th July 1572, before the two Diets that had met after that of Lublin had regulated the multiple questions that the election of his successor presented. We know that by law the throne of Poland had become elective since the distant epoch of the founder of the Jagiellonian dynasty. But, as long as this dynasty had lasted, nobody seriously considered electing a king outside it. It is, therefore, not without reason that tradition only regards our kings as freely elected from the time of 'the first interregnum' that followed the death of Sigismund Augustus. And it is only from this moment that the dangerous consequences of the right of a free election made themselves really felt.

We must not exaggerate these dangers. The Polish nobility, matured by a long and active participation in public life, in 1572 succeeded in fixing the principles which ruled that life during the interregnums, and, in fact, they asked nothing more than to find a new dynasty which, under the form of successive uncontested elections, would, in practice, become hereditary like that of the Jagiellos. This was, indeed, the case with the Vasas, who, since the election of Sigismund III in

1587, occupied the throne for eighty-one years until the ab-
dication of the last descendant of their Polish branch. The
election of the young Prince of Sweden, who, moreover, was
descended through his mother from the never-to-be-forgotten
Jagiellos, was preceded by two others, those of Henri de Valois in 1573 and Stephen Bathory in 1575, neither of which
could give us a durable dynasty, since the first of these kings
left Poland for France after only a few months, while the
second died without leaving children.

In spite of these rapid changes and in spite of the troubles
of the second and third interregnums, during each of which
an Austrian candidate, elected by the partisans of the Hapsburgs, had first of all to be put aside, the end of the sixteenth
century still constitutes a very brilliant epoch in our past and
is a worthy close to that 'golden century.' We can best be convinced of this fact by following as a guiding line the activities
of a personality of the very highest order, who laid the basis
of the definitive organization of the Republic, decided the
result of the first three elections, and did not lose his active
influence until the eve of his death on the threshold of the
following century. We allude to John Zamoyski, the faithful
collaborator of the greatest of the three kings of this epoch, a
typical representative of that nobility which had just taken
the direction of the State into its hands and was identifying itself with the whole of the nation, a politician whose career
seems to symbolize, in one brief epitome, the destiny of modern Poland.

No essential transformation, however, distinguished this
new Poland from that of the Jagiellos, which also had, with
increasing frequency, been designated by the name of Republic in the Latin and very general sense of that term. Yet
we see the 'republican,' or rather the democratic, character of
the State immediately emphasized, even though it had not

ceased to have a king at its head. For on the one hand it was admitted during the first interregnum that every man of noble birth had the right to take a personal share in the election, and even to be elected himself. And on the other hand, the traditional parliamentary institutions were then surrounded with new guarantees, completing these general rules by special conditions imposed since the time of Henri de Valois on every candidate elected: the famous *pacta conventa*.

All this system, which lasted to the eve of the Partitions, was in great measure the work of John Zamoyski, who played the part of a veritable 'tribune of the noble plebs.' This comparison is a very apt indication that the young statesman who then emerged from the ranks of the lesser nobility was inspired, not only by the national traditions of which he had a remarkable knowledge, but also by those of the ancient Roman Republic, with which the Polish Republic at the time of the Renaissance was frequently compared. The general tendency of these regulations was inspired by the fear of seeing a liberty, acquired at the cost of long efforts, violated by a king following the example of the other sovereigns of an epoch when absolutism was making such rapid progress in the rest of Europe. This fear was by no means a delusion. Given the absence of a serious national candidature, the elected king would, of necessity, be a foreign prince, and among these candidates there were, on one side, representatives of the House of Austria, which had so rapidly liquidated the ancient liberties of Bohemia and Hungary, and on the other—strange paradox!—Ivan the Terrible himself.

But the French candidature which triumphed at the first unanimous election could also inspire similar apprehensions. St Bartholomew's Day was but of yesterday; the accounts of which alarmed not only the Protestants in Poland, but all those who, by the terms of the celebrated Confederation of

Warsaw in 1573, had reciprocally guaranteed a general religious peace in spite of all their disagreements on the subject of their faith. Nevertheless, the idea of a lasting *rapprochement* with France, an idea which was born in the time of the Jagiellos, and which seemed now as though it would resolve in the most efficacious manner all the difficulties of the political situation, emerged victorious over these hesitations. A Polish embassy went to Paris to fetch the brother of the King of France, and on 21st February 1574 he was crowned in the Vavel.

Unfortunately, before Henri de Valois was able to familiarize himself with his new surroundings, on receiving the news of the death of Charles IX he fled precipitately from Cracow, thereby inflicting a sharp blow upon Franco-Polish sympathies. Faced with the evidence that, having inherited France, he had no intention of ever returning to Poland, the Poles were obliged to declare the throne vacant; and disconcerted by a first discouraging experience, on this occasion they offered Europe the dismal spectacle of two conflicting elections: that of the Emperor Maximilian II, the candidate of the aristocratic party, and that of his Hungarian adversary, the Prince of Transylvania, to whom it was decided to marry the last Jagiello's sister. This candidate of the majority came with haste to Poland in the beginning of 1576, and soon the death of his rival made his election unanimous.

Stephen Bathory justly ranks among the most glorious of our kings. He first broke the resistance of Danzig which, under the pretext of remaining faithful to the party of Maximilian II, had attempted to acquire a semi-independent position. He then completed the political work of Sigismund Augustus by at last repulsing Ivan the Terrible, and ensuring to the Republic the undisputed possession of the whole of Livonia which the tsar, profiting by the troubles at Danzig, had once more invaded. Of his campaigns, which were organized with all Stephen's strategic talent, the first, that of 1579, recaptured the town and the region of Polock. The two following, in 1580 and 1581, penetrated into Muscovite territory, where the tsar himself was menaced and the town of Pskov besieged. The treaty of 1582 restored to Lithuania her frontier prior to 1563 and enabled the king to organize the administration of Livonia on a durable basis.

The Holy See, which had entrusted the Jesuit Antonio Possevino with negotiating the peace between Stephen Bathory and Ivan the Terrible, hoped in vain to win Moscow to the union of the Churches. Soon, however, its attention was turned by the King of Poland to a project of capital importance for Christendom. Contrary to the last Jagiellos, who remained sceptical in regard to plans for a league against the Turks, Bathory, anxious to save his native Hungary, conceived his own similar plan. On the death of the tsar in 1584 it was his intention to subject Moscow to his sovereignty; but he saw this only as a means of organizing an expedition against Turkey which would have banded all eastern Europe in a coalition.

In these ambitious projects, the realization of which was prevented by Stephen's premature death, the personal initiative of the king is evident. It seems to have been less exclusive in the campaigns against Ivan the Terrible, where it is difficult to distinguish between the merits of the king and those of John Zamoyski, the Grand Hetman of Poland. On the other hand, the latter, loaded with honours, married to a cousin of Bathory, was also Grand Chancellor, and his influence was still more considerable in politics than in military questions. There was, however, complete agreement between the king and his minister. In their diplomatic relations they both remained resolute adversaries of the Hapsburgs. In their

internal policy they applied one and the same method with
the object of settling the problems that Sigismund Augustus
had left open.

In religious affairs they were like Sigismund, partisans of a
prudent tolerance. They were none the less attached to the
Catholic faith and anxious for a good understanding with
Rome. It was in Bathory's time that the decrees of the Council
of Trent were introduced into Poland and that the activity
of the Jesuits developed: the latter's college at Wilno was
even raised in 1579 to the rank of a university. But the most
delicate internal problem was that of establishing a just equilibrium between the principle of liberty on which the whole
Polish constitution rested and that of the royal authority,
more and more limited since the Jagiellonian epoch. King
Stephen, of foreign, and comparatively speaking, modest
origin, was, nevertheless, firmly determined to exercise his
power in an effective manner, and he found unreserved support in John Zamoyski. For the latter saw clearly that the
Royal Republic, such as he had conceived of it from the beginning of his career, had more need than an absolute monarchy of a scrupulous respect for the laws and a solidly established internal order.

At the beginning of the reign great progress was realized in
this direction by the creation of tribunals, or rather courts of
appeal, in 1578 for Great and Little Poland, and in 1581 for
Lithuania. Hitherto the king himself had been the supreme
judge; but naturally he could not give his personal attention
in the time required to all the affairs which had not been settled by the district tribunals, and his authority suffered
thereby as much as the public order. Henceforth, the nobility
itself could elect the judges of the new central tribunals, and
it hailed with satisfaction a reform which guaranteed the
more rapid and regular conduct of justice.

But the good relations between the court and the nobility were soon troubled by the unfortunate affair of the Zborowskis. This powerful family had largely contributed to the election of the Prince of Transylvania, and was now highly displeased at seeing Zamoyski occupying a quite exceptional position. Incapable of competing with him, the Zborowskis entered into very suspicious foreign relations, notably with the House of Austria, and then believed themselves strong enough to brave openly the king and the chancellor. After Samuel Zborowski was executed in 1584, in conformity with the law but with an unusual harshness in its application, the one thought of his brothers was to avenge him, and they appealed to all the nobility. The proceedings which were instituted against them ended with a severe sentence upon the one most guilty among them. But a minority of the deputies then broke up the Diet of 1585 in a manner which was at that epoch still exceptional, and in spite of all his energy the king, in the end, suffered great discouragement. Hence, in spite of all the brilliant successes of this reign of ten years, the kingdom was profoundly divided when he died in the following year.

The consequences of this division made themselves felt during the third interregnum. In opposition to John Zamoyski, under whose influence a strong majority had elected Sigismund of Sweden, the Zborowskis succeeded in getting the Austrian candidate, the Archduke Maximilian, brother of the Emperor Rudolf II, proclaimed as king. Passions were so excited that it was necessary to have recourse to arms. It was not till the beginning of 1588 that the victory of Byczyna, won by Zamoyski over Maximilian and his partisans, assured the throne to the Vasa.

His reign, which lasted till 1632, thus began under gloomy auspices. And the most serious of these was that the new king

soon deceived the hopes of those who had put forward and
defended his candidature, in particular those of John Zamoyski. Generally speaking, historians have been inclined to be
severe towards Sigismund III, whom it is, in fact, difficult to
compare with his predecessor and the great Jagiellos whose
memory he evoked. To-day, however, we are beginning to
find out that the reproaches made against him have often
been exaggerated; and, in any case, we must distinguish between the two parts of his long reign: before and after the
critical events of 1605–6.

John Zamoyski, who, in fact, died in 1605 after having
played in the last period of his life the role of a leader of the
opposition, reproached Sigismund above all else for his increasingly intimate relations with the Hapsburgs. The
chancellor, who had always combated their influence and who
had wished to exclude them for ever from the throne of Poland, was indignant when he saw that the new king retained
no resentment against the dynasty which had contended with
him for the crown. But what most disquieted him was Sigismund III's clandestine negotiations with a brother of Maximilian, the Archduke Ernest, who was attempting to get Poland spontaneously ceded to him by the Vasa. At the Diet of
1592, called the 'Diet of Investigation,' the king protested his
loyalty, but he had no intention of abandoning his policy of
drawing close to Austria.

No doubt Zamoyski went too far in considering that this
policy was, under every circumstance, incompatible with the
interests of Poland. There was, in reality, no cause of conflict
at that time between the two Powers, which were, moreover,
both threatened by the advance of the Turks. If Sigismund
gave a favourable reception to the projects of an anti-Ottoman league which Austria, in agreement with Rome, proposed to him, he was only taking up Stephen Bathory's plans

again under another form. And Zamoyski, who, towards the end of the sixteenth century, intervened with success in the affairs of Moldavia and even of Walachia, himself came near to a rupture with the Porte, although he attempted at all costs to avert it.

To explain Sigismund III's Austrian sympathies historians are accustomed to insist upon his religious sentiments. It is true that he was unreservedly devoted to the Catholic Church, and that he never forgot this in his general policy. But, in our opinion, he by no means deserves the reproach of fanaticism, for which he has become almost a byword in public opinion. Certainly he made a mistake in not having repressed with sufficient energy the 'tumults' which broke out from time to time in the large towns, when the mobs, hostile to the 'heretics,' attacked their places of worship. Yet, in spite of these regrettable incidents, it would be absurd to speak of a religious persecution comparable to what was then going on in other countries. The king even confided the highest offices to Protestants, although these latter only constituted a small minority, spontaneous returns to Catholicism having multiplied during the last ten years.

As regards the far more numerous members of the Orthodox Church, Sigismund III showed himself favourable to the project of religious union with Rome, realized in 1596 at the Synod of Brzesc. But in thus acting in agreement, moreover, with John Zamoyski, he was only encouraging a movement which had originated among the Ruthenians themselves and the flower of their clergy. This return to the traditions of the Union of Florence, which had here survived the fall of Constantinople, raised the intellectual and moral level of the Ruthenian Church, withdrew it from the influences of Stambul and Moscow, and completed the political union concluded at Lublin. It is true that a party of the Ruthenians, led for personal motives by Prince Constantine Ostrogski, rejected the Union, so that it gave rise to dangerous divisions. However, the first revolts of the Ukrainian Cossacks, which broke out about the same epoch, and to the consequences of which we shall have to return, had nothing in common with this religious problem. Hence it stands indisputably to the credit of the king and his collaborators that they worked for its solution on lines in conformity with the interests of the Church, as well as with those of the Republic and her Ruthenian population.

We can more truly reproach him with not having followed this up with sufficient consistency, preoccupied as he was with a problem which turned his attention in a completely different direction. Since the death of his father, John III, in 1592, Sigismund III was king of both Poland and Sweden. When he was raised to the throne of the Jagiellos, this personal union between the two Baltic Powers, or, at least, their close co-operation, such as had been prepared by Sigismund Augustus, was counted upon in advance. Here, again, the Vasa's electors experienced a great deception. Sigismund met with a far stronger opposition in Sweden than in Poland, dictated by the hostility of a fundamentally Protestant nation and by the ambition of his uncle, Charles of Sudermania, who ended by usurping the crown in 1600. Hence, instead of a Polish-Swedish alliance there was a war between the Vasas of Poland and those of Sweden which was to last sixty years. Sigismund III succeeded in interesting the Republic in this war by conferring Estonia, the object of disputes between the two countries, upon her, and Zamoyski distinguished himself once more in the conflict that began to rage in Livonia. Another military leader, younger than he, to whom he subsequently confided the defence of that province, John Charles Chodkiewicz, won a great victory in 1605 at Kirkholm. If neither

Poland nor Sigismund was able to profit by it, this was because a new conflict more serious than all the others was already preparing between the king and the nation.

After having suspected Sigismund of foreign intrigues, Zamoyski now accused him of intending to violate constitutional liberties and make Poland an absolute monarchy. The chancellor, who under Bathory had upheld the royal authority against the elements of disorder, considered it his duty to defend the traditional institutions of his country against a sovereign whom he never ceased to distrust. The reforms of which Sigismund dreamt were, in the main, useful. They corresponded to the ideas that the great preacher of the epoch, the Jesuit Peter Skarga, had developed with such eloquence in his celebrated political sermons. But, as in the time of Sigismund I and Bona Sforza, they were compromised by the manner in which the court wished to impose them. Fearing a *coup d'état* on the part of the king, Zamoyski profited by the Diet of 1605 to set forth his defence of his own conception of the Republic, based on the principle of liberty. His opposition, however, remained within legal limits, and consequently his death, which followed close upon this dissolved Diet, was an irreparable loss to Poland.

In spite of his grievances against the king, he had wished to avert the disaster of a civil war, and at the same time he placed the Polish nobility on its guard against a policy of adventure that a turbulent aristocracy was preparing in respect to Moscow. He departed without having been able to prevent either of these disastrous errors; and with him there departed not only an eminent statesman, but also a great humanist, the founder of a university in his own town Zamosc, a protector of letters and of arts; in a word, the most worthy representative of the last generation to know a wholly sound and prosperous Poland.

14

The Last Great Designs

THE project for the organization of Europe, known under the name of 'Henry IV's great design,' a project so characteristic of the political situation of the first half of the seventeenth century, gave a very honourable place to Poland. Among the three towns where the supreme Council of the 'most Christian Republic' was to sit, we find by the side of Paris and Trent our ancient capital Cracow, where our kings were always crowned and buried, even though their residence was now in Warsaw, the city where the elections and Diets were held. And Poland was considered as the 'bulwark and rampart' against Turks, Tartars, and Muscovites; in virtue of this title it was worthy of exceptional advantages.

In fact, until the date of 1648, as decisive in Polish as in general history, the Poland of Sigismund III and of his son Ladislas IV indisputably stood in the rank of a great Power which the whole of Europe regarded very seriously. Her role as the bulwark of Christendom even became more marked than ever, owing to the glorious battles then fought by the Polish armies, and the frontiers of the Republic had never been more extensive. It is not surprising that in Poland herself truly 'great designs' then made their appearance, which if they had been realized would have changed the destinies of eastern Europe, as the Polish-Lithuanian union had done in the past. Even the level of our culture, that had stood so high at the end of the sixteenth century, only declined slowly and imperceptibly; and if the Polish literature of the seventeenth century no longer equalled that of the 'golden century,' it does not, in reality, deserve the sharp criticism of which it has at times been the object.

Nevertheless, in the beginning of this new epoch of Polish history two events, so to speak, deflected the normal evolution of the Republic, creating evil precedents and grave menaces for the future. One of them disturbed the internal state of Poland, the other disorientated her foreign policy.

We have said that, until now, the historic evolution of Poland had been normal, and this applies equally to her constitution, which has been so much decried. The institution of a Royal Republic, sustained by a democracy of nobles, opposing a genuine cult for liberty to the absolutist rule of its neighbours, had certainly been, from the outset, a bold experiment which created a peculiar position, difficult and delicate, for Poland among the other states. But, in spite of the critical and pessimistic voices which were raised in our country in the sixteenth century—as, in fact, in every country and in every epoch—nothing foretold a fatal issue to this experiment, so long as a certain practical equilibrium was maintained between the royal authority and the rights of the nobility, and so long as the latter remained conscious of its duties and responsibilities.

In spite of the mistakes which he may have committed towards the end of his career, John Zamoyski had always admirably understood this. After his death two men, formed under his influence, believed themselves destined to continue his work. One of them, Nicholas Zebrzydowski, Palatine of Cracow, desired, like Zamoyski, to defend the liberties of the Republic. But, lacking the talent and prudence of his model, in 1606 he provoked a civil war, unhappily famous under the name of Zebrzydowski's rebellion. Starting from an interpretation of the Polish constitution according to which a king, accused of having violated that constitution, had no right to the obedience of the citizens, the Palatine gathered all the malcontents round him. A very devout Catholic, he allied himself with the leaders of the Protestants, who were only too eager to denounce obedience to the protector of the Jesuits and the ally of Austria. The revolt was crushed in 1607 in a fratricidal battle by Stanislas Zolkiewski, then Vice-Hetman of Poland. It is in this second personage that we see the man who really carried on the policy of John Zamoyski. He did not attempt to shut his eyes to the faults committed by the court, and his opinions differed in many respects from those of Sigismund III. But this great patriot nevertheless held it his duty to defend the lawful sovereign and to put an end to a scandalous rebellion, which, however, did not prevent him from subsequently recommending a general amnesty, voted, in fact, in the Diet of 1609.

In spite of this peaceable conclusion this first rebellion in Polish history had sinister consequences. Royalty lost, to a great extent, the moral prestige it had enjoyed in the time of the Jagiellos, which alone could compensate for all the constitutional limitations of its power. The insurgents, even though vanquished and compelled to implore pardon from Sigismund III, nevertheless gained their cause; for the Polish constitution was henceforth regarded as sacrosanct and the king had to renounce not only the idea of making any far-reaching changes in it, but even any reform which, without touching its principles, would have improved the functioning of parliament and ensured to the Republic the financial and military measures that were necessary to her.

This was the more serious, as in the course of these highly disturbed years Poland had become engaged in a vast enterprise, contrary to the pacific and prudent traditions of the Jagiellos, contrary even to the bolder but always definite and clear ideas of a Stephen Bathory. In the conflict with Moscow, a conflict which since the Union of Lublin had concerned the whole of the Republic, the aggressions until now had been on the part of her eastern neighbour, against whom Poland attempted nothing further than to recapture the territories which the other had seized. But this time an impostor found encouragement in Poland which enabled him to inaugurate a period of troubles in Moscow, in the course of which the Poles overran the whole of Russia without being able to agree among themselves upon the object of this intervention.

The lamentable history of the false Demetrius is well known. In 1598 the Tsar Feodor, son of Ivan the Terrible and the last of the line of the Ruriks, was succeeded by a simple boyar, Boris Godunov, who was suspected of having caused the death of another of Ivan's sons, Demetrius. Some years later a Russian of obscure origin appeared in Poland, asserting that he was this Demetrius who had escaped from the assassins and demanding assistance to ascend the throne of his fathers. Like Zamoyski, who lived to see the beginning of this affair, Sigismund III was distrustful, and all official support was refused to the pretender. Nevertheless, the latter won the co-operation of some Polish lords, notably George Mniszech, whose daughter he promised to marry as soon as he had overthrown Godunov. This came about in 1605, and with Demetrius and his wife Polish influences of every kind penetrated into Moscow. The following year this new regime was, in its turn, overthrown, and Prince Basil Shuiski took possession of the crown. But scarcely had the first false Demetrius perished when a new pretender presented himself whose imposture was still more evident. This did not prevent the ambitious Marina Mniszech from acknowledging him as her husband, and a great number of Poles, for the most part former combatants in Zebrzydowski's revolt, from supporting him against Tsar Basil. The latter allied himself in 1609 with Charles of Sweden, Sigismund III's chief adversary, thus hastening the official rupture with Poland.

It is useless to follow all the vicissitudes of the war. What concerns us is the project of submitting all Russia to Polish domination, a project which soon assumed two different forms. The king dreamt of a conquest of Moscow, which would accept him as tsar and be converted to Catholicism. Stanislas Zolkiewski, whose fame as a military leader was always on the increase, regarded this as a dangerous chimera. He covered himself with glory, winning in 1610 the battle of Kluszyn, and bringing Tsar Shuiski and his brothers to Warsaw as prisoners of war. But he would have preferred to gain Moscow by a freely conceded union, like that formerly concluded with Lithuania. Thanks to his spirit of conciliation, the son of the King of Poland, young Prince Ladislas, was elected tsar by the boyars, to whom Zolkiewski guaranteed that their Orthodox faith should be respected. However, this project, more in conformity with the Jagiellonian traditions, proved as impossible of realization as the other. Sigismund III only accepted it with reservations which discouraged his son's partisans, and, moreover, the differences between the two countries, which the Poles desired to unite by perpetual bonds, went far too deep not to provoke a violent reaction in Moscow against any foreign appropriation. After the second false Demetrius had been assassinated, this reaction turned exclusively against the Poles, whom the Russians saw occupying the

Kremlin. In 1613, after the election of another tsar in the person of Michael Romanov, the founder of a second national dynasty, the projects of the king, as well as those of Zolkiewski, were doomed to certain failure.

The only positive result of a whole series of campaigns was the capture of Smolensk, which surrendered in 1611, after a siege of nearly two years, and which was yielded by Russia under the terms of the truce of 1618, as well as Czernihow, which had been formerly torn from Lithuania before the loss of Smolensk. After the death of Sigismund III, Ladislas, who still continued to claim the title of tsar, delivered that hotly contested town from a fresh Muscovite siege, and it was not until 1634 that a treaty of peace confirmed the territorial clauses of 1618. But Russia, humiliated in the epoch of disturbances and invasions, only awaited the moment to take her revenge, and thus the memories and the distant consequences of all this war, which was prolonged by designs of too ambitious a nature, were to affect the relations between the two neighbours in a deplorable manner.

The latent danger for the Republic which resulted from this was the more serious because, even while avoiding a direct participation in the Thirty Years War, she saw her conflict with Sweden aggravated and the dreaded war with Turkey at last break out. Her relations with the latter had already been marred during the Moscow campaigns. Since 1612 the inopportune interventions of some Polish nobles, notably of the increasingly influential Potocki family, in the affairs of Moldavia where they supported their cousins the Moghilas, as well as the maritime expeditions of the Ukrainian Cossacks who penetrated up to Trebizond, had threatened to bring about a rupture with the Ottoman State. Zolkiewski succeeded in delaying this by the treaty of 1617; but on the one hand, the Cossacks did not attempt to respect the pledges given by the Government, and on the other, despite the similar pledges of the Porte, the Tartars, who depended on the latter, continued to stir up the Ukraine. Poland, therefore, found herself faced with a veritable vicious circle, and in the borderlands of the Republic with a chaotic situation which could not last.

The catastrophe was precipitated by the attitude taken by Sigismund III at the outset of the Thirty Years War. Without heeding a strong current of opinion hostile to the Hapsburgs, and hesitating to profit by their difficulties to recapture Silesia, the king sent the Emperor reinforcements against the Hungarian Protestants who, under Gabriel Bethlen of Transylvania, were threatening Vienna. The Sultan Osman, whose help was invoked by Bethlen, readily profited by this pretext to launch a long-meditated attack against Poland. Zolkiewski, who saw his prudent policy fall to the ground, had only very insufficient forces with which to defend the frontiers of the Republic against the Mussulman invasion that had been foreseen for more than a hundred years, and that now became a terrible reality. Abandoned by the Cossacks, whose undisciplined forays had greatly contributed to provoke the Porte, the old Hetman died heroically in the autumn of 1620, during a disastrous defeat in the vicinity of Cecora. This defeat was redeemed the following year by a not less courageous and more effective resistance that the Poles, commanded by John Chodkiewicz and this time assisted by the Cossacks, opposed to the sultan himself at the battle of Chocim.

Peace was restored on this side; but in the same year, 1621, Gustavus Adolphus, who had succeeded King Charles in Sweden, profited by Poland's struggles against the enemy of Christendom to invade Livonia. He took possession of Riga, and subsequently occupied in succession the chief ports of Prussia. East Prussia, Poland's vassal duchy, was as much a victim as Royal Prussia; but the situation on the side of the

Baltic was the more complicated for Poland inasmuch as, after the death of the son and last heir of Albert of Prussia, his duchy had passed into the hands of the Elector of Brandenburg in conformity with the concessions made to the Hohenzollerns since the reign of Sigismund Augustus. As Duke of Prussia the Elector paid homage to the King of Poland in the critical year of 1621; but the fact that Königsberg and Berlin, separated from each other by Polish territory, now belonged to the same prince naturally held great danger for the future.

The war against the Swedes, carried on by land and sea, was signalized by several victories, owing, chiefly, to Stanislas Koniecpolski, one of the great leaders in whom Poland at that epoch was not lacking, owing also to the Polish fleet which was organized by his advice. Nevertheless, the treaty concluded at Altmark in 1629 left provisionally to Gustavus Adolphus all his conquests on the south coast of the Baltic, and enabled him to turn upon the Emperor.

Thus the alliance with the House of Austria had brought about disastrous results, which explains why Ladislas IV, who was elected without any difficulty after the death of his father in 1632, attempted also to approach France. The latter, seeing that the Hapsburgs alone profited by the hostility between Poland and Sweden, had, since the days of Henry IV, played the part of mediator between those two Powers several times. The truce of 1635, like that of 1629, was concluded with the co-operation of French diplomacy. It restored to Poland the towns of Prussia that were occupied by the Swedes, but the latter kept Livonia as far as the Dvina, and the dynastic question, which was the basis of the whole conflict, remained in suspense. The son of Sigismund III was no more willing than his father to renounce his rights to the throne of Sweden, whose Diet had definitely disinherited the Polish line of the Vasas.

The new king was far more popular in Poland than his father, who was always looked upon as a foreigner. In fact, Ladislas IV ensured one last period of peace and prosperity to the Republic. He was full of initiative and remarkably gifted; nor was he lacking in vast projects which, if they had succeeded, could have given back to Poland her old power, which had been so manifestly shaken since the first years of the seventeenth century.

Within the state, the king, conscious of the dangers presented at this epoch by religious dissensions, attempted to pacify the minds of his subjects by a policy of wide tolerance. In view of the fact that a great part of the Ruthenian population remained opposed to union with the Roman Church, Ladislas IV, at his accession, sanctioned the re-establishment of an Orthodox hierarchy side by side with that of the Uniats. An Orthodox college, founded at Kiev by the eminent Metropolitan Peter Moghila, a native of Moldavia, became an important centre of culture, open to western influences, and at the same time shedding its light beyond the eastern frontiers of the Republic. Uneasy also at the attitude of the Protestant minority, the king cherished the hope of re-establishing religious unity by means of amicable discussions, by the famous *Colloquium Charitativum*, which was held at Torun in 1645.

The atmosphere of the Thirty Years War, which was still raging in the vicinity of Poland, was by no means favourable to such a project. It failed completely. But, and this was more serious, the king was no more successful in fixing the guiding line of his foreign policy in the conflict which continued to ravage central Europe. Without sufficiently taking into account the inflexible rivalry which Richelieu's policy then opposed to that of Ferdinand II, Ladislas IV oscillated between France and Austria, avoiding a decision, although he was even given a hint of the possibility of obtaining the im-

perial crown. In 1637 he even preferred to return to the
alliance with the Hapsburgs, forgetful of his father's unfortunate experiences. He, too, in his turn married an arch-
duchess, and hastened to conclude a treaty with the new
Emperor Ferdinand III to help him to conquer Sweden.
It was not till 1645 that his second marriage to Louise Marie
de Gonzague, Princesse de Nevers, marked a revision of his
policy and a new friendliness with France, encouraged by the
most eminent of Ladislas IV's collaborators, the Chancellor
George Ossolinski.

About this time it seemed as though the last of the king's
great projects was to be realized. Deceived in his hope of
re-establishing the domination of the Vasas in the country
of their origin, he decided to turn his whole strength against
the Mussulmans. The beginning of this project, prepared by
Ladislas IV in agreement with Ossolinski and Koniecpolski,
dates, in fact, back to the first years of his reign. Here, again,
we maintain that his policy was not so fundamentally different from that of his father as has been long supposed. His
plan of an anti-Ottoman league was, however, distinct from
that which had been formerly considered by Sigismund III.
This time it was not a question of an Austrian initiative with
which Poland was to be closely associated. In accord with the
Holy See the king intended to take command of this new
crusade upon himself, ensuring the support of Venice and
even that of Moscow. Antagonism against the latter was to
have given way before a common action against the Tartars
of the Crimea, while the King of Poland, avenging the hero
of Varna whose memory his name recalled, would not only
have restored to the Republic her access to the Black Sea,
but also delivered the Balkan populations, possibly even
driven the Turks out of Europe, and given the Holy Land
back to Christendom.

It is easy to perceive all the grandeur but also all the Uto-

pian features of this plan. Where the Jagiellos in the period
of their greatest power had failed, the Poland of the seventeenth century, still great but weakened and menaced on every
side, could have no real success. And Europe, such as we see it
on the eve of the Treaty of Westphalia, was far less disposed
to lend Poland effective support than even Renaissance Europe. On the other hand, it is true that the project of Ladislas
IV had some chance of success as regards its direct and immediate object, the establishment of order and security in the
southeastern borderlands of Poland, but under the condition
of obtaining the adherence of the whole nation, which would
have had to accept very heavy sacrifices. But the king, foreseeing some resistance, fell into the mistake which had caused
so many equally happy initiatives of his predecessors to mis-
carry: he attempted to impose his plan in an arbitrary manner, disregarding the consent of the Diet, and overstepping
his constitutional authority. The opposition which inevitably
followed ended by discouraging Ladislas himself, who was,
moreover, mourning the death of his only son, and weakened
by a mortal sickness.

But what contributed the decisive factor was that public
opinion had not grasped the chief positive advantage which
the crusade dreamt of by the king could have ensured to
Poland. The nation was not yet aware of all the gravity that
the Cossack problem was assuming, a problem which would
have found a natural solution if all the Ukrainian Cossacks
had been mobilized against the Moslem world. The abandonment of Ladislas IV's great design had as its immediate
consequence a Cossack insurrection, infinitely more violent
than all those preceding it, and which, breaking out on the
eve of the king's death in the spring of 1648, was to destroy
the work of all his life, at the same time inflicting an irreparable blow to the prestige of Poland.

15

The Deluge

THE most penetrating historical intuition has found only
the one significant word 'deluge' with which to characterize
the series of catastrophes which, from 1648 onwards, shook
the foundations of the Polish State. Thanks to the vital forces
of the Polish nation the Republic emerged therefrom bat-
tered and mutilated, but independent and capable of pro-
longing her existence for more than a century. But if, as there
was every reason to fear, she had succumbed in the middle of
the seventeenth century to the enemies who were invading
her and were prepared to partition her, the cause of her fall
would have been easy to name: Poland would have been
blotted out from the map of Europe because she had been
unable to solve the problem of the Ukrainian Cossacks. It is,
therefore, all the more necessary to explain who these Cossacks, of whom we have spoken with increasing frequency in
the preceding pages, really were.

Since the end of the fifteenth century this name of Tartar
origin was given to a class, difficult to define, of the population which gradually formed in the 'Ukraine,' that is to say, on
the borders of the Jagiellonian State, under the exceptional

conditions which were created there by the perpetual danger
of the neighbourhood of the Tartars. Remaining outside the
normal organization of society and of its traditional classes,
rebellious against all authority, recruited among the Ruthenian inhabitants of the border provinces, but also among the
newcomers of every social class, these Cossacks had only one
means of livelihood: that of fighting the Mongolian invaders
while at the same time imitating their proceedings, and, in
return, making adventurous inroads as far as the Crimea and
the Ottoman strongholds on the shores of the Black Sea. Disciplined and organized, they could have rendered service to
the Republic, the more valuable since the defence of the
frontiers, entrusted to the armies of the State, always left
something to be desired. Hence projects of utilizing this
heterogeneous element, which was concentrated in the steppes
beyond the rapids of the Dnieper, make their appearance in
the middle of the sixteenth century. Sigismund Augustus and
Stephen Bathory had attempted to make part of the Cossacks,
enrolled into regiments and subject to the military authorities, into a species of army corps charged with the defence of
the frontiers. But it was impossible to admit into this organization the whole of a social group which, in peace time, had
no motive for existence; so that even the enrolled Cossacks
paid little heed to the official treaties with Turks and Tartars,
and instigated new invasions on their own account.

Naturally, no State could tolerate such a situation, which
perpetuated the disorder that reigned in the Ukraine: an ap-
pellation which more particularly signified the Palatinates of
Kiev and Braclaw. But to remedy it, the Republic, on the one
hand, would have had to guarantee to these provinces adequate security from the Tartar side, and, on the other, gradually to assimilate the Cossacks with the thousands of members
of the gentry, with whom their military occupations formed

a bond, as had been done by progressive stages with the old Ruthenian boyars. Hesitating between risky concessions and severe repressions with the object of converting the majority of the Cossacks into peasant serfs, Poland saw the repetition from the end of the sixteenth century onwards of increasingly frequent and savage insurrections. They were all the more dangerous as they inflamed provinces which differed in faith and the ethnical origin of their inhabitants from Poland proper. This explains why the social character of the problem was increased twofold by a religious or even national aspect, i.e. why the Cossacks, who were highly indifferent to the ecclesiastical point of view, became defenders of Orthodoxy, and why, at a given moment, a purely separatist movement was capable of arising in the Ukraine.

This moment arrived in 1648 when the Cossacks had found a leader of the first rank in the person of Bohdan Chmielnicki, who was himself a member of the gentry, but was anxious to avenge personal wrongs he had suffered, and when the Polish armies, hitherto generally victorious in their battles with the insurgents, experienced several shameful defeats. It was at this precise moment that Ladislas IV, who enjoyed a great reputation among the Cossacks, died, and of his two brothers, the only serious candidates for the crown, the elder, the weak' and undecided John Casimir—he had first embraced an ecclesiastical career—became King of Poland.

The new monarch was won over by the Chancellor Ossolinski to a programme of compromise with the revolt. But it was too late for a policy of concessions. Chmielnicki himself would no longer have been able to master the movement that he had unchained. The masses of the people, carried along by the Cossacks, would have nothing more to do with the nobility, the clergy, or the Jews, whom they included in one same passion of hatred; and in the midst of a social revclution, the more sanguinary inasmuch as Chmielnicki had allied himself with the Khan of the Crimea, a programme of national independence was born, which placed the Orthodox Ruthenians in opposition to the Polish Republic, and which broke with the long traditions of a common life.

The aristocracy of the revolting provinces, in great part itself of Ruthenian origin, as was notably its undisputed head, Prince Jeremy Wisniowiecki, was therefore not mistaken when it remained sceptical in regard to equivocal negotiations with Chmielnicki. The atrocities committed by the Cossacks and their allies were retaliated by hardly less cruel reprisals, and soon the richest regions of the Republic were in ruins. Wisniowiecki, whose strategic talent far surpassed that of the commanders nominated by the king, distinguished himself by the heroic defense of Zbaraz, where a small Polish garrison resisted the assaults of many thousands of Cossacks and Tartars during six weeks of Homeric combat. The royal army, which at last advanced, allowed itself to be caught in a position from which there was no exit. It was therefore necessary to conclude, in 1649, an agreement of doubtful worth, which granted considerable concessions to the Cossacks, without, however, satisfying the ambitions of their chief or the appetites of the masses he had mobilized.

The most disquieting factor was that this agreement had been negotiated with the help of the Tartars, who, as it appeared, had passed over to the side of the Poles. In reality, the whole Moslem world had resolved to profit by the civil war in the Ukraine to crush the last rampart of Christendom. The battle of Beresteczko, which lasted three days, from the 28th to the 30th June 1651, was, therefore, of decisive importance for the whole of Europe. The king, who had at last succeeded in assembling a new army, gained a brilliant victory over Chmielnicki, who with his Turkish and Tartar reinforcements commanded forces three times superior in number. But, like so many other Polish victories, this military success had no sequel. Neither the king nor the nobility, divided by factious rivalries, showed sufficient perseverance and energy to put an end to the chaos which continued to reign in the Ukraine.

At last, in 1654, Chmielnicki, who, on the eve of Beresteczko, had not hesitated to place himself under the suzerainty of the sultan, took a decision still more serious for the future of his people. By the terms of the Treaty of Perejaslaw he placed the Ukraine under the suzerainty of Alexis, the Tsar of Moscow, who promised it a large autonomy. This promise was not kept. On the contrary, Great Russia took advantage of this rash act of the Cossack leader to attach the Little Russia of Kiev as closely as possible to herself and to resume her old programme of aggression against her western neighbour. In the same year the Muscovite invasion, a tardy retaliation for the Polish intervention at the beginning of the seventeenth century, tore Lithuania's White Ruthenian borderlands from her, including Smolensk, and the following year, in the summer of 1655, Wilno itself fell into the hands of the enemy.

Some ten days after the sanguinary sack of the capital of the Grand Duchy, Princes Janusz and Boguslas Radziwill, instead of defending Lithuania, treacherously handed her over to another invader. For the tsar had not been the only one to profit by the misfortunes of the Republic. Charles Gustavus, Palatine of Zweibrucken, who had been King of Sweden since 1654, had without scruple broken the truce with Poland so as to ensure his share in a partition that seemed imminent. Aiming, above all, at the occupation of Prussia in order to secure all the Baltic coast for Sweden, Charles Gustavus was helped at the outset by the policy of the Elector, Frederick William, who was determined to take this unique opportunity of freeing himself from the bond of vassalage which united East Prussia to Poland. But, what was far worse, the treachery which, declaring itself in Lithuania, intended to replace the Jagiellonian union by an improvised union with Sweden, also delivered Poland proper to the new aggressor.

A magnate who had fallen out with the king, the Vice-Chancellor Radziejowski, had encouraged Charles Gustavus to take the field. Another, the Palatine Opalinski, after having sought the Elector's protection, brought about the capitulation of the whole of Great Poland to the Swedish army. The veterans of the Thirty Years War took Warsaw on 8th September 1655; a few weeks later Cracow, in its turn, was obliged to surrender. The lawful king, abandoned and discouraged, took refuge on the borders of Silesia, and all the provinces, one after another, rendered homage to Charles Gustavus. Only a miracle could save the Republic.

At the height of the disaster this miracle was effected. Like a Noah's ark in the midst of the deluge, the monastery of Czestochowa resisted the enemy. The prior, Augustine Kordecki, gathered a handful of soldiers round the picture, venerated for centuries, of the Black Madonna; and after a forty days' siege the Swedes were, for the first time, forced to beat a retreat. This was on the day after Christmas. Faced with this unheard-of fact, which seemed like a legendary tale, the nation recovered itself. It mattered little now that in the beginning of 1656 the Great Elector, consummating his disloyalty, allied himself with the King of Sweden and declared himself his vassal in his capacity of Duke of Prussia. Some days later the Confederation of Tyszowce united the immense majority of the Polish nobility and gentry round John Casimir, who had returned from exile, and the whole country in a unanimous outburst of reviving patriotism rose against the foreigner. The chief traitors disappeared, struck by death that seemed a judgment of heaven, and courageous and disinterested leaders, Stephen Czarniecki in Poland, Paul Sapieha in Lithuania, placed themselves at the head of the movement of liberation.

The king himself, mediocre as he was, then lived the great hours of his life. He, too, yielded to the inspiration of religious enthusiasm which had rekindled love for a native land, and to the exalted moral convictions which called the nation to the expiation of inveterate faults. When he reached Lwow, that ever faithful city which had just repulsed Cossacks, Tartars, and Muscovites, John Casimir solemnly made a double vow.

In the name of the whole nation he first proclaimed that the Blessed Virgin should henceforth be venerated as 'Queen of the Crown of Poland.' The Polish nation was never to be false to that promise. The cult of Our Lady remained its supreme consolation through epochs the anguish of which surpassed that of 1655.

At the same time John Casimir swore that when once his native land was freed, the peasant population should in its turn be liberated from the serfdom by which it was oppressed. This serfdom was no heavier in Poland than in other contemporary States, including her neighbours. But in a country which boasted of being a land of liberty it was peculiarly unjust to limit that liberty to a single class which identified itself with the nation. This identification was now more than ever arbitrary, considering that the nobility had so ill fulfilled the task of defending the country, which mission was the only justification of its privileges. Moreover, in a country where the bourgeoisie had never had the same importance as in the west, and was being increasingly effaced, it was all the more regrettable that the peasants who constituted the immense majority of the population should be deprived of all their rights. And even when they saw their position growing steadily worse since the economic transformations of the sixteenth century that were felt in Poland as elsewhere, the Polish peasants never reacted by revolts, so frequent in other countries. It was in vain that the Cossacks attempted to gain them over to the civil war directed against the nobility. Their propaganda won only insignificant results in the purely Polish provinces, whose rural population distinguished itself, on the contrary, in the nation's struggles against foreign conquerors, above all against the Swedes.

In spite of all this, this second promise of John Casimir's was unfortunately not respected. Nothing was done all through the following century to ameliorate the lot of the Polish peasant. And this may be the basic reason why the war of liberation did not realize its initial hopes, and did not mark a real regeneration of the Republic.

This war, moreover, dragged on for several years, during the course of which each success was followed by a fresh reverse of fortune. Charles Gustavus, threatened in the spring of 1656 with total defeat, escaped with the bulk of his army. On the 30th June Warsaw was liberated, but a month later an unsuccessful three days' battle caused her to fall once more for several weeks into the enemy's hands. The alliance concluded with Austria ensured indispensable reinforcements to Poland, and so ameliorated her diplomatic situation that she was able to gain another ally in Denmark. But this did not prevent the King of Sweden from building up new plans for the partition of the Republic, and even a prince with as little power as George Rakoczy, of Transylvania, believed he could attack her with impunity in order to claim his share. He was defeated, and ended by losing his own principality, and soon the Elector of Brandenburg, kept in play by the Hapsburgs, found it convenient to become reconciled with John Casimir. But his alliance with Poland had to be paid for by the Treaty of Wehlau, on the 19th September 1657, which put an end to Polish suzerainty over East Prussia, with the result that a veritable foreign wedge dependent on Berlin was established between Polish West Prussia and the Grand Duchy of Lithuania.

In 1658 and 1659 the war with the Swedes, of which so many romantic details have been described for us in the celebrated memoirs of John Chrysostom Pasek, was obviously drawing to its end. But in these same years the last project of agreement with the Cossacks collapsed. Since the death of Bohdan Chmielnicki in 1657, the moderate element, disposed to enter into an understanding with Poland, seemed to be uppermost in the Ukraine, and John Wyhowski, having secured the rule during the minority of Bohdan's son, concluded a very important treaty with the representatives of the king, the Union of Hadziacz, ratified by the Diet of 1659. This union ought to have happily completed that of Lublin by creating a Ruthenian duchy similar to the Grand Duchy of Lithuania, and, like it, placed on an equal footing with the Republic of Poland. It was to be limited to the Ukraine proper, that is to say, the Palatinates of Kiev, Braclaw, and Czernihow; but this solution was, in any case, far more favourable to the Cossacks and the Ruthenians in general than their subjection to Moscow had been. Unfortunately, this treaty could not take effect in an atmosphere of reciprocal distrust. Among the Cossacks, themselves divided, the party of young George Chmielnicki proved itself the strongest. The tsar, whose support he sought, imposed conditions upon the Ukraine that were of great danger to her autonomy, and once more attempted to conquer Lithuania also, from which country he had been driven back during the course of the preceding years.

The year 1660 at last brought the greatly needed peace with

Sweden, and on tolerable conditions. It was only a case of renouncing Livonia on the north of the Dvina, which since the days of Gustavus Adolphus had been practically lost. The work of the Congress of Oliva which reconciled the two nations was placed under the guarantee of Louis XIV, who, like his predecessors, had played the part of mediator between Pole and Swede. In this same year appreciable defeats were inflicted on the armies of the tsar and George Chmielnicki, but the hostilities on that side were indefinitely protracted. Tartars and Turks again threatened to profit by the struggles that were tearing the Ukraine, and finally Poland and Russia, signing in 1667 the Truce of Andruszow, divided between them the country which had dreamt of a more or less complete independence. The Republic was forced to abandon to the tsar, with Smolensk and Czernihow, all the territories beyond the Dnieper, and even the greatly coveted town of Kiev on its right bank. The latter was only yielded provisionally for two years, but it was easy to foresee that it would not be given back to Poland.

As a final result, it was thus that the Ukraine and the national aspirations of the Ruthenian people were ruined by the movement started by Bohdan Chmielnicki. Poland was saved, but at the price of desperate efforts and sinister concessions which she was obliged to make to the gain of Berlin and Moscow. These concessions were the more inevitable because, without waiting for the end of the war on the eastern boundaries of the Republic, a new internal conflict had broken out. The history of this conflict offers striking analogies with the constitutional crises that we have encountered in the course of the preceding years. The project of a reform, more than ever necessary, but propagated by the court in an inopportune manner, again provoked a violent reaction which, as under Sigismund III, reached civil war.

The most deplorable abuse to have deformed Polish parliamentarism was, beyond all doubt, the too famous *liberum veto,* which permitted any deputy to dissolve the Diet, even annulling the decisions taken before his intervention. This absurd consequence of the principle of unanimity, a principle long applied in a reasonable fashion, had developed as time went on, and it is not accurate to date it from the Diet of 1652, dissolved by the deputy Sicinski. But the application of the *liberum veto* had never before been of so revolting a nature. Neither had it ever been so clear that the member of the gentry who put himself forward as the champion of democratic liberty, was only the miserable instrument of one of the great lords who, in spite of the dogma of absolute equality among the nobility, in reality exercised an increasingly dominating influence on their less fortunate 'brothers.'

To the project of remedying this vice of parliamentary life, that was ceaselessly discussed since the darkest days of the Deluge, there was added, in the same epoch, the often renewed plan of avoiding the troubles of a 'free' election after the death of a childless king by nominating his successor during his lifetime. This plan especially appealed to the queen, that same French princess Louise Marie who, soon after the death of her first husband, Ladislas IV, had married his brother, gaining an extraordinary influence over John Casimir. It goes without saying that she wished to give him a French successor and, in agreement with Cardinal Mazarin, she chose the Duc d'Enghien, son of the Great Condé.

The opposition which arose against this project, and which had the Grand Marshal of Poland, George Lubomirski, at its head, exasperated the queen to the point of resorting to corruption, to conspiracies, and even to a *coup d'état,* which she prepared in secret. On the other side, Lubomirski had not hesitated to encourage a purely revolutionary movement among the disbanded troops, who were in vain demanding their pay. At the Diet of 1664, the defender of the threatened liberties found himself sternly condemned under the influence of the court, and it was then that, imitating Zebrzydowski, he placed himself at the head of a second rebellion, which ended in 1666, in exactly the same way as the first. After fratricidal combats, a mournful epilogue to the Deluge, Lubomirski asked pardon of the king, who, on his side, was obliged to renounce all his plans of reform, including the idea of altering the law of free election.

Yet the election of John Casimir's successor took place before his death. For, disillusioned and worn out by his many trials, and foreseeing the future partitions of the Republic, the last Vasa only waited for his wife's death to abdicate the following year, in September 1668. Four years later he died in France, where he had retired to the abbey of Nevers; and his heart, which during his life had never known rest, found it at last under the aisles of the church of Saint-Germain-des-Prés.

16

John Sobieski

At the election of 1669 all the foreign candidates, representing the most diverse dynasties, presented themselves in vain. This time the recent memory of the many invasions and the many intrigues at the court of the last Vasa brought about the realization of an idea which had been discussed since the first free election: that of raising to the throne a compatriot belonging to the ranks of the Polish nobility, a new 'Piast.'

Unfortunately, the unanimous choice fell upon a completely insignificant personage, a young man who had nothing to recommend him to the electors except his father's name. Michael Wisniowiecki was the only son of that Prince Jeremy who had covered himself with glory by opposing almost alone the mounting flood of the Cossack insurrection, and who had died prematurely. But King Michael bore no sort of resemblance to this much admired hero. Neither the tradition which maintained that his family was descended from a brother of Jagiello, nor his marriage with a sister of the Emperor Leopold I, could enhance his authority. As regards internal affairs, he showed himself incapable of controlling the scandalous rivalries between the partisans of France and those of Austria. He was still more feeble in the face of the sanguinary troubles which were perpetual in the Ukraine and which, at last, provoked the most dangerous intervention of the epoch, that of the Sultan Mahomet IV, to whose suzerainty the Cossack leader Doroszenko had submitted. In 1672 the fortress of Kamieniec in Podolia was taken by the Turks, to whom an ignominious peace surrendered the whole of that province as well as all that was still left to Poland of the Ukraine.

But at the side of an indolent king there stood the great figure of a leader in war who had already distinguished himself under John Casimir in battle with the Mussulmans. It was he who the following year carried off the second victory of Chocim, a more brilliant one than the first, which in 1621 had avenged the death of Stanislas Zolkiewski. John Sobieski, who was, moreover, a great-grandson of the hero of Cecora, thereby saved Poland from a new Ottoman invasion, and at the same time gained the royal crown. For Michael Wisniowiecki died on the eve of this victory, and when the triumphant victor appeared at the election of 1674 he was elected in an outburst of general enthusiasm.

This time no better choice could have been made. The noble who accepted the succession to the Piasts and the Jagiellos was entirely worthy of it. In the whole history of the ancient Republic there is no name more popular in Poland, better known abroad, than that of Sobieski. And we know to-day that the traditional prestige which had not ceased to surround his memory is fully justified in the light of critical research.

He was not only a great military commander. Like the most eminent of his predecessors, he concerned himself as much with the eastern problems which had a passionate interest for him as the defender of Christendom, as with the political possibilities which an alliance with the France of Louis XIV opened to.him in the west and on the Baltic. This alliance was concluded in 1675 by the new king of Poland, who had married a Frenchwoman of Queen Louise Marie's court, the beautiful and tenderly loved Marie Casimire de la Grange d'Arquien. This Franco-Polish alliance was directed, in the first place, against the Great Elector, Frederick William of Brandenburg, with the definite object of recapturing East Prussia, which was, in fact, very discontented under the absolutism of Berlin. This plan, which would have redeemed a long series of Polish political mistakes reaching as far back as that of Conrad of Masovia, preoccupied John III for several years. In 1677 he concluded a new alliance to this effect with Sweden by a treaty signed at Danzig. But soon a complete and sudden change seemed to come over the king's foreign policy. The king, who had supported the Hungarian insurgents against Austria and had even thought of reclaiming Silesia which had so long been lost, gradually approached the Emperor, and instead of pursuing the project of a coalition against the Elector of Brandenburg he took the initiative in forming a Christian league against the Turks. This new policy, which began in the Diet of 1678–9, ended in 1683 with the memorable campaign which was to save the capital of the Hapsburgs.

The relief of Vienna holds so considerable a place in universal history that it.is necessary to grasp, as clearly as we can, the complex reasons which determined this unlooked-for orientation of Polish policy. For it was by no means the result of a lack of firm decision on Sobieski's part any more than of the caprices of his wife, of which so much has been said. On the contrary, this change of attitude is to be explained, not so much by the diplomatic adaptability of the king as by his qualities as a clear-sighted statesman who, in addition, perfectly understood the nation who had entrusted him with power.

John III's original plans could not have succeeded unless they had been unreservedly supported by Louis XIV. Now the latter never came to the point of ensuring that security to Poland on the Turkish side which was indispensable before she could undertake an action of wide scope on the coast of the Baltic. The efforts at conciliation attempted by French diplomacy did not prevent new Ottoman attacks in 1674 and 1675, attacks which were only repulsed owing to new victories on the part of the king, and which, in spite of his brilliant defence of the city of Lwow, were repeated in 1676. This time French mediation contributed to· the signing of the preliminaries of peace, which, however, were unsatisfactory for Poland since they left the·greater part of Podolia with Kamieniec to the Turks. The co-operation with Moscow on which Sobieski had for a time counted proved to be still more illusory, inasmuch as the new Tsar Feodor soon concluded a long truce with the Porte. Under these conditions the Mussulman danger took precedence for the moment over all others.

Sobieski was aware that the danger from the side of the Hohenzollerns might in the future become still more disquieting. But the Great Elector succeeded, in 1679, in himself forming an alliance with Louis XIV, and found French diplomats to help him in upholding the opposition directed in Poland against the king. This opposition was composed chiefly of partisans of Austria and conducted by magnates jealous of Sobieski's elevation and unscrupulous as to the means they employed. It had, from the outset, created innumerable difficulties for the king and paralysed the work of the Diets, so that every bolder initiative in foreign relations became a risk. At one moment John III had wished to march against Brandenburg without waiting for the approval of the

Diet, and to take possession of East Prussia for his family as the basis of a dynastic policy. But, unwilling to alienate the sympathies of his people, he renounced the idea, and looked for some object that he could pursue with the support of the nation.

It goes without saying that the alliance with Austria was only a means to an end. Sobieski was not ignorant of the fact that if thereby he tranquillized the partisans of the Hapsburgs, at the same time he created a new opposition, composed of the partisans of France. But, very skilful in his relations with the great lords, whose susceptibilities he knew how to spare, and of whom only one, the Grand Treasurer Morsztyn, went so far as treason, John III aimed, above all, at rallying to himself the great majority of the gentry and rekindling the enthusiasm which had decided his election. This enthusiasm, evoked in 1674 by the victorious defence of the Republic against the Mussulman invasion, could only be reawakened in the presence of an equally great reason. A war designed to occupy East Prussia would have had the appearance, at least, of a war of aggression and conquest, and consequently would never have gathered the whole nation, which had little knowledge of Berlin's diplomatic intrigues, round the king. On the contrary, every member of the Polish gentry understood the nature of the situation, both humiliating and perilous, which the Mussulman advance created for his country. An appeal for the defence of the Republic and Christendom, in conformity with age-long traditions, was sure to meet again with a universal response.

Moreover, the king had no intention of a co-operation only with Austria. The Peace of Nimeguen, concluded in the beginning of 1679, appeared to remove the obstacles which had opposed the formation of a league of all the Christian Powers against the common enemy. To realize this project that

Sobieski had had in consideration for several years, Polish ambassadors went not only to Vienna, Venice, and Rome, but also to France, England, and the Low Countries. It was, however, easy to foresee that, apart from the Holy See, only the Emperor would receive the Polish initiative favourably, as he also was directly threatened by the Ottoman power. This menace became all the greater when, in 1682, Tököly, the leader of the Hungarian opposition, made his submission to the Turks. John III's negotiations with Leopold I, there-fore, ended in a complete agreement. All that remained to be done was to gain over the Polish Diet to a treaty of al-liance with Austria, which especially provided that, in the case of an attack directed against the capital of one of the contracting parties, the other would go immediately to its help; a clause evidently dictated by Vienna's dangerous situ-ation.

It was then that Sobieski exercised all his energy and all his skill to obtain unanimity of public opinion. He succeeded admirably. On 31st March 1683, the Diet authorized the sig-nature of the treaty, which demanded of Poland, exhausted by many wars, an extraordinary effort; and the whole country showed a readiness which shrank from no sacrifice and which recalled the best hours of the past. Poland once more rose to her feet, conscious of a historic mission to fulfil.

In the July of the same year the case provided for in the alliance, that had hardly been as yet concluded, became fact. One hundred and thirty-eight thousand Turks, commanded by the Vizier Kara Mustafa, laid siege to Vienna, the fate of which seemed desperate. Responding to the appeal of the Pope and the Emperor, the King of Poland immediately pro-ceeded to mobilize, and rapidly led an army of thirty thou-sand men into Austria. The Austrians had also obtained rein-forcements from most of the princes of the Empire, with the exception of the Elector of Brandenburg. Their forces, which numbered forty-six thousand soldiers, were commanded by Prince Charles of Lorraine, who a short time previously had considered contending with John Sobieski for the Polish crown. Happily, no personal rancour hindered the collaboration of the two leaders, and by unanimous agreement the supreme command was entrusted to the king, who with his own hand drew up the plan of campaign. The unique experience he had acquired in the course of his glorious battles with Turks and Tartars secured unreserved acceptance of his orders, and this same experience made the presence of the flower of the Polish knighthood doubly valuable.

It was, in fact, the latter which decided the great battle of the 12th of September 1683. Descending from the heights of the Wienerwald, its terrible charge broke the furious resistance that the enemy was opposing to the German troops. By the evening, the immense Ottoman army was in flight, and amidst the enthusiastic acclamations of a population delivered after great sufferings, the King of Poland entered the walls of Vienna as its saviour. The victims of Varna and Mohacs were avenged, the advance of Islam arrested for ever, and before the eyes of the whole Christian world a last ray of glory shone upon the twilight of the Republic.

In the face of such a spectacle we almost hesitate to reckon up in cold blood the advantages that Poland reaped from this campaign. It has sometimes been regarded as an act of useless generosity, even dangerous in its consequences, since it served the interests of a State which a hundred years later shared in the partitions of the Republic. The most competent of our historians have refuted this superficial and narrow point of view. We know to-day that Sobieski's decision, generous as it was, was also justified by the circumstances, and by the fact that the fall of Vienna would have had for Poland also incal-

culable consequences. Independently, besides, of any immediate advantage, the victory of 1683 had a moral bearing of
the first order and of lasting value. It recalled the traditional
role of Poland in the history of Christian Europe; it showed
that the Republic, in spite of all her weaknesses, was still
capable of worthily filling that role; it became a symbolic
memory whose value increased with the misfortunes which
were again to fall upon our country.

We have all the more reason to ask ourselves another question, more disturbing and more difficult to determine. Why
did not the second half of the reign of John III, which followed that unparalleled but short-lived triumph, realize any
of the hopes of 1683? Why, on the contrary, did it know only
lamentable failures, inaugurating the period of the deepest
decadence of the Royal Republic? This turn of events is the
more surprising as Sobieski cannot be reproached with the
want of perseverance and consistency which prevented so
many other Polish victories from being turned to good account. Without being discouraged by the cold and haughty
reception to which Leopold I, on his return to his capital,
treated him, the king, before he went back to Poland, took
part also in the beginning of the campaign in Hungary, faced
new dangers there, and distinguished himself by new feats of
arms; and the following year, on 5th March 1684, he formed
with Austria, the Holy See, and Venice, that 'Holy League,'
whose obligations never ceased to direct all his foreign policy.
But the reproach commonly levelled against him is precisely
that of having made himself, so to speak, the slave of that policy of the league, of having continued to serve only the
interests of his allies, exhausting the Polish forces in sterile
undertakings.

In our opinion, the problem has been badly stated. To
make the Republic benefit by the *beau geste* of 1683, it was
indispensable to pursue the war against the Turks, and this it

was quite impossible to carry out otherwise than by co-operation with Austria and the other western Powers with which
even France seemed ready to associate herself. It was no less
natural that, leaving the Austrians to recapture Hungary
from the Ottoman Porte, the King of Poland should have
started his subsequent campaigns from Podolia, where Kamieniec still remained in the enemy's hands, and that he should
have directed them towards the Black Sea so as to restore
access thereto to the Republic. But he seems to us to have
committed a serious mistake in his choice of the route which
was to lead him to that sea, as well as of the territories which
were to be the reward of his efforts. From 1684 to 1691, Sobieski incessantly renewed his attempts to conquer Moldavia
and even Walachia, and thus to reach the lower Danube and
its mouth. To gain this object he was obliged to fight, not
only the Turks, but also a Christian population, hostile to
his intervention, and at the same time he impaired his relations with the Hapsburgs, who desired to re-establish the
former Hungarian influence in these regions. Devoting all
his forces to a series of expeditions fully as unfortunate as
many other Polish campaigns in Moldavia—it is enough to
recall that of 1497—losing his prestige of an invincible leader,
the king at the same time lost sight of the essential problem
which presented itself to Poland from the side of the Black
Sea: that of re-establishing her domination over the steppes
between the Dniester and the Dnieper, reaching the coast
between their mouths, and putting an end to the continual
invasions of the Tartars of the Crimea.

John III, who knew how to treat the remaining Cossacks
with such wise moderation, and who made the work of the
union of the Churches progress peacefully, seemed admirably qualified to solve the question of the Ukraine and to
repair the errors of the past there. Unfortunately, he re
signed himself to concluding the treaty of peace with Mos-

cow in 1686 which perpetuated the surrenders of the truce
of 1667, including that of Kiev, in the hope that the tsar
would, on his side, give his support to the Holy League, and
would, in particular, take upon himself the struggle with the
Tartars. This illusion was no less deplorable than that which
at one moment led the king to seek the alliance of the Khan
of the Crimea himself, whose hordes were ceaselessly penetrating into the very heart of Polish territory, again threatening Lwow. The opportunity of making Poland benefit
from that enfeebling of the Ottoman power to which her
king had contributed in so decisive a manner, was thus definitely lost.

The plan of conquering Moldavia which for so long en-
grossed John III is chiefly explained by his desire to make of
it a sovereign principality for his son. Is this dynastic motive
an additional reason to criticize the project? We think not.
From the outset of his reign Sobieski had cherished the ambition of founding a dynasty. This ambition was not only
justified by the desire of sparing the Republic the danger of
a new interregnum after his death; it was also the essential
point of a whole programme of constitutional reforms envisaged by the king. Here, again, he proceeded with a good
deal of prudence, and while doubtless inspired by the example of Louis XIV, he had no intention of imposing an
absolute monarchy on the Polish nation, but rather of gradually eliminating the abuses which had vitiated the parliamentary regime and made the principle of the free election
of the kings one of increasing danger.

Sobieski would, perhaps, have succeeded here had his military glory lasted. Losing the ascendancy which he owed to
his victories, he could not surmount the double obstacle
which presented itself in his path. On the one hand, the
neighbours of Poland, who had every interest in maintaining
internal disorder there, united at this epoch in impeding

every reform capable of consolidating the Royal Republic. Without ignoring the steps that Frederick William of Brandenburg took to this effect, attention should be drawn to the treaty concluded in 1676 between Austria and Russia, who undertook to defend Polish liberties against the projects of the king. On the other hand, it is undeniable that this attitude of foreign Powers could not have embroiled the internal life of the Republic had it not been that those Powers found blind instruments in the persons of many of the great lords, in the pay of foreign courts, who were mutual rivals, but who, above all else, acted in stubborn opposition to John Sobieski. We have seen him triumph over their proceedings on the eve of the Vienna campaign. He was less fortunate in this respect on the eve of his death, the more so because this time the opposition had found particularly violent leaders in the Sapieha family.

But what gave the finishing stroke to the ageing king's discouragement was dissension in the bosom of his own family. The queen was certainly justified in attempting a new *rapprochement* with France, and the treaty that she negotiated with Louis XIV in 1692 seemed to promise Poland a solid support against Austria, Russia, and Prussia combined. Unfortunately, the treaty was never put into force; and, moreover, all Maria Casimira's policy was dictated by her personal ambitions and by her hatred of her eldest son James, who, married to a sister of the Empress, allowed himself to be influenced entirely by the court of Vienna. Under these conditions, although there was some question of the candidature of James's younger brother Alexander, who was more worthy of the crown, it was with no hope of leaving the throne to his descendants that their father died in 1696. The hero of 1683 departed with the mournful presentiment that nothing could now avert the ruin of the Republic.

17

The Decay

ACCORDING to the argument of one of our most distinguished historians, the epoch of Polish independence came to an end in 1696, and the hundred years which preceded the Partitions constitute, with the century that followed them, an epoch of struggle to re-establish that independence. Under a paradoxical appearance this idea contains a good deal of truth. It is, at least, true that the four kings who succeeded John Sobieski were imposed on their electors by foreign Powers. This affected fatally all their foreign policy, and at home the nation was no longer free to proceed with the most indispensable reforms, because its neighbours saw in these an obstacle to their plans of partition. These plans, which we have seen appear at different critical moments of Polish history, became at the end of the seventeenth century an almost permanent spectre, and for long—unhappily, too long —the Poles were unable to find the forces necessary to react against the tragic conclusion which was visibly approaching.

Fortunately, this melancholy story does not apply to the whole of the last century of the Republic. We shall see that the last third of the century repaired many errors. Nothing on the contrary is more depressing than the history of the sixty-six years that the rule of the kings of the House of Saxony lasted in Poland. A great part of the responsibility for this falls, without doubt, on these two kings. But how can we explain the fact that the Polish nation, so jealous of its right of free election, should have twice accepted foreign kings whose candidature had only been upheld by a minority? And, above all, how can we explain the fact that this nation, accustomed for centuries to oppose every abuse, real or apparent, of the royal power, should have tolerated the arbitrary methods, unscrupulous and lacking in greatness, of an Augustus II, as well as the revolting indolence of an Augustus III?

We see here, in the first place, a proof that the part of the king in our former Republic was by no means so insignificant as the text of the constitution would have led us to suppose. But we must also admit that the Polish nation was then passing through the most profound moral crisis that it had ever undergone. The share of responsibility that falls to it was far more the result of a failure of moral sense than of the obstinacy with which it defended its traditional institutions. We have stated that the experiment of the Royal Republic, such as it emerged from the first interregnum, could only succeed if its structure, bold and at the same time delicate, was sustained by moral principles orientating its political life. We have noted on several occasions the signs of a weakening, at least transitory, of the moral forces of the nation, showing itself in the unpardonable faults committed by its leaders. But the reason which eventually led to the breakdown of the forces of a whole people was the long series of almost uninterrupted wars, including those particularly pernicious episodes of civil strife, which filled the Polish seventeenth century.

Far longer, taken altogether, than the Thirty Years War, the consequences of which for Germany are well known, almost recalling the Hundred Years War which came near to destroying France, these wars had internal consequences for Poland still more disastrous than their territorial losses. Fought out in great part on the still very extensive territory which remained to Poland, they ruined her economically. Absorbing the flower of the nation, they made us pay for even our victories, not only by our best blood, but also by a halt, if not a backward step, in the development of our civilization.

The consequences were to be felt even in the religious sphere, from which the source of Poland's life had sprung for centuries. Religious exaltation, so often in the seventeenth century the decisive factor in Poland's struggles with Mussulmans, schismatics, and heretics, could not last. What replaced it was, unhappily, not the sentiment of daily duty, inspired by the Christian understanding of life, but a sentiment which attached itself, above all, to the exterior forms of devotion, and which was too often manifested in a negative way by the ill will which accumulated against all the Dissidents. It was, therefore, incapable of triumphing over another sentiment which appears to have hovered over the whole of this epoch: that of an extreme lassitude which was the basis of the worst weaknesses, and which tolerated the most degrading adventures in public and private life.

Under these conditions the Poland whose regeneration by her own strength John Sobieski had not succeeded in effecting, had imperative need of the support of another state. This support could not come to her from any of the neighbouring countries, which were only too anxious to profit by her weakness. Against this there was another state, very distant, it is true, but united to Poland by ever closer bonds of intellectual affinities and influence, a state which had every interest in making the Royal Republic, duly consolidated, a sure ally in the east of Europe. This was France, who had already so often negotiated with Poland on the subject of such an alliance, and who precisely at this epoch was living the great century of her history. In fact it was a French candidature, put forward in spite of the preceding failures at the election of 1697, the candidature of Prince François Louis de Conti, that seemed this time to have the most chances of success. Among the other candidatures, as usual very numerous, it was the only one that corresponded with the interests of the country, and for which an indisputable majority declared itself. But hardly had the Primate of Poland proclaimed Conti's election when a minority opposed him with a candidate who had appeared nearly at the last moment, Frederick Augustus I, Elector of Saxony, who hastened to have himself crowned King of Poland under the name of Augustus II.

The Poles had never wished for a king of German origin. Accordingly, they had in the past discarded candidates who were worth much more than Augustus the Strong. His despotic ways, which with his physical strength had gained him this surname, were assuredly not of a nature to win the sympathies of the Polish nobility. The descendant of a Protestant dynasty, he had recently embraced Catholicism; but every one knew that this conversion was only inspired by the desire of becoming King of Poland. He was able to secure the throne of Poland thanks only to the unanimous support of the Powers who eventually brought about the Partitions. That of the new tsar was particularly efficacious, as Peter the Great did not content himself with the corruption practised by the other courts: he also applied a method which the tsars and their ambassadors were to follow through the whole of

the eighteenth century, that of intimidation. Nevertheless
two years were needed to break all resistance. The Prince de
Conti even attempted to disembark in Poland, and it was
only when discouraged by the hostility of the Danzigers that
he returned to France. But it was not till the Diet of 1699,
called the Diet of Pacification, that his partisans acknowledged Augustus II as their lawful king.

This same date marks the liquidation of John III's political programme and the inauguration of that of his successor.
The latter began by gathering the tardy fruits of Sobieski's
victories, when the Peace of Karlowitz restored the fortress
of Kamieniec to Poland with the rest of the Podolian borderlands occupied, until then, by the Turks. He then launched
out into an enterprise that was directly contrary to the interests of his new kingdom. Poland had imperative need of
peace. Augustus II dragged her against her will into a new
war, which completed her ruin. She had no more implacable
enemy than Peter the Great; the king made him his intimate
ally. Since the Treaty of Oliva every reason for a conflict
with Sweden had disappeared. The king's project of attacking that country, in concert with Denmark and Russia, rekindled that conflict. The only advantage of an eventual victory would have been the recovery of Livonia; but Augustus
II promised his Russian ally and Frederick I of Prussia, who
was soon to assume the royal title, and even Austria, territorial compensations in advance which were equivalent to as
many projects for the partition of Poland.

The great northern war began, however, in 1700 by a defeat of all the allies, and it was Poland who paid the cost by
becoming the territory where the epic of Charles XII was
enacted. The Poles in vain declared that they were in no way
parties to the aggression that their king had perpetrated
against Sweden. Charles, in his turn, invaded Poland, and in

1702 the greater part of the country, including Warsaw and Cracow, found itself, as in 1655, in the hands of the Swedes. From the outset their young king had laid down as the condition of peace the deposition of Augustus II. In 1704 he, in fact, caused the election of a new King of Poland. The candidate he nominated, after having first considered a son of John Sobieski, was the Palatine of Poznania, Stanislas Leszczynski.

This national king beyond doubt deserved general esteem. His subsequent career, although abounding in disillusions, proved him infinitely more worthy of the crown than Augustus of Saxony. But the first election of Leszczynski was still less legal than that of his rival had been. Its consequence, furthermore, was to divide the nation into two opposite camps, one of which endured all the caprices of the Swedish conqueror, while the other humiliated itself before the Russian despot. After having effected the coronation of Stanislas I, Charles XII, wearying at last of sterile battles in Poland, in the autumn of 1705 turned directly upon Saxony, and in the following year imposed upon Augustus II the Treaty of Altranstadt, which compelled him to renounce the throne.

The King of Sweden had now only one adversary left, but that one was the most formidable of all. As we know, his war with Peter the Great, in which he counted on the support of the Cossacks of Mazeppa, the defender of Ukrainian autonomy, ended, on 8th July 1709, with the catastrophe of Poltava. This battle likewise decided the fate of Poland. Leszczynski naturally had to depart into exile, and Augustus II was re-established. But it has been rightly said that it was the tsar who then became the real master of Poland. It is true that in 1711 he suffered an unexpected check in his campaign against the Turks, with whom Charles XII had taken refuge, and who seemed suddenly to become allies of Poland.

However, all they were in reality intending was to seize the opportunity of recapturing the Polish Ukraine; and, moreover, Peter the Great knew how to extricate himself at very little cost from the blind alley in which he had involved himself. Understanding that as yet it was too soon to dream of the partition of the Ottoman Empire, he preferred to profit by the decline of Poland, not to partition her as the King of Prussia then suggested, but to subject her entirely to his scarcely disguised domination.

The king himself soon offered him an excellent pretext to make his influence decisively felt there. Augustus the Strong believed the moment had come in which to realize the project that had haunted him since his election to the throne of Poland, that of making it by a *coup d'état* the throne of an absolute monarch. This plan, which had not even the merit of involving serious and positive reforms of the Polish constitution, naturally came up against a furious opposition which in 1715 ranged the great majority of the nobility, coalescing in the Confederation of Tarnogrod, against the Saxon army of Field Marshal Flemming. In this conflict between the king and the nation it was the ambassador of the tsar who played the part of arbitrator. The agreement which he negotiated, and which was ratified by the 'Dumb Diet' of 1717, claimed to pacify the Republic. In reality it signified the most profound humiliation for her. It limited her army to the ridiculous figure of twenty-four thousand men, a figure that the provisions relating to the maintenance of the troops did not even permit of its actually attaining. From that moment Poland found herself disarmed in the midst of the military powers who surrounded her on all sides.

Augustus II himself had had enough of his ally by now. The prodigious success of the tsar, who was preparing to assume the imperial title, was, moreover, beginning to arouse considerable uneasiness in Europe. In 1719 the king was consequently enabled to enter into an alliance against him with the Emperor Charles VI and even with England under conditions very favourable for Poland. Considering the indignation which roused the whole of the latter country against the Muscovite design, the hour seemed at last propitious for an understanding between the king and the nation, inspired this time by the vital interests of the Republic.

This moment, unique in the long reign of Augustus II, was unfortunately lost. The king could scarcely be surprised that he met with no confidence, for until now he had done nothing to deserve it. But he was assuredly not wrong in reproaching the Poles for the shameful weakness which in 1720 led them to renounce every effort that could have delivered them from the supremacy of the tsar. The latter, on his part, concluded with Prussia the first treaty directly aimed against the existence of Poland, and designed to prevent in advance any project of recuperation. A year later, in 1721, the Peace of Nystadt, imposed on Sweden soon after the death of Charles XII, ended the northern war to the sole advantage of Peter the Great. Until his own death in 1725 the latter did not cease to work for the ruin of the Republic, and as she no longer counted in the general policy of Europe, he and his successors meddled all the more boldly in her internal life.

During all the rest of Augustus II's reign only one event attracted foreign attention to Poland. But it was of a nature to alienate the sympathies of many from her, and seemed to justify the interference of her neighbours. We know that Polish public opinion, gradually departing from the wise traditions of religious tolerance, had become increasingly hostile to the Dissidents. The most radical sect, that of the Arians, had been expelled in 1658. Later, though without attacking the liberty of conscience of the Protestants and the Orthodox Church, the stage was reached of excluding them from public offices. Yet there had never been a sanguinary persecution for religious opinions in Poland. But in 1724, because the municipal authorities of Torun had not prevented the odious excesses of the mob against the Jesuit College, the mayor of that town and nine other Protestants were condemned to death. The severity of this sentence was so excessive that even the Apostolic Nuncio attempted to intervene in favour of the accused. Nevertheless, the king ordered their execution. This did not add to his popularity in Poland, while in non-Catholic countries a violent propaganda, exaggerating the regrettable but isolated incident, was immediately set on foot against the Polish nation. Russia and Prussia, who had inspired it, soon profited by it to renew their alliance, mutually guaranteeing their right of protecting the religious minorities in Poland.

Augustus II concerned himself little with this growing danger. The 'great design' which preoccupied him towards the end of his life had in reality only one object: that of securing absolute power for himself in Poland as in Saxony, and of transmitting it to his son Frederick Augustus who, like himself, had become a Catholic with a view to his future election to the Polish throne. To effect this, the old king counted, above all, on one of the parties which had formed among the Polish aristocracy, and was briefly entitled 'The Family.' It was led by the Czartoryski princes and their brother-in-law Stanislas Poniatowski, a former partisan of Charles XII, of very modest origin, but who, owing to exceptional qualities, had attained to the highest offices. The other party, gathered round the Potockis, was so fundamentally opposed to the court that there could be no question whatever of gaining it over to the candidature of a second king of the House of Saxony. The opposition had, moreover, a candidate ready in the person of Stanislas Leszczynski, whose chances had become far more favourable since his daughter Maria had, in 1725, married the King of France, Louis XV.

The advantages of his re-election were so evident, and the indignation provoked by the rule of Augustus II so general, that after the latter's death in 1733 the two parties which were directing the whole of the nobility united to exclude every foreign candidate from the throne, and to elect, on 12th September, Leszczynski, who obtained more than thirteen thousand votes. This time the election of Stanislas I was indisputably legal, and to assure his rule he no longer counted on the orders of a foreign conqueror, but on the support that Louis XV would give to his father-in-law and to a Poland desirous of freeing herself from German and Russian influence.

Unhappily, the neighbours of the Republic, who had first had the idea of imposing a Portuguese Infante on her as king, had agreed with each other to uphold, at all costs, the Elector of Saxony. They gained for him a minority of three thousand electors who, protected by Russian cannon, gave their votes, on the 5th October, to the son of Augustus II. Unfortunately also Cardinal Fleury, who was then directing French policy, did not provide the efficacious help to his rival which the latter had anticipated. With the Primate of Poland and the French ambassador, Leszczynski vainly waited for succour from his son-in-law in the town of Danzig, which this time gave a fine example of devotion to the lawful king. The heroism of the Comte de Plelo, who died for the freedom of Poland and the honour of France, did not prevent the capitulation; on 29th May 1734, the king was obliged to take refuge in Prussia.

The war which had resulted from the double Polish election was finally decided, not by the attitude of the immense majority of the nation who in the Confederation of Dzikow had declared themselves in favour of Stanislas I, but by the great European States, among which eighteenth-century Poland no longer held her former place. In 1735 the Peace of Vienna obliged Leszczynski to abdicate and to content himself with the Duchy of Lorraine, while Augustus III definitely remained King of Poland.

He spent the thirty years of his reign almost exclusively in Saxony, abandoning his kingdom to the mercy of his favourites, among whom the Saxon Bruhl and his son-in-law, the Pole Mniszech, acquired an unenviable celebrity. This scandalous hegemony was able to continue, as the apathy of the king, the most unworthy sovereign that Poland has ever had, seemed as though it had taken possession of the whole nation. Under the impression of the dreary monotony which those thirty years reveal, we almost end by asking ourselves whether Poland, condemned to a more and more passive role, had indeed at that time any history of her own worthy of the name.

In any case, she had no longer any foreign policy. Considering that the War of the Polish Succession had been liquidated without the Poles, we are scarcely surprised to see Poland remaining neutral in all the succeeding conflicts which roused the passions of Europe: in the war against the Turks from 1735 to 1739; in the War of the Austrian Succession which broke out the following year, and even in the Seven Years War which synchronized with Augustus III's last seven years. But, which was much worse, the Republic could no longer even make her neutrality respected, and became accustomed to see foreign armies violate her territory. It has been possible to liken the former rampart of Christendom to a roadside inn, serving, above all, the Russian armies which were thus enabled to make their appearance on the battlefields of central Europe.

On the other hand, the great majority of the Poles were not aware of the immense danger that the policy of Frederick the Great represented to their country. His attack directed against Austria in violation of the most solemn engagements should have been a warning, the more serious because it decided the fate of Silesia, formerly Polish, now separating Poland from Saxony, and the annexation of which by Prussia caused all the western provinces of the Republic to be surrounded by that country. Not having known how to profit by those years that had seen Prussia and Russia in two hostile camps, Polish diplomacy hesitated between two equally dangerous alternatives, seeking by turns the support of each of these formidable neighbours against the other. It ended by Poland finding herself faced with a close alliance between these two Powers, an alliance inaugurated by the Tsar Peter III and, in spite of the *coup d'état* that overthrew him in 1762, continued by Catherine II.

We have mentioned Polish diplomacy. Rather we should say the foreign relations maintained by the two factions which, under Augustus III, had recommenced disputing with each other for the highest public offices and the influence they carried with them. This unscrupulous rivalry had the deplorable result that no Diet under this king could carry through its work normally, and that the second half of his reign offers, in this respect, a still more wretched aspect than the first. The 'Family' of the Czartoryskis had, beyond doubt, far more political foresight and a more definite programme than the party of the Potockis. They had even begun by an attempt at collaboration with the court with a view to bringing about a reformation of the internal situation. Having failed in their plans, seeing themselves removed from

power, and finding no serious support from the western
Powers, including France, the Czartoryskis went so far as to
prepare a *coup d'état* in agreement with Catherine II. The
death of the king, on 5th October 1763, released them from
a highly equivocal situation, but it seemed only to aggravate
that of the Republic. In her state of decadence a fresh interregnum was, in fact, only a fresh pretext for interference by
the Empress of Russia and the King of Prussia.

18

The Regeneration

THE epoch of our Saxon kings has been compared to a
night which fell upon Poland, and we all know that under
their successor this night was followed by the partitions
which signified her death. The conclusion might easily be
drawn that the crime of these partitions was justified, or, at
least, explainable, by the century of incurable decay which
had preceded it, and that, in any case, the ruin of the Royal
Republic was inevitable. But this opinion, very prevalent
among foreigners, in no way corresponds with historical
truth.

Since the internal history of Poland under Stanislas Augustus has been thoroughly studied, and the latter's part in
the history of Polish culture clarified, it has been necessary
to revise the too hasty judgment which had weighed so long
on the last of our kings. To-day we know that, in spite of all
the failures of his foreign policy, his reign constitutes an
epoch of genuine national regeneration, a regeneration
which could not avert the final catastrophe, but which for-
bids us to see in that catastrophe the immediate and fatal
consequence of the decay that had preceded it.

But this is not all. The most penetrating analysis of the night of the Saxon epoch enables us to perceive through its darkness the rays of a dawn, which was breaking, rich in promise, on the horizon of the future. Briefly, it is true, the character of that most dreary epoch whose history we have sketched is in keeping with the most striking external facts, but it would remain incomplete and superficial if we did not at the same time endeavour to point out certain signs which then foreshadowed the complete change brought in by Poniatowski's reign.

Moreover, let us not forget that Stanislas Augustus did not only succeed Augustus III, the docile puppet of foreign States, but also Stanislas I, the lawful king who, from his distant residence in Lorraine, never ceased to follow the fortunes of his country. In the papers of this exiled king a vast plan of perpetual peace has recently been found, based on a new organization of Europe, a plan which arouses our admiration for its broad views on international policy, and for its generous ambitions, worthy of the finest traditions of Poland. But what had a more concrete and direct influence was the role which he filled, until his death in 1766, of an educator of the Polish nation, giving his protection to the young compatriots whom he received at his court at Lunéville, and lifting his authoritative voice in political writings of high value, which indicated the road that should be followed to preserve the liberty of the Republic, once it had been wisely reformed.

This voice had such a hearing in Poland, it found such a lively echo in other publications appearing in the country, that we perceive here in the middle of the eighteenth century the germ of all the salutary ideas which were subsequently to expand and be realized under Poniatowski. What is particularly significant is the fact that the author of a most remarkable political treatise, Father Stanislas Konarski, of the Piarist Order, was at the same time a great practical educator, a real reformer of the educational system which was then in force and the results of which left so much to be desired. This explains why the political reforms which aimed at ensuring to Poland a stable government, well ordered finances, and an army comparable with that of her neighbours —reforms attempted in vain by a group of the best of the generation under Augustus II—could be successfully resumed by the following generation which, formed by a more adequate education, raised itself to a higher level of culture.

To this new generation belonged the son of that Stanislas Poniatowski whom we saw raise himself to the rank of the most powerful aristocrats and marry a Czartoryska. Born in 1732, Stanislas Augustus shone among his contemporaries by a refined culture which he owed to innate gifts, a careful education, and long sojourns in the west. First Vienna, then chiefly Paris and London, familiarized him with all the currents of eighteenth-century European culture, and prepared him for his future role of a Maecenas of letters and arts, an enlightened protector of industry and commerce, and a renovator of the political ideas of the nation. All that was accomplished during his reign in these very diverse spheres bore the stamp of his initiative, and he had, in addition, the merit of getting the best minds of his epoch to work together around his fascinating person. This new epoch of our civilization, recalling in certain respects the golden age of the Jagiellos, lives in history as that of Stanislas Augustus, whose name remains linked with the new style of Polish architecture as also with the great constitutional reforms now at last realized.

Unfortunately, the moral strength, which alone could have made young Poniatowski the king that Poland needed in the tragic hours that awaited her, formed no part of that accomplished intellectuality. Supple and benevolent, he was wanting not only in the energy which had assured his father's amazing career, but, above all, in the moral principles which were then being reborn in the tormented souls of many other Poles. This explains why, attracting talents as he did, he numbered among his adversaries, side by side with the jealous and the reactionaries, the most generous hearts and the most ardent patriots. Some would remind him of the modest origin of his family and the quite secondary position from which he was raised to the throne. Others reproached him with far better reason for many culpable weaknesses in his private and public life, beginning with the manner in which he had gained the crown of the Piasts and the Jagiellos.

At the election of 1764, which was preceded by troubles of evil augury, and which was unanimous only because of the armed intervention of Russia, Poniatowski, like his Saxon predecessors, was imposed on the nation by Poland's worst enemies, Frederick II of Prussia and Catherine II of Russia. But what gave a peculiarly disgraceful character to this proceeding was that Stanislas Augustus owed the empress's decisive support to the notorious fact that during his diplomatic missions in Petersburg he had been her lover. This scandalous origin of his elevation to the throne lay heavy on all his reign, and his sentiments of gratitude and attachment to Catherine II warped all his foreign policy. Even the internal reforms which constitute his chief merit suffered from the illusion that made him endeavour to carry them through successfully in agreement with Russia and using her support.

These reforms, thanks to the initiative of the Czartoryskis, had been begun at the Diet of Convocation which, according to usage, preceded that of the election. In amelioration of

the parliamentary regulations, the decision had been reached
for the first time to limit the principle of unanimity, the
rigour of which, hitherto absolute, had clogged all progress.
Modest beginnings of administrative, economic, and social
reforms had also taken place. Stanislas was only too willing
to carry on this immense work immediately after his coronation, celebrated in Warsaw on 25th November 1764. He at
once came up against unlooked-for difficulties. Even the
Czartoryskis, who had hoped to obtain the crown for a member of their old princely house, descended from the race of
the Jagiellos, showed little alacrity in supporting the nephew
who had been so favoured by fortune. On the other hand,
the king soon provoked the anger of his protectress by showing himself less docile than she had anticipated, and by even
seeking a *rapprochement* with Austria and France, Powers
which at the election had favoured the House of Saxony, but
whose support now seemed indispensable. Frederick II hastened to notify Catherine II of these plans, so that they had
only one result, that of strengthening the understanding between Russia and Prussia, both of whom were firmly resolved
to oppose everything that could favour the revival of Poland.

The king had proof of this at the Diet of 1766. He had
not thrown away the two years which had passed since his
accession. Permanent commissions, genuine ministries, were
functioning ever more satisfactorily. A council of ministers,
ensuring the continuity of the nation's policy, was in process
of being formed. Financial and monetary reforms enabled
the budget to be balanced. In collaboration with his cousin,
Adam Czartoryski, Stanislas Augustus founded an excellent
military school. Assisted by the chancellor, Andrew Zamoyski, he showed great solicitude for the urban population.
And he hoped that the first Diet of his reign would develop
these beginnings, and, above all, bring in a new limitation

of the principle of parliamentary unanimity. But hardly had this delicate problem been approached when the diplomatic representatives of Catherine II and Frederick II protested, going so far as to threaten the Republic with a declaration of war.

On their side they raised the question of the equality of the rights of the religious minorities, Orthodox and Protestant. Under an appearance of liberalism which deceived Europe, this manœuvre was designed to create new internal difficulties for Poland, to exasperate the conservative opposition, and, above all, to embroil the latter definitely with the king, who was ready to compromise in the matter. Prince Repnin, the Russian ambassador, in fact succeeded in thus stopping all the practical work of the Diet, and from this moment it was really this foreign diplomat who, with frank brutality, dictated his will to the Poles.

In 1767 the opposition to the parvenu Poniatowski formed the Confederation of Radom which, deceived and subsequently terrorized by Repnin, requested the Empress of Russia to guarantee the former Polish constitution. At the Diet of this same year, the ambassador had two bishops, a senator, and a deputy, who had dared to protest against these demands, arrested and deported to Russia; and despite certain useful reforms voted by this Diet the independence of Poland now seemed pure fiction.

But it was precisely now that Russia perceived that she was no longer dealing with the decadent Poland of Saxon times. On the 29th February 1768, in the small Podolian town of Bar, a new confederation—and this one was spontaneous—courageously took up the struggle for freedom. This desperate struggle lasted four years until the eve of the first partition, for which it served as a pretext. It recalls the war for independence which had saved Poland at the epoch of the Deluge. Again the nobility took up arms in the name of their threatened faith and country, and again all the provinces of the Republic rallied, one after another, to this movement which saved the honour of Poland.

But why did it not save Poland herself? Why was the sanctuary of Czestochowa, which, as in 1655, served as the rallying-point for the reviving patriotism, finally compelled this time to capitulate? Why do the exploits of these courageous knights of Christ and His Mother resemble, not the campaigns of independent Poland, but rather the future insurrections of partitioned Poland? Their ardour was, indeed, checked in the first year by the atrocities of a popular revolt in the Ukraine, where Russia, although she subsequently assisted in its repression, was not without her share of responsibility for the outbreak. It is also true that the confederates did not find the foreign support on which they had counted. Turkey entered into war with Russia, but was herself beaten, and France only sent Poland a handful of soldiers, who all distinguished themselves, but whose counsels were not always happy ones. But what decided the failure of the movement was the impossibility of securing union among all the Poles, including the king. The latter made at that time serious mistakes which roused the indignation of the confederates, and subsequently caused them to repulse all his overtures. On their side they committed the great error of proclaiming, in 1770, the deposition of Poniatowski, and in the following year going so far as an attempt upon his person. Even if we deplore the spirit of faction which divided the confederates among themselves, still we must render homage to their disinterested leaders, such as the Krasinskis, and, above all, the Pulaskis, the most heroic of whom, Casimir, unable to save the freedom of Poland, died for that of America.

The Confederation of Bar was crushed by the Russians.

The hour, therefore, seemed to have arrived in which to realize the plan of Catherine II and her minister Panin of subjecting the whole of Poland to Russian domination. But Frederick II had his own plan which he had been patiently developing since 1768 and with which he acquainted the empress in 1770. He succeeded in gaining Russia to the idea of a partition of Polish territory, and at the same time he hinted to Austria, who at one moment had seemed to support the confederates, the advantages of a share in this act of violence. It was, indeed, the Austrians who, in spite of Maria Theresa's scruples, were the first to penetrate into Polish territory.

On the 5th August 1772 Poland's three neighbours entered into an agreement, and proceeded immediately to occupy the provinces which they had arrogated to themselves. Russia's share was the most extensive, comprising all that still remained to the Republic beyond the Dvina and Dnieper. Austria appropriated a territory hardly less large with a still more considerable population, the whole of the future Galicia as far as the Vistula; but it was Frederick the Great who secured the most valuable acquisition, obtaining West Prussia which had separated East Prussia from the rest of his possessions, and, if he was obliged to renounce provisionally the towns of Danzig and Torun, he took in return the north of Great Poland.

Exhausted by her preceding struggles, Poland could not prevent these annexations. But the partitioning Powers were, in addition, anxious to obtain their ratification by the Polish Diet. This Diet, assembled in April 1773, did not close its labours until April 1775. It yielded, like the king, to the peremptory argument that in the case of refusal further territories would be detached from Poland. Let us pass over in silence the names of the miserable men who facilitated this

blackmail. Rather let us record that of the deputy who protested the most courageously, Thaddeus Reytan.

But the most cheering feature of the story is the fact that
this first spoliation was not able to arrest the great movement
of national rebirth. Russia, who, like Prussia, saw in the
partition of 1772 only the first stage of the project for the
integral destruction of Poland, intended on this occasion to
impose upon her an internal administration, which would
have cut short every attempt at reform, perpetuated the
causes of her weakness, and limited still more strictly the
royal power by a Permanent Council. Now it was precisely
this council that Stanislas Augustus and his collaborators succeeded in making into a highly useful institution. All the
administration of the State was concentrated in its five departments, and the king, who presided, secured considerable
influence there for himself. Thanks to this stable government, which gained by degrees in authority, a vast work of
organization was accomplished in a dozen years. These years
are certainly not brilliant in the political history of Poland,
and her role in Europe seemed increasingly reduced; but 'in
the shadow of the proconsul'—that is to say, of the Russian
ambassador Stackelberg—Poniatowski was patiently preparing a better future. Without suffering himself to be discouraged by inevitable failures such as that of the industrial
enterprises of the too ambitious grand treasurer, Anthony
Tyzenhaus, or by the rejection of the project for a code prepared by the chancellor, Andrew Zamoyski, the king strove
above all to raise the intellectual level of the nation by developing reforms in the sphere of education, reforms whose
modest beginnings we have pointed out above.

In this respect the lamentable Diet which had been forced
to sanction the first partition created in the course of its

labours, in 1773, an extremely valuable institution, the celebrated Commission of National Education. The Jesuit Order having been dissolved by Clement XIV, Poland assigned the funds that had thus become at her disposal to the foundation and functioning of this new organization, which has been justly compared to a ministry of public instruction, the first in Europe. The whole of Polish education, from the primary school to the Universities of Cracow and Wilno, was reorganized by this commission with as much competence as moderation and good method. Among the inspirers of this movement we must mention at least the devoted secretary of the commission, the Rev. Gregory Piramowicz.

Moreover, without waiting for the result of his other efforts, Stanislas Augustus succeeded at once in creating what has been called his 'kingdom of Parnassus.' He gathered round him, in particular at his famous 'Thursday dinners,' the flower of Polish intellect who, while still cultivating the sciences and arts, also gave birth to a new period of Polish literature, resuming the fine traditions of the sixteenth century. Among the poets who made his reign illustrious the first place is undoubtedly held by Ignatius Krasicki, a mediocre bishop but an incomparable author of fables and satires. By his side, writers as different as Stanislas Trembecki, a sceptical and satirical courtier, and Francis Karpinski, a sentimental poet of religious and national inspiration, were all distinguished for their high culture and the classical perfection of their language. Contrary to their predecessors of the 'golden century,' they wrote exclusively in Polish, although strongly influenced by French literature. One of them, Bishop Adam Naruszewicz, was also an eminent historian who, assisted by the king, organized vast researches in the archives in order to give a scientific basis to the knowledge of the past. His work remained unfinished, but the documents he gathered together are still used by the Polish historians of to-day, as also is the magnificent library formed shortly before by another bishop, Joseph Andrew Zaluski, one of the deported senators of 1767.

It is impossible to enlarge here upon the beginnings of the Polish theatre and press, which belong to this same epoch. Instead, let us emphasize that the efflorescence of belles-lettres was now accompanied, as in the sixteenth century, by quite as remarkable a development of political literature. And let us note the significant fact that its most illustrious representative, Stanislas Staszic, gave the first of his works, which appeared in 1785, the form of *Observations on the Life of John Zamoyski*. This essentially modern writer, of plebeian origin and liberal tendencies, thus recalled the memory of the founder of the Royal Republic in order to stigmatize the later distortions of his work, and to establish a complete plan of reforms, which were especially bold in the social department. Together with Staszic, it was also Hugo Kollataj, known first as the reorganizer of higher education, who, surrounded by a staff of friends, prepared and stimulated by his writings the work of effective reforms which was at last accomplished by the Four Years Diet, the Polish 'Great Parliament' which sat from 1788 to 1792.

Without entering into details of its activities, let us first point out its immense difficulties. In the midst of political preoccupations, the gravity of which we shall consider later, this Diet had to convert all the wise and generous ideas, which had come to the fore in the course of the preceding years, into legislative acts. These ideas still met with opposition from a turbulent minority which, conducted by a few reactionary magnates, prevented unanimous decisions. The Diet, therefore, constituted itself into a Confederation, which permitted it to abide by the majority of votes. To reinforce

its authority it made an appeal in the midst of its labours to
the public opinion of the country. Doubling the number of
the deputies by new elections it became thereby a genuine
national assembly.

Inspired by the tendencies of the French Revolution, and,
like it, proclaiming the rights of man and the citizen, our
constituent Diet succeeded, however, in avoiding all violence
and in following the lines of Poland's historical evolution.
Let us, moreover, observe that all the reforms which it
adopted exacted considerable sacrifices from those who voted
them. The nobility which alone was represented at this assembly was obliged, in the general interest, spontaneously to
renounce traditional privileges and many of the principles
which were dear to it. It began by decreeing, in 1788, this
time unanimously, the creation of an army of a hundred
thousand men, which involved heavy financial burdens. It
then made important concessions to the 'third estate,' the urban population whose delegates, assembled in Warsaw, were
insistent in formulating their claims. At last it accepted, by a
crushing majority, the celebrated Constitution of the Third
of May 1791, the anniversary of which is still in our days kept
as the Polish national feast day.

This constitution ratified the rights accorded to the burghers, giving them access to public offices and to Parliament,
and thus breaking down the barrier which had hitherto
separated them from the nobility. It placed the peasant population under the protection of the Government, not going
so far as to abolish serfdom, but encouraging and guaranteeing individual contracts between the gentry and the peasants,
contracts which became more and more frequent and ameliorated the situation of the latter. Perfecting the central administration and the management of the finances, the new
constitution resolutely abolished the right of *liberum veto,*

as well as that of the 'free' election of the king, a right which had ended by imposing upon the Republic the candidates of foreign Powers. It decreed that after Poniatowski's death the throne should be hereditary in the House of Saxony.

It is easy to criticize the choice of this dynasty. It is equally regrettable that, in view of the protests of a dissatisfied minority, it was considered necessary to have the project of the constitution adopted almost by surprise. This does not affect the fact that from the moment of its promulgation it evoked a refreshing enthusiasm, and that this grand result of a loyal collaboration between the king and the patriotic party, among whom was the Speaker of the Diet, Stanislas Malachowski, permitted the belief that this time the Royal Republic, happily adapted to the needs of the hour, was definitely saved.

19

The Partitions

CONTRARY to all hopes, the Constitution of 1791, eloquent witness to the national rebirth, was followed in 1793 by the second, and in 1795 by the third partition of Poland. These last partitions, which erased our country from the map of Europe, are essentially different from the first, which was, in reality, only a mutilation of our territory. Poland's neighbours who, in 1772, had thought it necessary to justify their annexations by appealing to historical rights—easy, however, to refute—did not even put themselves to the trouble of invoking any kind of right when they proceeded to the complete partition. And while at the first partition they had been able, with a certain show of reason, to denounce the internal troubles which had then been seething for several years in Poland, no such argument could serve them after the reforms accomplished without the slightest disturbance of order by the Four Years Diet. The accusation of Jacobinism, raised against the new Poland, was in such obvious contradiction to the spirit and methods of that Diet, that no one could take it seriously. Under these conditions, even the immediate origin of the partitions of 1793 and 1795 raises highly com-

plex problems that we shall attempt to solve before analysing
the deep-seated causes of the catastrophe.

During the years of her internal work following the first
partition, Poland had sedulously avoided everything that
could have provoked a new conflict, either with Prussia, or,
above all, with Russia. Stanislas Augustus, always filled with
admiration for Catherine II, was all the more convinced of
the necessity of a good understanding with the empress because she had lately carried off a fresh success of 1783, by
annexing the Crimea and putting an end to the existence of
the last Tartar khanate, which had formerly been so dangerous both to Russia and to Poland. In 1787, on the eve of the
Great Diet, the two sovereigns met at Kaniow, on the
Ukrainian borders of their states, and, in agreement on this
point with the most reactionary group of the Polish aristocracy, the king himself showed favour to the project of a
Russo-Polish alliance, directed against Turkey.

On the other hand, the alliance between Russia and Prussia,
which had had such fatal consequences to Poland, came to an
end in 1788, and Frederick William II, who had succeeded
Frederick the Great, appeared to be embarked on a policy
hostile to the empress. This explains why the Polish patriots,
directed by Ignatius Potocki, believed the moment had come
to profit by the rupture between the two principal adversaries of Poland. They calculated that, instead of allowing
the dominating influence of Russia to be perpetuated over
the whole of the territory which still remained to the Republic, it was more advisable to conclude a defensive alliance
with Prussia which would guarantee both the integrity of
that territory and its complete independence.

Prussia attempted on this occasion to have the greatly
coveted towns of Danzig and Torun ceded to her. Her
minister, Hertzberg, even foresaw diplomatic combinations

which would have restored Austrian Galicia to Poland by way of compensation. These projects turned out to be unrealizable, but the Polish-Prussian alliance was, nevertheless, signed on 29th March 1790, the king having rallied to the foreign policy of the party with whom he was collaborating with a view to constitutional reforms. This alliance provided that in the case of aggression against one of the contracting parties the other would come to its assistance, so that the safety of Poland seemed assured.

This was unhappily a pure illusion. For Prussia this transitory alliance with Poland was merely a tactical move which she was willing enough to use as long as her antagonism with Catherine II lasted, but which she was ready to renounce as soon as a new opportunity presented itself of extending her frontiers to the detriment of Poland. The latter was anxious to gain some years of peace by maintaining a part of passive neutrality, in the hope that the diplomatic support of Prussia would enable her to escape Russian appropriation of her country. But it was easy to foresee that in the event of real danger this support would entirely fail her, and it was still more evident that the empress, indignant at the policy of the Great Diet which had emancipated itself from her tutelage, was only waiting for a pretext to interfere more energetically than ever in Polish affairs.

She was, unfortunately, provided with this pretext scarcely a year after the adoption of the new constitution by a handful of Polish nobles, who, dissatisfied with that reform, did not hesitate to invoke the help of Catherine II against the lawful government of their own country. The empress only waited for the signing of peace with Turkey before she invaded Poland, in response to the appeal of a new confederation which a few traitors had formed at Targowica, after it had been carefully prepared in Petersburg.

At the outset of the campaign of 1792 the Polish army, which, thanks to the recent reforms, numbered more than sixty thousand men, well equipped and disciplined, gained some important successes under the command of two eminent leaders: young Prince Joseph Poniatowski, nephew to the king, and General Thaddeus Kosciuszko, who had distinguished himself in the American War of Independence. But when Prussia flatly refused to keep her engagements and to uphold the independence of Poland, the king, and with him the majority of the most influential politicians, lost courage. Stanislas Augustus, therefore, put a premature end to all military resistance and, believing in the possibility of reconciliation with Russia, he himself adhered to the Confederation of Targowica.

The results of this capitulation surpassed the worst antici pations. Not only did the Russians enter Warsaw and force the abolition of the work of 3rd May 1791, but Prussia, seeing that the whole of Poland was falling into the hands of Catherine II, suggested a new partition, which she had inaugurated by occupying Poznan. This time Austria took no part in the scheme, but neither had she any intention of opposing it, in her desire of securing Prussian collaboration in her war against Republican France. Russia, who the confederates of Targowica had intended should march against Prussia, quickly came to an understanding with the latter, and, in the beginning of 1793, the agreement between these two Powers were effected. The new frontiers that they drew up between them, purely artificial and almost rectangular, assigned to Prussia the whole of Great Poland and part of Masovia as well as Danzig and Torun, and to Russia all the eastern part of the former Grand Duchy of Lithuania and the rest of the Ukraine, including Podolia and a part of Volhynia. The Republic retained no more than a mutilated fragment, incapable of subsisting as an independent State.

As had been the case after the first partition, a Diet, this time assembled at Grodno, the last Diet of the old Poland, was forced to consent to this new spoliation, a far more grievous one than that which had preceded it. It was in vain, that the parliamentary resistance now showed more energy. The Russian ambassador Sievers broke it by violence, and did not desist until he had obtained the ratification of the treaties of partition, first with Russia, then also with Prussia. But, nevertheless, he obtained nothing beyond a desperate silence which a dishonourable deputy interpreted as a unanimous consent.

The honour of Poland was saved by the insurrection of the following year. Prepared since the second half of 1793 by conspiracies in Warsaw and by overtures to revolutionary France, which, however, remained without result, this insurrection found a leader, full of devotion and courage, in the person of Thaddeus Kosciuszko. The conditions in which he undertook his task were by no means favourable. For this reason he put off moving until the moment when the Russians proceeded to the compulsory reduction of the Polish army, prescribed by the Diet of Grodno. The resistance that several generals opposed to this disarmament which was dictated by the enemy put an end to all hesitation. On the 24th March 1794, Kosciuszko swore in the great square of Cracow to fight until the end for the liberty, the integrity, and the independence of his native land. It was assuredly no fault of his that this object was not gained.

It is easy to reproach the insurgents with the fact that their action, undertaken without due consideration, merely hastened the third partition, as the Confederation of Bar had accelerated the first. In any case, Kosciuszko has the high merit of having, for the first time, interested all classes of the population in the national cause. Having at the outset only four thousand soldiers at his disposal, this member of the Polish gentry did not hesitate to make his appeal to the peasants, armed only with their scythes. It is thanks to them that, on the 4th April, he won the battle of Raclawice, and a few days later Warsaw was delivered from the Russian occupation by a popular movement, inspired by the shoemaker Kilinski. Kosciuszko then energetically opposed the excesses of the mob, which was beginning to rise against certain magnates suspected of treason. But, convinced that only the participation of the masses could secure victory to the insurrection, he published, on the 7th May, the Manifesto of Polaniec, which proclaimed the principle of the liberty of the peasant and freed immediately from serfdom those who had taken up arms.

Kosciuszko's insurrection, which had begun at Cracow, rapidly gained all the provinces of the Republic. Wilno, led by General Jasinski, rid itself of the Russians as Warsaw had done, and the war for independence, which had repercussions even in Danzig and Courland, was particularly violent in Great Poland, where, directed by John Henry Dabrowski, the general who afterwards became so famous, it caused grave anxiety to the Prussians.

The Prussians had not failed to enter the war against the insurgents, even though the latter had, at the outset, only fought the Russians. The unexpected appearance of a Prussian army decided Kosciuszko's first defeat at the battle of Szczekociny, and it was the Prussians who took Cracow, subsequently to besiege Warsaw side by side with the Russians. The responsibility for the final defeat of Maciejowice has been much discussed. What is certain is that the insurrection was broken by this disastrous battle, as Kosciuszko, seriously wounded, fell into the hands of the Russians. The horrors of the sack of Praga, a suburb of the capital, where Suvorov's army massacred thousands of its inhabitants, brought about the capitulation of Warsaw itself on 5th November 1794.

The only task left for the victors was to fix among themselves the conditions of the final partition of the Republic. As in 1772, Austria hastened to secure her share without having participated directly in the campaign of 1794. On 3rd January 1795, she made an agreement with Russia, obtaining the territory included between the Pilica and the Bug, the prolongation of Galicia towards the north as far as the centre of Poland. But it was Prussia who once more succeeded in securing the best part for herself, gaining, with Warsaw, the very heart of the former Republic by the treaty of 24th October in the same year. Having concluded the Peace of Basle with France, she had her hands free on the eastern side, and even Russia was obliged to reckon with her. However, Catherine II, as usual, obtained the vastest regions: all that was still left of the former Grand Duchy of Lithuania and of Volhynia.

A month later the last king of Poland, who had not known how to take any firm decision in the tragic hours of 1794, was forced to abdicate at Grodno, and departed to die in Russia. The Prussians, when they left Cracow, which had been allotted to Austria, carried away the royal insignia from the Vavel; and, finally, on 26th January 1797, the three partitioning Powers, believing they had liquidated the Polish question forever, completed their territorial settlement by the reciprocal pledge never to use a title which could recall the existence of a kingdom of Poland. After eight centuries of a history, so often a glorious one, the Poland of the Piasts and the Jagiellos had disappeared, and the experiment of the Royal Republic had finished in utter failure.

Having reached this extraordinary break in the historical evolution of Poland, we think it incumbent on us to recall what we have emphasized in our introductory remarks: it would be an exaggeration, especially in our days after the re-establishment of Polish independence, to envisage all that evolution from the standpoint of the Partitions, as if for centuries she had been making her fatal way towards that catastrophe, and as if the continuity of our history had been broken only to be resumed later under entirely different forms. It is, however, quite reasonable to seek for an explanation of so exceptional, not to say unique, an event in general history. It is true that even in the history of modern Europe many States have more than once had to face a partition similar to that of Poland; but all, without excepting Turkey, who has been particularly threatened with such a revenge on the part of the Christian world, have escaped total destruction. Why had Poland alone suffered that cruel fate, the consequences of which she endured for more than a century?

In regard to the direct and immediate causes which brought about the solution of 1795, we have just shown how dangerous was the course in which Poland involved herself by allying with Prussia in 1790, what illusions induced her to lay down her arms prematurely in 1792, and, finally, how full of risks was the renewal of the struggle in 1794. Yet is it not a certainty that a contrary decision on Poland's part at each of these critical moments would have had consequences fully as deplorable for her? In 1790 Russia assuredly was deserving of no greater trust than Prussia; a prolonged resistance in 1792 would only have made the defeat of that same year a more honourable one; a more prudent attitude in 1794 would only have condemned the Republic to a slower and more ignominious death. But we have had enough of hypothetical suggestions. It suffices to state the brutal fact that nothing could then have saved Poland from two adversaries who were firmly resolved to finish her, and who had each at their separate disposal forces three or four times superior to those of Poland, thanks to their military and financial resources.

But how were these two neighbours of Poland thus enabled to abuse their forces, and why did they turn them only against Poland? When we come herewith to the essential causes of the partitions, far more interesting and instructive than the occurrences of her last moments, the answer to the first of the two questions that we have set ourselves is a very easy one. Those partitions which later opinion, even that of the nations responsible, was to stigmatize, at least, in theory, as crimes against international morality, were calmly accepted by an epoch in which that morality no longer existed even in theory, and was perpetually violated with impunity in practice. Together with the last memories of Christian solidarity, the conceptions of an international society and of a common good superior to the individual interest of particular states had completely disappeared. The idea of European equilibrium was incapable of replacing them, and in the case with which we are dealing this idea did nothing beyond adjusting itself to the advantages which the two chief enemies of Poland were seeking, and encouraging Austria, who was less directly interested, to demand an equivalent compensation.

The future was to prove that even the political equilibrium of Europe was far better ensured by the existence of an independent Poland. In any case, no one has ever been able to claim that she had threatened that equilibrium and constituted a danger for her neighbours. On the contrary, those who have been anxious to cast the responsibility for her fate upon herself have never reproached Poland with being too strong, but, on the contrary, with being too weak, and consequently incapable of maintaining her own life. This reproach would have had some show of reason if the destruction of Poland had immediately followed her decadence in the first half of the eighteenth century. It falls to the ground from the fact that the national rebirth had begun before the first partition, which attempted in vain to stop it, and that it was effected before the other two partitions, which did not allow it time to bear all its fruit. Before she perished the Royal Republic provided the proof that the course of constitutional development which she chose in the sixteenth century could result normally, without passing through the hard school of absolutism or through that of revolutionary upheavals, in a government which was as good as that of other contemporary states. A constitution which enabled Poland to remain for so long a great Power, to traverse subsequently a long period of wars and trouble, and, finally, to remedy by law the abuses which had deformed her, such a constitution could not have caused the fall of the Republic, as has long been asserted.

Rather, it is thanks to her institutions that the State, based on the Jagiellonian traditions, was capable of triumphing over the difficulties which might have resulted from the differences of nationality and religion among its inhabitants. On the eve of the partitions the assimilation of the Grand Duchy of Lithuania with the kingdom of Poland had become so complete, that the Four Years Diet could discard the dualism of the central administration, which no longer corresponded with any actual need. This same Diet pacified, with no disturbance and to the general satisfaction, the question of the religious minorities, artificially magnified by foreign interference at the time of the first partition. The Cossack question, once so serious, no longer presented itself at the time when Poland disappeared, as the principal part of the Ukraine already belonged to Russia, who had suppressed the last remnants of its autonomy. Ethnical individualities, therefore, no longer existed in the Republic except among the peasant population, which counted for nothing from the political viewpoint. This fact may be deplored; but, at the same time, we must bear in mind that the lot of that population was infinitely harder in the empire of the tsars and was scarcely beginning to be improved in Austria and Prussia.

Does it follow that Poland had in no wise contributed to her own ruin, and that the covetousness of her neighbours was alone responsible? We claim nothing of the sort. Without renouncing the constitutional principles peculiar to her, Poland could have secured to herself, within their own military organization and on her vast territory, far more considerable forces, and thus have more efficaciously resisted external dangers, if her citizens, rich in privileges as they were, had shown more devotion to the public cause, and if their spirit of sacrifice had not only shown itself at exceptional moments. A still heavier responsibility than this one of a general nature is the individual responsibility of the leaders of political factions who, from the rebels of the seventeenth century to the inspirers of the Confederation of Targowica, at times went as far as high treason.

In both cases it is a question of moral responsibility, and it is on the moral plane that we must, in fact, consider the problem of the partitions—in regard to the Poles as well as their adversaries—if we wish to understand it fundamentally. From this standpoint even the builders of the renascence in the time of Stanislas Augustus, including the king himself, cannot escape bitter reproach. While they revived Polish culture and reformed Polish institutions, they did not arrest the decay of morals, and they were, for the most part, of too feeble character themselves to regenerate the national character.

The Poles of the eighteenth century could not remedy this situation, because they had no longer the deep religious faith which had animated their ancestors when they tried the great experiment of the Royal Republic and defended the frontiers of Christendom. Hence, Providence sent them a great ordeal which was to purify the national soul and give their sons to behold in the humiliation of expiation a new historic mission, worthy of a great past.

Part IV

THE ORDEAL

20

Napoleonic Poland

Poland is still living
While we are alive.

SUCH was the cry of defiance which on the morrow of the Partitions was proudly flung in the name of the Polish nation to those who had recently brought about the disappearance of the Polish State; it was a simple song of the legionaries, contemporary with the *Marseillaise,* and destined to become our national hymn.

This song of victory was composed in Italy, far from the territory of the old Poland. A heavy oppression was then weighing down that territory, and evoking a profound discouragement and an almost general apathy. Under the Prussian and Austrian rule this oppression was the more dangerous inasmuch as it was at the same time a systematic Germanization. Under Catherine II the violence of the conqueror had made itself felt in a still more brutal manner; but the empress only survived the third partition by a year, and under her son Paul, as under Alexander, who succeeded his assassinated father in 1801, the Poles were treated in a far more conciliatory manner. Prince Adam Czartoryski, nephew of the last King of Poland, who had become one of the tsar's ministers, was, therefore, not only able to make the University of Wilno a more powerful centre than ever of Polish culture, but could even envisage the possibility of a reconstruction of the kingdom of Poland by the Emperor of Russia.

If, however, this ambitious illusion was able, twenty years after the last partition, to become a modest and transitory reality, it is because in that interval the Polish question, scarcely as yet condemned to silence, had again risen before the whole of Europe, thanks to the Napoleonic epic. We use this traditional phrase designedly, because the Napoleonic epoch was for Poland, as for France, a veritable epic. It is easy to contend that the relations, which have been so closely studied, between Napoleon and Poland were, at bottom, a long series of deceptions and misunderstandings from which the Poles often suffered cruelly, and which the emperor regretted at St Helena. It is none the less true that the former Republic, now partitioned, was almost immediately replaced by what we can call Napoleonic Poland, a glorious vision which haunted the enslaved nation, disquieted her masters, covered the timid and ephemeral creation of the Duchy of Warsaw with its splendour, and still set its imprint on the 'kingdom' of 1815.

Thanks to Napoleon, Poland, instead of foundering in oblivion, lived years of true grandeur beyond the tomb; and it is this that the Poles will never forget.

In the midst of the sad symptoms of indifference and servility which unhappily were multiplied in the three mutilated sections of Poland, attempts for liberation were certainly not lacking. But they inevitably took the form of conspiracies, often almost puerile, which could have no chance of success. The most clear-sighted patriots had at once understood that only a general overthrow of the European order, of that artificial order based upon the agreement between the partitioning Powers, could create conditions favourable to the resurrection of Poland. When the moment should arrive this overthrow, opening the way to a new era of history, could only come from the side of France, against whom the enemies of Poland were in coalition, who had been enabled to breathe more freely when their attention was concentrated on the problem of the Partitions, and whose tricolour flag seemed to announce the liberation of all oppressed peoples. Hence the Polish emigrants, who from that time gathered together in Paris, were anxious to interest the Directory in the project of forming 'Polish Legions' in the service of France as the nucleus of an allied army.

It was Bonaparte alone who understood the importance of this idea. During the course of his first Italian campaign, in January 1797, he authorized General Dabrowski, the former collaborator of Kosciuszko, the latter of whom was now maintaining a strict reserve, to form these legions in the service of the Lombard Republic. The Poles who enrolled in them hoped that, marching with Napoleon against Austria, they would soon pass from Italy into Poland and would thus be fighting for their own country. They were profoundly disappointed by the Peace of Campo Formio, concluded some months later, as well as by the Peace of Lunéville in 1801; neither the one nor the other touched upon the Polish question, with the result that there seemed no reason for the existence of the legions. In 1802 the First Consul even sent a detachment of them to San Domingo, where these unfortunate Polish soldiers were compelled to fight against the negroes, and perished *en masse*.

However, these first sacrifices were not entirely sterile. The crushing victories that Napoleon achieved from 1805 to 1807 in central Europe broke in succession the forces of the three Powers which had partitioned Poland. A unique opportunity was thus presented of liberating her, an opportunity of which

Dabrowski made use to launch, in 1806, an appeal for a general insurrection. What was left of his legions could at last go to Poland to constitute there the framework of a national army, and the emperor only seemed to be awaiting its definite formation before proclaiming the independence of Poland. Nevertheless, in spite of the considerable part played by the Poles towards the end of the Prussian campaign, the Peace of Tilsit, on 7th July 1807, again deceived their hopes.

Why was Poland, whose re-establishment they expected, reduced to a small buffer state between Russia and Prussia: a state that only included the territories annexed by Prussia on the occasion of the two last partitions—without Danzig, which was established as a free city—and that received the artificial title of Duchy of Warsaw? The reason is very simple. Napoleon was then anxious to enter into an understanding with Alexander I in order to divide his adversaries, and the Polish question had consequently become a subject of barter between the two emperors. Inevitably the result was a compromise of which the Poles had to pay the price.

Nevertheless, the creation of the new duchy was still a first and very important step towards the restoration of Poland, a part of which, at least, became free and independent. This independence was certainly limited by the fact that the duchy remained entirely subject to the will of Napoleon, who dictated its constitution, eploited it economically, and even employed a part of its army at the other end of Europe in fighting the Spaniards. Also, the organization of the Duchy of Warsaw departed in many respects from Polish traditions, for example, in imposing upon it an administration of a bureaucratic character on the model of France, as well as the Napoleonic code. But taken as a whole the Constitution of 1807, albeit essentially different from that of 1791, repeated certain of its leading ideas in raising the House of Saxony to the throne in the person of Frederick Augustus, grandson of Augustus III, in strengthening the executive power, and in extending the rights of the third estate and of the peasant class. It went much further than the Act of the Third of May in the provisions which limited the jurisdiction of the Diet and the privileges of the nobility, and which ensured, at least, full liberty of their persons to the peasants. And, in spite of the dissatisfaction that this constitution provoked among the conservatives on one hand and the republicans on the other, in spite even of the mistakes committed by the King of Saxony, the ruler of the duchy, the duchy gave proof of an astonishing vitality, even at such a dangerous moment as that of the campaign of 1809.

Attacked by the Austrians, the Duchy of Warsaw not only succeeded in defending itself and in creating a diversion useful to the Napoleonic army, but, in addition, Prince Joseph Poniatowski, at first obliged to abandon the capital to the enemy, soon took a brilliant revenge, occupying the two Galicias with Lwow and Cracow. The Poles could once more hope that the victory of Napoleon, to which they had contributed useful assistance, would bring them decisive advantages. But the Peace of Vienna, 14th October 1809, was one more disappointment. Its eplanation is to be found, as in 1807, in the equivocal role played by Alexander I, on whom Napoleon counted the more this time, inasmuch as the Russians had been at least formally, his allies. They opposed the project of joining to the Duchy of Warsaw all the territories that Austria had taken from Poland at the first and second partitions. She was only obliged to cede to the duchy her acquisitions of 1795, including Cracow, keeping the Galicia of 1772, of which a frontier district was assigned to Russia, as had been the case with a district of Prussian Poland in 1807.

However, the Polish question, which it was attempted to

solve by half measures, remained one of the essential causes which made the decisive struggle inevitable between the two monarchs who were then the most powerful in Europe: the Emperor and the Tsar of Russia. The latter, while preventing a restoration of Poland by his rival, at the same time was luring the Poles by promises which surpassed those of Napoleon. A few nobles of the former Grand Duchy of Lithuania allowed themselves to be gained over by the prospect that Alexander I would, first of all, proclaim the re-establishment of that Grand Duchy, would then reunite it to the Duchy of Warsaw, and become king of a Poland as great as Poland before the Partitions. But even Prince Adam Czartoryski no longer placed any trust in the tsar's tortuous policy, and when the latter attempted to win Joseph Poniatowski, that always loyal soldier repulsed what with good reason seemed to him a treacherous offer, and hastened to warn Napoleon of the danger which threatened him from the side of Russia.

Seeing that it was in vain that he was attempting to conciliate that state, the emperor then envisaged new aggrandizements of the Duchy of Warsaw, and, when war with Alexander I at last broke out in 1812, he did not hesitate to call it his second Polish campaign. On the other hand, he hesitated in determining in advance what solution he would give to the Polish question, and even in encouraging an insurrection which would have been directed against both Austria and Prussia, then his allies. All that he permitted was the summoning of an extraordinary Diet in Warsaw, a Diet which proclaimed the re-establishment of Poland within her historical boundaries, and which, following tradition, formed a 'general confederation' of the nation. He refrained, however, from officially sanctioning this proceeding when he received the delegates of the confederation at Wilno. Among vague promises he imposed upon them the condition that they should wait for the former Polish provinces, which were still under the domination of Alexander I, to adopt a similar attitude.

His distrust, to a certain extent justified in respect of a part of the aristocracy of these provinces, was, on the contrary, by no means justified as regards the great majority of the Poles. As Adam Mickiewicz was later to recall in a magnificent evocation of the Napoleonic legend, in all the regions of the former Republic, and more particularly in that historic Lithuania through which the imperial army passed, the beautiful spring of 1812 had inspired not only hope but wellnigh certainty that the tragic episode of the partitions was nearing its end, and that the country, faithful to the spirit of the Four Years Diet and closely associated with the triumph of the emperor, was about to rise again.

Realizing at last the decision of the Great Diet, the Polish army now numbered a hundred thousand men who had distinguished themselves on every battlefield: at the capture of Smolensk as at Borodino, and even at the tragic crossing of the Beresina. Especially the corps commanded by Joseph Poniatowski sacrificed itself unreservedly, although Napoleon had only entrusted a third of the Polish forces to that leader, who had covered himself with glory, while the rest of those forces had been dispersed among the whole of the Grand Army. He placed, on the contrary, too great confidence in his German allies, which, together with the rash advance in the depth of winter into the interior of Russia, against Poniatowski's advice, contributed to the fatal issue of the campaign.

It was fatal, above all, for the Poles. As might have been foreseen, an alliance was soon effected between the Russians, who occupied Warsaw in the beginning of 1813, and the

Prussians and Austrians who had only marched with Napoleon against their will. Napoleon having hastily returned to Paris, the Poles once more found themselves at the mercy of their reunited enemies. Under these conditions it is not surprising that a mass levy of the whole nation should have proved impossible, and that the Government of the Duchy of Warsaw should have sought its chances of salvation by negotiating with Alexander I. The conduct of the Polish army in remaining faithful to the emperor, even in this last extremity, and fighting under his drooping banners to the end, is all the more meritorious. The Napoleonic epic ended for that army on 19th October 1813, when Prince Poniatowski, who had repulsed all Russia's offers and had been named Marshal of France, perished in the waters of the Elster.

Even after Leipzig, many Poles, attached to the person of the vanquished emperor, followed him to the bitter end. But the fate of the nation was to be decided at the famous Congress of Vienna which, meeting in October 1814, interrupted by Napoleon's return from the Isle of Elba and the campaign of Waterloo, ended in the formation of the Holy Alliance on 26th September 1815.

The Polish question was determined there by a series of treaties which bore the date, rich in memories, of 3rd May. The signing of these had been preceded by thorny negotiations. For it was necessary to find a compromise between the interests of the victors and the principles of right and liberty that they proclaimed, between the desire of re-establishing the state of affairs that Napoleon had just overthrown, and the necessity of taking into account the *faits accomplis* which marked his passage. Among these none was more striking than the abolition of the frontiers drawn up by the partitions of Poland, and the creation of a nucleus of a new and independent Poland with an army which, in spite of recent defeats, still represented a considerable force. Alexander intended to profit by this to resume his programme of a Poland restored under his sceptre and closely bound to Russia, and as he was undeniably the master of the hour, the Prussian project of returning to the conceptions of 1795, though for a moment even supported by England and France, had to be abandoned. But as all the members of the congress opposed a solution which, under the form of a reconstitution, more or less fictitious, of an integral Poland, would have increased inordinately the power of the tsar, his original intentions, which had impressed Czartoryski and even Kosciuszko, underwent essential modifications. He became 'King of Poland,' but of a 'kingdom' which did not even include all the former Duchy of Warsaw. Prussia, who had not succeeded in annexing the whole of Saxony, received by way of compensation the 'Grand Duchy of Posen,' while Cracow became a free city.

These dispositions have often been likened to a fourth partition of Poland. She was, in fact, again cut into pieces by artificial frontiers which persisted, except in the region of Cracow, down to the Great War of 1914. This partition even went further than in 1795, because this time Poland was divided into five parts: the little Republic of Cracow, whose independence was only an illusory symbol as it was placed under the protection of its three powerful neighbours; Austrian Poland, officially called the 'Kingdom of Galicia and Lodomeria'; Prussian Poland, comprising the provinces of Poznania and West Prussia; the 'Kingdom of Poland,' attached to Russia by the person of her sovereign and by a common foreign policy; and, finally, the Lithuanian-Ruthenian 'governments' which remained, as after the partitions, an in-

tegral part of the Russian Empire, although Alexander I long
encouraged the hope of the Poles that he would reunite these
provinces to the 'kingdom.'

The essential and durable difference between the solution
of 1815 and that of 1795 lay in the fact that the partitions of
the eighteenth century had been far more favourable to Poland's German neighbours, who had then secured all the
regions that were purely Polish from the ethnical standpoint, while the part assigned, in one way or another, to
Russia was now a preponderant one. This fact was to influence all the Polish policy of the following century, directing our patriotic aspirations in the first place against the
empire of the tsars.

On the other hand, the decisions of the Congress of Vienna
secured two undeniable advantages to Poland. On the morrow of the partitions her enemies had believed that it was
possible to efface the very name of Poland, and to erect insurmountable barriers between her three sections. In 1815,
Russia, Prussia, and Austria each engaged to guarantee to
their Polish subjects the maintenance and development of
their national individuality by institutions proper to the
purpose. At the same time they recognized the economic
unity of Poland's territory prior to 1772, promising to facilitate communications and transit over the whole extent of
that territory.

Although these promises were not observed, yet they constituted an official and international recognition of Poland's
historical and national rights, a very valuable recognition,
which the Poles owed solely to the events of the Napoleonic
epoch. They likewise owed the full autonomy granted to the
'Kingdom of Poland' to those very recent memories. It was
the constitution of the kingdom, promulgated on 27th November 1815, and based upon the Napoleonic constitution of

the Duchy of Warsaw, that was to differentiate her distinctly from Russia. It even developed the latter constitution in a more liberal sense, enlarged the authority of the Diet, and transformed the regional administration in a direction more in conformity with Polish traditions and with the Constitution of 1791. As in the Duchy of Warsaw, all the public offices were reserved to Poles, and it was a Pole—albeit a bad choice—in the person of General Zajaczek, who was nominated as the emperor-king's viceroy.

Under these conditions one part at least of Poland seemed as though, with its own national institutions and army, it could develop freely. Considerable progress was, in fact, soon effected there, notably in the domain of intellectual and economic life. In 1818 a university was opened in Warsaw; the activities of the Society of Sciences, which had existed there since 1800, took new impetus; literature by its extraordinary development recalled the days of Stanislas Augustus, and, under such an eminent minister of public instruction as Stanislas Potocki, the work of the Commission of National Education, interrupted during the years of crisis and of war, was resumed. Another minister, Prince Xavier Lubecki, energetically carried through the task of placing the finances of the kingdom on a sound footing, and assured her economic prosperity, albeit sacrificing the interests of the peasant population.

But even if the Poles had contented themselves with intense internal labours under the political tutelage of Russia, they would have had likewise to pay another sacrifice, that of their ideas of independence and of national unity. Those men were rare exceptions who, like Lubecki, resigned themselves to seeing the future of Poland lie in the collaboration of one relatively favoured part of the nation with the Russian power that dominated it. And this prospect was becoming intolerable in proportion as Russian influence penetrated even into the internal life of the kingdom, threatening the constitution, and inflicting humiliations of an ever-increasingly painful description on the national dignity. This began in the first years of the existence of the Congress Kingdom, preparing Polish minds for a new epoch of armed struggles in the name of the same ideas that had inspired Napoleonic Poland.

21

Romantic Poland: The Insurrections

THE Napoleonic wars which had rekindled the hopes of partitioned Poland and the First World War which realized them are separated by the saddest century in the whole of our history. From its sombre background there stand out the unforgettable scenes of the Polish risings. The November Rising—or rather the Polish-Russian war of 1830–1—the Polish participation in the revolutionary movements of 1848, and, finally, the January Rising of 1863, have each their place in the general history of Europe. The conspiracies and plans of action which filled the intervals between these dates are less known, such as notably the tragic attempt at a general insurrection in 1846. And a particularly interesting revelation in the light of recent researches may be found in the vast network of diplomatic overtures which, emanating from the Polish emigration in Paris, endeavoured at that period to interest the whole of Europe in the Polish question, and to remind it without ceasing of the international character of that question.

Of all our insurrections in the nineteenth century the first had, beyond doubt, the best chance of success. Studying its beginnings, which of themselves explain the causes of its failure, we shall at once grasp the character, the strength, and the weaknesses of all the struggles for Polish independence.

With this object we must revert to the conditions under which, after the Congress of Vienna, the 'kingdom' which it had created developed. We have already drawn attention to the positive aspect: the advantages and the possibilities that the solution of 1815 offered to that central part of Poland. Let us now look at the reverse of the medal.

The idea of a Polish-Russian union, upon which this solution was based, had shown itself to be unrealizable even in those epochs when the partitions of Poland, and the part that Russia had played in them, had not yet dug an abyss between the two countries, and when there had still been a certain equilibrium between the strength of both. To the irreconcilable differences of mentality and culture which resulted from a completely divergent historical evolution were now added the bitterness of the conquered and the conqueror's mistrust. The latter enables us to understand why the Polish army was placed under the command of a brother of Alexander I, the Grand Duke Constantine, well known for his brutality and his incalculable caprices, of whom Russia herself wished to be rid. Owing to this same mistrust a commissary of the Russian Government, the too famous Novosiltsov, was imposed upon the Polish Government. While Constantine himself, morganatically married to a Polish lady, ended by becoming attached to Poland and the soldiers over whom he tyrannized, Novosiltsov was the incarnation of all the hostility of the tsarist bureaucracy against the constitutional liberties of the kingdom.

Fearing lest their influence should make itself felt in the eastern provinces of the former Republic, for whose reunion with the kingdom the Poles hoped in vain, Novosiltsov began by persecutions directed against the University of Wilno. It was then that Mickiewicz and his colleagues were deported to Russia.

However, secret societies were also formed in Warsaw, and the severe sentence upon Lukasinski, who had been at the head of this movement, could not stop it. It is true enough that these conspiracies were encouraged by foreign examples, as the absolutist reaction which had followed the Congress of Vienna was exciting analogous movements at the same moment in nearly every country in Europe. The influence of freemasonry is likewise undeniable. But even this took on an essentially patriotic aspect in Poland, and the revolutionary tendencies which were spreading among the youth of the kingdom were in reality but the echo, still clandestine but all the more violent, of the constitutional struggles of which the Diet had from the outset become the arena.

Alexander I, irritated by the liberal opposition which he met there, had already, above all towards the end of his reign, ceased to respect the constitution which he himself had granted to the Poles. Nicholas I, who succeeded him in 1825 with a very decided conception of autocratic power, took up the course of repression with even greater determination. Accusing the Polish opposition of complicity with the Russian revolutionaries, he was indignant when the tribunal of the Diet treated the Poles who had conspired against his rule with indulgence. The war that the tsar declared against Turkey this same year, 1828, as well as the rivalry with Austria which resulted from it, led him for a moment to seek Polish sympathies. But he lost them finally when, in 1830, it was learned in the kingdom that the Polish army was intended to march with the Russians to crush the Revolution of July in France, and to prevent the Belgians from acquiring their independence.

In the face of this odious prospect, and in the intolerable atmosphere that reigned in Warsaw, the insurrection at last broke out there on the night of 29th November 1830. At the outset it was the work of young enthusiasts, in particular the students of the School of Cadets led by the sub-lieutenant Wysocki. Their attack against the residence of the Grand Duke Constantine aroused the enthusiasm of the populace, and at once gained all the elements of the Left. The Moderates, not less patriotic but more prudent, had the merit of controlling this initiative, a spontaneous and generous one but incalculable in its consequences, and of opposing, through all the duration of the rising, the acts of violence which threatened to compromise it. They had, however, too little faith in final victory and too little firm decision at the critical moments.

This reacted, above all, on the military action of the rising. All the army of the kingdom soon rallied to the insurrection, which extended even to the former Grand Duchy of Lithuania and penetrated into Volhynia. This army was not lacking in courage, a courage often reaching heroism, nor in eminent tacticians who elaborated strategic plans of high value. But the execution of these plans was brought up against the weakness of the supreme command, which passed from hand to hand. Chlopicki and Radziwill, Skrzynecki and Krukowiecki—all these generals were, without any doubt, excellent patriots who freely risked their lives, but none of whom knew how to lead his soldiers to victory. The most important battles remained undecided like that of Grochow, or finished in defeats like that of Ostroleka.

But it was not only on the battlefields, made illustrious, moreover, by acts of gallantry which enabled the resistance of the Poles to last ten months, that the fate of the rising was decided. The Diet in Warsaw sat permanently, and political parties disputed both within and without it. This Diet, which unfortunately did not succeed in solving the question of the complete emancipation of the peasant population, showed itself more resolute in dethroning Nicholas I, on 25th January 1831, and thus repulsing projects of compromise, which served no purpose. It placed at the head of the National Government a personality who possessed a unique experience and an indisputable authority in Poland as well as in Europe— Prince Adam Czartoryski. But even this distinguished diplomat was unable to appease the irresponsible extremists inside the country who were banded together in the Patriotic Society, or to gain for insurgent Poland the support, if only diplomatic, of the foreign Powers. It was in vain that the idea of offering the royal crown to an Austrian archduke or to the Duke of Reichstadt was considered; and neither England nor even France moved any more than Austria.

Under these conditions the overwhelming forces at Russia's disposal, which at the end of the war were commanded by Field Marshal Paskevich, inevitably gained the ascendancy. After a defence which again was signalized by fine examples of devotion, Warsaw capitulated, and in the beginning of October 1831 the remains of the Polish army saw themselves compelled to lay down arms.

European opinion, favourable to the vanquished who had fought for the liberty of all nations, did not prevent Nicholas I, while in certain respects saving appearances, from revenging himself upon them. The amnesty, as a matter of course, excluded the leaders of the insurrection and all the emigrants, who lost their property, as well as the inhabitants of the provinces situated beyond the frontiers of the kingdom. It was then that the brutal Russification of the eastern borderlands of the former Republic began, by confiscation of landed estates, deportations to Russia and, above all, to

Siberia, the persecution of the Uniat Church, carried so far as its total suppression, and, finally, by the closing of Polish schools, including the University of Wilno. But scarcely less severe measures were applied to the kingdom itself, where the University of Warsaw shared the fate of that of Wilno. Under the deceitful form of a new 'organic statute' the tsar, in 1832, suppressed the constitution and replaced it by a fictitious autonomy which no longer provided for a Polish Diet or army. Paskevich, the victor of 1831, rewarded by the title of Prince of Warsaw, remained for many years the real master of the country; and a strong citadel, built at the gates of Warsaw, became, with its filthy dungeons and its cannon directed against the town, the symbol of the new rule.

During the whole of the epoch which was thus inaugurated, the eyes of all Poles were turned to Paris, which then became the centre, not only of Poland's intellectual life, but also of her national policy, that of the emigrants. These thousands of emigrants, among whom the flower of a whole nation was to be found, had, unfortunately, two rival policies. Under the impression of the defeat, for which the members of the Right were held responsible, the Radical Left gained the upper hand, and it was from its Democratic Society that the initiative of new revolutionary movements soon started. Wherever similar movements showed themselves in Europe, Polish emigrants took an active part in all of them, convinced that the sacred cause of liberty was common to all nations. But it goes without saying that the emissaries of the emigration laboured, above all, to prepare a new insurrection in Poland itself. Many among them attempted to resume a conflict with the Russians and, arrested by the latter, were executed in Warsaw or Wilno. However, during the course of the years which followed the war of 1830–1, it was to be foreseen that the conflict would be waged also against the other two Powers which had dismembered Poland: Prussia and Austria.

This is explained, not only by Poland's desire of reuniting the whole of the national territory, but also by the fact that the lot reserved to the Poles in those two States was becoming increasingly hard. The Prussian Government, which, on the morrow of the Congress of Vienna, had shown itself more or less conciliatory, changed its attitude after the November rising. In spite of the sympathy that the insurgents found among the German people, the King of Prussia helped Nicholas I to crush them, and then began an active policy of Germanization. At this epoch President Flottwell employed the same methods in Poznania that Bismarck was to apply later, not even shrinking from a conflict with the Catholic clergy. Moreover, the king, like the tsar in 1833, entered into an understanding with the Emperor of Austria to co-ordinate the repressions directed against their Polish subjects, and shortly afterwards they made an agreement to send garrisons of the three Powers into the free city of Cracow. We must not forget that Austria was then governed by that Prince Metternich who inspired the reactionary policy of all the European monarchies, and whose rule of bureaucracy and police aimed also at stifling the national and liberal aspirations of the Poles in Galicia.

In fact, it was in Galicia that in February 1846 the new Polish insurrection at last broke out, which was to have begun simultaneously in the three sections of Poland. Insufficiently prepared, in spite of long years of propaganda, it was prevented at Poznan by the arrest of Mieroslawski and the other leaders of the conspiracy, and nothing could be attempted in Russian Poland. Cracow alone succeeded in liberating itself from foreign occupation, and the insurrection spread from there into the neighbouring regions of Galicia.

The Austrian Government then struck back by a proceeding which, even in the tragic history of partitioned Poland, remains unique in its horror. This time the insurgents, who were all of very advanced democratic leanings, although for the most part of noble birth, had immediately proclaimed complete freedom for the peasants, to whom they promised full possession of their lands. Before their proclamations were sufficiently known, Austrian officials succeeded in persuading the peasants in certain districts of western Galicia that the insurrection, led only by the nobility, was designed to enslave them. They organized well-paid bands who turned upon the nobles and, by means of hideous massacres, helped the Austrian army to stifle the opening of the insurrection in blood. The insurrection, moreover, served Austria as a pretext to annex the Republic of Cracow, in spite of the protests of France and England.

Yet hardly had this last vestige of a free Poland disappeared when a revolutionary movement, more violent than all those which had preceded it, began in Europe; and the Poles believed they could make use of it to resume, with greater chances of success, their struggle for national independence. In 1848, that year full of enthusiasm and of hope, we see them making their appearance wherever the political order from which they suffered so cruelly was shaken. In Prussia they first of all fraternized with the German revolutionaries who, in March 1848, freed Mieroslawski and the other Poles that had been imprisoned for two years. But the hope that the King of Prussia would see himself forced to grant a large autonomy to his Polish provinces was far from realized. In spite of some successes gained by Mieroslawski, the insurrection which had broken out in Poznania and had even gained Pomerania was easily crushed, and the constitution granted to

Prussia brought no change to the situation in that part of Poland.

The role of the Poles was more considerable in the Austrian revolution. Their representatives participated in the Slav Congress assembled at Prague; others fought against the Hapsburgs under the flag of the King of Sardinia. And when the struggles waged in Cracow and Lwow finished with the bombardment of those two towns, the Poles played a large part in the revolt of the Viennese and, above all, in the Hungarian insurrection. The Polish General Bem, after having directed the defence of Vienna against Windischgrätz, distinguished himself, together with many other Poles, in Kossuth's army. Their appearance in Hungary gave Nicholas I an increasingly plausible argument for Russian intervention, and, in fact, it was Paskevich, the governor of the oppressed 'kingdom,' who, in 1849, put an end to the struggle for Hungarian independence. We know that his victory inaugurated a new period of reaction in all the empire of the Hapsburgs, including, of course, Galicia. In the empire of the tsar no serious revolutionary movement had been able to show itself.

The policy of the Polish Left, which had closely linked the fate of the nation with the cause of European democracy, had, therefore, only led to fresh failures. It remained to be seen whether the Right of the Polish emigration would be more fortunate in its projects. From the beginning it had had at its head the leader of the National Government of 1831, Prince Adam Czartoryski, whom the Polish monarchists were pleased to consider the king *de facto,* and who, indeed, had his diplomatic representatives in different European capitals. The Poles of this group, sceptical and reserved in regard to the revolutionary movement, counted more upon a European war which would place the Polish question, supported, as they hoped, by France and England, once more upon the order of the day. These calculations seemed confirmed when in 1854 these two Powers went to war with Russia, and when at the same time Napoleon III revived the imperial legend, basing his policy on the principle of nationalities, always invoked by the Poles.

Moreover, the Crimean War opened all the more favourable prospects to the latter inasmuch as certain of their military leaders, including General Bem, had found a refuge in Turkey. Hence Czartoryski's chief collaborator, General Ladislas Zamoyski, intended to form a new nucleus there of a national army. It was to remove the difficulties which beset this plan that Adam Mickiewicz went himself to Constantinople, where he died in 1855. But it was already easy at that moment to foresee that the Congress of Paris which was to wind up the Crimean War would not so much as touch on the Polish question. In the course of hostilities, the creation of a Polish State, if only within very reduced limits, was considered, notably in England; but the opposition of Prussia and Austria, whom the allies desired to gain over to their cause, soon brought about the abandonment of this idea, of which there could no longer be any question when it was a case of reconciliation with Russia.

Thus the peace of 1856 only perpetuated the tragic situation of Poland, which seemed more desperate than ever when Czartoryski died in Paris in 1861. Even in 1859, when the principle of nationalities had once more come forward, there was no thought of applying it to our territory, where the following year William I and Francis Joseph met the tsar in Warsaw in order to emphasize the complete understanding between the masters of Poland.

However, the tsar who received them was no longer Nicholas I. His son, Alexander II, who had succeeded him in 1855, warned the Poles against any 'dreams,' but showed himself, nevertheless, less uncompromising than his father. The concessions that he was ready to make on points which were, however, secondary ones, encouraged one of our most vigorous politicians, the Marquis Alexander Wielopolski, to make an attempt at collaboration with the tsarist regime. He actually obtained certain appreciable results. The administration of the 'kingdom' again became Polish; the University of Warsaw was opened under the title of 'Principal School'; he himself was placed, in 1862, at the head of the Government. But his programme of autonomy perpetuated the bond with Russia and seemed to abandon definitely all hope of independence. Also Wielopolski remained isolated. Even the Conservative party—the 'Whites'—with their universally respected leader, Count Andrew Zamoyski, were hardly ever at one with the marquis, who has been erroneously termed 'the last Polish noble.' For, in spite of his aristocratic tendencies which prevented him from solving the agrarian question and encouraging the development of the towns, he had broken with the time-honoured traditions of the Polish nobility, enamoured as it was of freedom and at the same time deeply attached to the national idea.

As a matter of course those on the Left, the 'Reds,' were still more hostile to Wielopolski. The patriotic manifestations that they organized and which, since 1861, had produced sanguinary repressions on the side of the Russians, seemed, with good reason, the prelude to a new insurrection. In the course of the year 1862 this party formed itself into a 'National' Government co-existent with that over which Wielopolski presided, and when the marquis attempted to stifle the movement which was preparing, by allowing the young men who were indicated by the police to be enlisted in the Russian army, the rising broke out openly on 22nd January 1863.

It had assuredly no chance of success. Nevertheless, this act of despair has left a memory sacred to every Pole. No sacrifice for the national cause had, in fact, ever been so disinterested and of so moving a nature. Never had such large classes of the population rallied to a movement which, unlike that of 1830, did not possess even the skeleton of a regular army. On the other hand, even the 'Whites,' who at heart disapproved of a conflict undertaken under such conditions, adhered to it as proof of their patriotism. And, as always, Lithuania rose simultaneously with ethnographic Poland.

The January Rising, as it is usually called, lasted even longer than the November Rising. The last insurgent was only executed in 1865. But the fate of Poland was in reality decided when France, England, and Austria, for whose intervention she had hoped, contented themselves in June 1863 with sending diplomatic notes to the tsar in favour of the Poles. Again the latter had universal sympathy, notably that of Napoleon III and Pius IX, but no one in Europe contemplated going to war with Russia, who, on the other hand, found unreserved support from Prussia. Hence Russia succeeded without any difficulty in annihilating, in the course of a number of successive encounters, the forces of the insurrection, which were insufficient, scattered, and badly armed. The last Polish 'dictator,' Romuald Traugutt, died on the scaffold on 5th August 1864.

Examining the situation of Poland on the morrow of this new defeat, we could easily reach the general conclusion that all the armed struggles for Polish independence were nothing but a series of gross political mistakes. But if we would judge that policy fairly, a policy genuinely romantic, and difficult of application to practical realities, we are unable to isolate it from the other manifestations of the national life. The conflicts, apparently useless, which were waged by the Poles at the epoch of the insurrections, only show their true meaning when we consider them in their relations with Polish thought of those same years.

22

Romantic Poland: Her Poets

THREE times in the course of Poland's history her culture has reached a particularly high level, each time participating in the powerful currents of European thought. Her role was never limited to that of passively submitting to western influences, nor even to spreading these in eastern Europe. Each time also Poland's creative activity in the intellectual sphere was in close relation to her political situation. In the epoch of the Renaissance, the first expansion of our national culture, favoured by the heritage of the last Piast and by the triumphs of the Jagiellonian dynasty, facilitated, in its turn, the creation of the Royal Republic. Under Stanislas Augustus the parallel between the progress of the intellectual order and the work of political reform is entirely obvious. There is, on the other hand, a striking contrast between the desperate situation of Poland at the time of the insurrections and the simultaneous development of her spiritual forces. And, what is more, this third efflorescence of Polish culture is, beyond all doubt, the most brilliant and most original.

It is true that again it benefited from an intellectual movement common to all Europe, that of Romanticism. In its beginning, which was purely literary, Polish Romanticism, reacting as elsewhere against the rigidity of Classicism, followed the model of its foreign inspirers fairly faithfully. To understand how it was subsequently transformed it is enough to recall a symbolic scene from one of the best-known works of Adam Mickiewicz. In the dungeon where he had been thrown by the Russians, the hero, in whose personality that of the poet himself is reflected, inscribes on the walls those often quoted words: 'Obiit Gustavus, natus est Conradus.' Gustavus is the unhappy lover, the Polish Werther; Conrad, the persecuted patriot who suffers for millions of brothers.

But the evolution of Polish Romanticism did not stop at this transition from a personal drama, half imaginary and modelled on many others, to the national tragedy which exalted a cruel reality, unique in the world. The Christian name adopted by the transfigured hero is that of Konrad Wallenrod, in whose person Mickiewicz, on the eve of the November Rising, had glorified a pagan and savage patriotism—to-day we should call it nationalism in the derogatory sense of that term—which does not recoil even before treachery should such a means serve its end. What a difference between this primitive conception of patriotism and that which was to be enunciated by the same poet some ten years later! He will revolt no more against the sufferings of his people which once led him to improvise the most violent of blasphemies. He now believes that, like Christ, Poland suffers for the salvation of the world, to redeem the sins of all the nations so that they may become worthy of freedom.

This, it may be said, was another extreme, not less dangerous and erroneous than the first; another aberration of national idolatry. But if we disengage Polish Messianism from the exaggerations that, like Mickiewicz himself, it owes to Towianski's extravagant mysticism, and essential basis remains which may be summed up in two ideas, both of them alike true and sublime: that of sacrifice in the Christian sense and that of the solidarity of the nations. And it is from them that a light which illuminates the whole political history of the epoch emerges. When Mickiewicz, while an emigrant in Paris, wrote his *Books of the Polish Nation and of the Polish Pilgrims* in biblical style, he was only translating into literary language what the insurgents of 1830 had dimly felt, what alone could unite the politicians of the emigration, and what was to prolong the conspiracies and insurrections of the following generation beyond all possibility of success.

What may seem obscure or pathetic in Mickiewicz's Messianic visions becomes clear for us, as it did for his contemporaries, thanks to the admirable national epic he has given us, which constitutes a commentary full of calm and simplicity upon those visions. The twelve cantos of *Pan Tadeusz* have been compared to those of Homer. Apart from the purely literary standpoint this comparison, which may seem a very daring one, is justified by the fact that in this epic, as in the Iliad or the Odyssey, the historical tradition of a whole people lives again. In Mickiewicz it is the tradition of a relatively recent past which already seemed legendary; a few scenes passing from the daily to the heroic life of the Polish nobility, of a generation which had still known the free and independent Republic, evoked the whole history of that Poland of other days, of which the emigrants gathered 'on the Paris pavement' [1] dreamt with a poignant homesickness.

The historic sense had never been wanting in the Poles. Hence Mickiewicz was sure of being understood in appealing to such memories. But what was far more rare in Poland, even in the epochs of her greatness and among the finest

[1] Translator's note: A quotation from verses intended by Mickiewicz as an introduction to *Pan Tadeusz*.

minds of the nation, was the philosophic sense. The leading ideas of Polish Messianism, as they had been formulated by this most celebrated of our poets, whose name is familiar even to foreigners, required to be gathered together in a Polish system of the philosophy of history. It was Sigismund Krasinski who took upon himself this task.

With him we reach the most sublime summit to which Polish thought had attained through the centuries. His patriotic exaltation certainly idealizes the past of Poland as no historian would dare to do. But he needed this starting-point as the guarantee, the promise that the risen Poland, whose dawn he foresaw, would fully respond to the ideal which he himself carried in his generous heart and in his conscience of a Christian. This Polish count was, it is true, an aristocrat who turned with horror from the scenes of social revolution that he had depicted in an *Undivine Comedy*. But this is because he foresaw, eighty years before Bolshevism, all the future excesses of the revolutionary movement. This patriot has left us the finest imaginable conception of the universal commonwealth; this man of conservative tendencies, like the greatest Poles of the preceding epochs, only sought the harmonious synthesis of the ideals of justice and liberty.

Like the other Polish poets of his time, Krasinski was from his childhood subject to the influences of western Romanticism, German, English, and French. But he was now to turn back to the Roman origins—classical, therefore, in the proper sense—of European civilization. Like other Polish philosophers with whom he collaborated, he was affected by the so-called idealistic philosophy of Hegel and his disciples. But he transformed this idealism in the light of the Christian doctrine to which he ended by submitting unreservedly. In this manner he was able to work the destiny of Poland, as it appeared to him, into the general plan of providence, being profoundly convinced that each individual nation—instrument of the Divine Will—had its own mission to carry out in the harmonious whole of this plan, to the benefit of all the others.

Krasinski, too, saw in his martyred native country the Messiah of the nations. But even the foreign reader will forgive him as he forgives Mickiewicz for this apotheosis, seeing that its actual work was to encourage all Poles to serve the cause of international society, of a lasting peace, based on justice, liberty, and charity. In union with all the Polish Romantics and Messianists, he firmly believed that this cause, which for him signified the advent of the kingdom of God upon earth, would triumph with the resurrection of Poland, inaugurating a new era in the history of humanity.

Krasinski's prose is full of vigour and poetic inspiration. But he himself suffered from the limitations of his talent as a poet. Such limitations were unknown to Julius Slowacki, the third of the great Polish poets of the epoch of the risings. None of our writers has attained to such perfection of language, which was his obedient instrument in expressing the most subtle emotions in melodious verse. He was in rivalry with Mickiewicz and had differences with Krasinski upon their political opinions. But, agreeing with both in regard to the mystical interpretation of Poland's sufferings, he has transmitted this to us in symbols of incomparable artistic beauty, thereby rendering it more accessible and more beloved to those who had not themselves lived through the experiences of his epoch. Slowacki found these symbols in every epoch of our history. It is sufficient to mention two: one placed by the poet's fancy in the shadows of prehistoric Poland; the other shedding an aureole of the purest beauty on the most appalling miseries in contemporary history. In the first he calls upon us to witness the extermination of a whole innocent nation, as though to imagine an example, if only legendary, of a still more cruel fate than that of modern Poland. In the other he has raised an imperishable monument to that other Polish emigration which, instead of disputing on the banks of the Seine, was slowly dying in its Siberian exile. The idea of expiation by guiltless victims has been expressed in no more moving manner than in *Lilla Weneda* and *Anhelli*. And it is, likewise, their author who has best succeeded in grasping the tormented mental outlook of the first insurgents of 1830.

The three men of genius who were the intellectual leaders of romantic Poland were not isolated. Their prestige, which still reacts on the Pole of to-day, was undisputed among their contemporaries. Nor were they isolated as poets, for we see them surrounded and followed by a whole phalanx of writers who shared their ideas and were subject to their influence. Many of these were not wanting in talent. If we do not attempt to enumerate them it is because it is not our intention to write a bibliographical work, but rather to set in relief the most representative individualities of the epoch. Yet none of those three inspiring writers was exclusively a poet. Hence the activities of each one of them were also united with other manifestations of Polish intellectual life, upon which they all impressed a poetical stamp.

The epic talent of Mickiewicz was also expressed in his work as historian. His masterly course on the history of Slavonic literature, which attracted so much attention when given at the College de France, is well known. But by the side of Michelet's friend we must hasten to mention the writer who was himself the Polish Michelet. Joachim Lelewel was a professor at the University of Wilno when Mickiewicz was studying there. After playing an important part at the time of the war of 1830–1, he too emigrated, and subsequently worked unweariedly in Brussels and Paris. He was a scholar of the first rank, who interested himself in questions of method as well as those of bibliography, in historical geography as well as the sciences auxiliary to the study of history. Nevertheless, this learned scholar, prudent as he was in analysis, allowed a large share of poetic imagination to enter into his attempts at synthesis. Democracy was for this inflexible Republican the supreme ideal that Poland had realized in the beginnings of her history as well as at the most brilliant moments of her evolution. Because she departed from it she perished. If she would be reborn she must rally unreservedly to the democratic and liberal movement of the nineteenth century. All the political programme of the Polish Left thus found its theoretical justification in this great historian.

Charles Szajnocha, who held the first place after him among the Polish historians of the Romantic period, and who only died on the morrow of the rising of 1863-4, did not follow Lelewel and his school either in their political doctrine or in their frequently arbitrary interpretation of the past. The works which he devoted to the most diverse periods of our history have retained their scientific value to our own days. No one had surpassed him, especially, in his skilful reconstruction of the great epoch of Jadwiga of Anjou and Jagiello. But it was not for nothing that he had begun his career as a poet. Even in his case, scrupulous though he was in the examination of texts, intuition now and then ran to imagination. This is precisely the reason why he has exercised so great an influence on all Poles, in reviving memories so different from the miseries of the present hour, with a brilliancy heightened by the author's poetical enthusiasm.

In the domain of historical sciences, it was a case of resuming a very ancient tradition reaching from Dlugosz to Naruszewicz. Polish philosophy had to be entirely created by the generation to which Krasinski belonged. This philosophy was first developed in close contact with the exact sciences, as we see in another professor of the University of Wilno, John Sniadecki, who surpassed his brother Andrew in the extent of his philosophical conceptions. But even those of our philosophers who, like Hoene-Wronski, started from mathematical problems ended in a doctrine which, in spite of all that distinguished it from that of our poets, was, like theirs, a poetical Messianism.

None of them was so closely associated with the work of Krasinski as his friend Augustus Cieszkowski. Under the form of a vast commentary on the Paternoster, he has left us a philosophy of history which entirely corresponds with the ideas of our romantic poets, determining the mission of Poland within the framework of the Christian universe. It is he who has most clearly predicted the institution of a new international order which, in the third and last period of general history, shall realize the Kingdom of God on earth. But what most interests us is that his theory was essentially a philosophy of action. Nothing is a better proof of this fact than the generous projects of social reform which he propagated as the practical consequence of his speculations. And, in spite of certain points on which his ideas swerved from Catholic orthodoxy, he, like Krasinski, contributed to the religious regeneration of Poland.

The names that we have just cited are not unknown abroad, thanks to the works that these historians and philosophers have written in French or German. Moreover, they, like the poets, wrote such beautiful Polish that their work is distinguished from others by its high artistic value. But at this epoch that was so rich in talent the artistic sense of the Poles was not only exercised in literature. It also saw the birth of a style of Polish painting infinitely superior to that of its modest beginnings in the preceding centuries, when the plastic arts in Poland had been a domain restricted chiefly to foreigners. By the side of the poetic images of a Slowacki, so perfect in form, so vivid in colour, pictures came into being which, for the first time, worthily reproduced every patriotic memory and perpetuated the mental emotions of the time.

Julius Kossak, who so perfectly understood the great Poland of the past, opened the way to John Matejko's magnificent historical pictures, the first of which appeared immediately after the January Rising. This insurrection itself was the subject of two series of pictures by Arthur Grottger, the one entitled *Polonia* and the other *Lithuania*. And let us not forget that this remarkable artist, who died young, devoted another series to *War*, to depict all its horrors, and in this way to send forth in the name of his bloodstained country a desperate appeal for peace on earth.

But the most illustrious Polish artist, inseparable from the great poets who were his contemporaries, is a musician who, in truth, belongs to the whole world: Frederic Chopin. Like the painters, he spoke a language understood by all nations. The sounds which he set vibrating, the echo of which is prolonged unceasingly, have evoked, and still evoke, better than the pictures of the painters, better than the most eloquent verses, all the glories and all the sufferings of Poland. The dream of the Romantics which at times seems no longer to affect the more recent generations when it is embodied in words, or even in pictures, appeals to them without a break as long as the Polonaises of Chopin resound in their ears, accompanied by the same immaterial emotions which once brought strength and comfort to the vanquished heroes of our insurrections.

Hence, is it too bold a claim that these insurrections, and with them the whole of Poland's romantic policy, are only comprehensible if, at the same time, we contemplate the romantic Poland of the poets? Like their heroes, the Poland of that most troubled epoch was a symbol for Europe. She represented all the great ideas which were then revolting in vain against an order based exclusively on force. She was admirably qualified to represent that idea of liberty which had been the leading idea of the whole of her history, and the apparent failure of which, even temporarily, was more painful for her than for any other nation. She was no less qualified to represent the idea of nationality: because by the very fact of her existence she bore witness how false and artificial a thing it is to identify the nation with the all-powerful state, since a nation could survive the destruction of her state and utterly refuse to be amalgamated with the victorious nations who dominated her politically. Finally, Poland was qualified to represent the idea of a new international order based on moral principles, not because she herself had been without reproach, as the Messianists claimed, but because she was expiating in the most terrible manner all the faults that she had committed.

This suggests our reply to the question why the insurrections, in spite of all their disastrous consequences, were indispensable to the history of partitioned Poland, and what their significance is in our historical evolution, taken as a whole. They were, with all the sufferings that they engendered, above all, an expiation, more complete than that for which the Partitions stood: because they were the sacrifice, freely consented to, which redeemed a long series of sins of omission, dictated by individual egoism or by an equally culpable class egoism. Finally, they gave proof that the beautiful language of the poets was by no means a matter of empty phrases, but responded to the sincere convictions of the whole nation, which no longer recoiled before the practical consequences of the principles professed by its finest sons.

23

Organic Work

THE last century of Polish history before the Great War is
divided into two halves of an entirely different character.
The epoch of insurrections and conspiracies in the course of
which the boldest hopes alternated with the most profound
disillusions, that epoch when the Polish question incessantly
reappeared in international politics, was followed by another,
dreary and monotonous, broken by no armed conflict, and
which seemed to envelop Poland in the shroud of oblivion.
Abroad she was spoken of less and less, and even those she
counted as her friends no longer believed in the possibility
of her resurrection. From the political point of view each of
the three parts of the national territory appeared to be living
its life apart; and if one happened to be more fortunate than
the others, the separation of their destinies was only the more
clearly accentuated. Polish culture remained one and indivisible, conscious of its individuality; but the enthusiasm of
Romanticism which had caused it to shine with such splendour was entirely at an end, and the new tendencies which
guided it were no longer of a nature to distinguish it from
those of other nations.

It would, however, be eminently unjust to pass over the results acquired during these fifty years, and to regard them as something resembling lost time. Such an interpretation would not enable us to understand how the reconstitution of Poland was prepared, indeed assured, in the shadow and silence of that epoch. It is generally termed that of organic work: a happy expression which reveals its secret. Two generations, the sons and grandsons of the insurgents, including those who had themselves fought in their first youth, confined themselves to carrying on practical work day by day. This was an expiation worth that of the wars for independence. No one will ever know how much this apparent resignation cost those who consented to it and even preached it to others. And, moreover, we shall see that this new attitude of prudence and loyalty in regard to the Powers which governed Poland did not spare her fresh persecutions.

But this is not all. Independent Poland had often failed in that spirit of patriotic sacrifice which partitioned Poland practised in the epoch of the insurrections. She had, however, failed still more, and during many years, in patience and continuity in systematic work. Her 'Slav unproductiveness' and her small talent for organization could have been made a reproach against her. In this respect, the years 1864 to 1914 were a valuable school which rendered us capable of providing later the immense effort of organization which a reborn State exacted after a disappearance of more than a hundred years.

Finally—and we cannot insist too strongly on this point—the experience of work in common, and respect for every sort of work which was its consequence, consolidated not only the economic bases of the Polish nation, but also, and above all, her social structure. It is not until this epoch of transition that there disappeared, once for all, the watertight compartments which had too long separated the classes: the nobility, composed of landed proprietors who had formerly believed themselves to represent the whole nation; the bourgeoisie, relatively neither numerous nor influential; and finally, the millions of a poor and ignorant peasant population.

We have seen that each insurrection, beginning with that of Kosciuszko, proposed to remedy this state of things. Each of them had a more democratic character than the preceding one. Unhappily, the very fact of their defeat prevented the insurgents from realizing their programme of social justice. And particularly tragic was the fact that the governments which were fighting against them hastened to forestall them on this delicate ground, and to offer concessions to the masses of the population which were aimed at detaching them from the national cause. This is how the peasants of Russian Poland were finally emancipated by Tsar Alexander II on the morrow of the rising of 1863–4 which had promised them the proprietorship of their lands.

However, in the course of the following years an ever closer collaboration was established between all the Poles. The nobility, always very numerous and active, did not cease to play a predominating part, proving that they could work as well as they could fight. But many of their descendants, impoverished by their participation in the risings and subsequently hit by innumerable confiscations, had lost their estates. They formed the nucleus of a middle class that had hitherto been lacking in Poland: the class of the intellectuals, which, little by little, came to comprise the most gifted sons of the Polish people.

In addition, two other phenomena of capital importance accompanied the social transformations of this epoch. On the one hand, owing to the development of industry and the influx of the rural population, an urban proletariat was formed in the towns which, as everywhere in Europe, was radical in its principles, while interesting itself far more than elsewhere in national claims. On the other hand, the rapid democratization of public life, stimulating the national consciousness of the masses, brought forward the ethnical differences in the midst of the population in the eastern borderlands of former Poland. This grave problem, which had first arisen in Galicia in the middle of the nineteenth century under the form of the Ruthenian question, was to prove still more complex in the vast regions of Russian Poland, from Lithuania to the Ukraine.

It was actually in Russian Poland that the slogan of 'Organic Work' was originally launched. It was a natural reaction against the immediate consequences of the last rising. These were even more terrible than those of the defeat of 1831. In the territory of the former Grand Duchy of Lithuania it was no longer a case of chastising only the insurgents and all those who were suspected of connivance with the culprits, but of exterminating the Polish population there and effacing all the traces of its centuries-old influence in those regions. The Governor-General Muraviev, who carried this programme into execution, was given by the Russians themselves the name of 'Hangman.' The Government went so far as to forbid the use of Polish in any and every public place, finally even in the churches, as well as all teaching, even in private, of that language. In the nine Lithuanian-Ruthenian provinces the Poles were forbidden to acquire landed property; what had been confiscated from the families of insurgents passed into the hands of Russian officers or officials.

But this time these severe measures did not stop at the frontiers of the 'Kingdom of Poland.' It goes without saying that all the concessions that Wielopolski had obtained were immediately withdrawn. But the Russianizers, determined to suppress everything that still distinguished that territory

from the rest of the empire of the tsars, did not stop there.
The ten provinces of the 'kingdom' lost their very name
which recalled the old Poland and which was replaced by
that of the 'Vistula Provinces.' Their administration was
completely assimilated into that of Russia, from which
crowds of officials, hostile to everything that was Polish,
streamed into the country. War was waged in the heart itself
of Poland against the national language, which was styled a
mere dialect, and the Russian Government preferred to
lower the level of the whole education of the country rather
than tolerate a Polish education. Finally, undeterred by a
rupture with the Holy See, it attacked the religious life of
all Catholics, and ended, in 1874, by suppressing, with the
greatest brutality, the Greek Uniat rite which, prohibited
for the last forty years in the eastern provinces, still subsisted
in the borderlands of the 'kingdom.'

This persecution, the severest that Poland had ever
known, enveloped the whole nation in mourning. Faced
with the impossibility of any sort of resistance and under the
influence of an understandable discouragement, increasing
numbers of voices were to be heard recommending a purely
realistic policy. Many Poles, especially in the more well-to-do
classes, considered that all that was left to them was at least
to profit by the possibilities of economic development that
its fusion with Russia offered to the former 'kingdom.' This
opened an unlimited outlet to Polish industry, which made
rapid progress, especially in the entirely modern town of
Lodz. The 'Positivists' who broke with the tradition of the
risings believed that by enriching themselves individually
they were contributing to the welfare of the nation, and in
order to secure modest but tangible advantages for it they
followed a policy of compromise with the tsarist rule. Even
the recrudescence of autocratic oppression under Alexander

III did not turn them from this course, and the more conciliatory methods that Nicholas II seemed to inaugurate confirmed them in their attitude.

Moreover, this was not entirely dictated by the situation in which Russian Poland was placed. The policy of the Romantics had always been fed on the illusion that the international situation would prove favourable to the Poles provided that they did not cease to struggle for their independence. No one could now delude himself with such hopes, since the policy of Bismarck and Prussia's victories in 1864, 1866, and 1870–1 had secured a predominating place in Europe for the new German Empire. From that moment France, upon whom Poland had so long counted, now herself vanquished, sought for a supporter in Russia. And Prussia, who had helped the latter to suppress all the insurrections, was enabled to resume more methodically than ever her policy of Germanization which was fundamentally, according to the admission of Bismarck himself, a programme for the extermination of the Poles under Prussia.

As in Russian Poland, German measures of repression were directed in the first place against the Polish language. They were first applied in Upper Silesia and West Prussia, where its disappearance, as was believed, would be effected more easily than in Poznania. Facts have proved this belief to be erroneous. In addition, Bismarck profited by the economic crises through which large properties were passing to bring about the purchase by Germans of the estates of the Polish nobility. The chancellor, however, made two mistakes. One was in wounding the religious feelings of the population. His battle with the Catholic Church at the time of the *Kulturkampf* naturally took on a particularly acute character in Polish territory. Mgr Ledochowski, Archbishop of Poznan and Gniezno, who had opposed the introduction of

the German language into religious instruction, was thrown
into prison in 1874, and soon other Polish bishops and
priests shared his lot. In 1886 a German succeeded him, and
Bismarck, having settled his conflict with the Holy See, believed he had triumphed. But it was precisely at that moment that his second mistake was laid bare. He had imagined
that only the Polish nobility was opposed to Germanization.
But the religious persecutions had turned the whole oppressed nation into a common front. The Polish population
of the towns, as well as the peasants in the country, both
admirably organized, showed themselves fully as attached to
their nationality as the nobility, and even more unyielding
than the latter to any idea of compromise.

Bismarck then ordered, in 1885, the expulsion of thousands of Poles who, though long domiciled in Prussian Poland, were originally Russian or Austrian subjects. The following year a fund of a hundred million marks was created,
designed to encourage German colonization in the Polish
eastern provinces of Prussia. But in thus supporting 'Hakatism'—as German nationalism was subsequently called after
the initials of its leaders—the chancellor only exasperated
the antagonism between the two nations, and gradually the
Poles began to realize that the Germans were fully as great
a menace as the Russians, against whom the principal insurrections had been directed.

The Polish policy in Prussia remained, notwithstanding,
a policy of 'organic work,' as that of the Russian Poles had
become. No one dreamt of an insurrection, and the most
ardent patriots, such as, for example, Father Wawrzyniak,
who for some forty years directed the co-operative movement
in Poznania, devoted themselves entirely to the economic
and social organization of their people, remaining within
legal limits. Thanks to them, the Poles under Prussian dom-

ination, hardworking and prolific, increasingly conscious of their nationality, were able to resist all the government measures as well as the efforts of the powerful German Association of the Eastern Marches, founded in 1894. Yet the danger grew, for the era of the concessions, very modest as these were, which had followed Bismarck's fall, had not lasted, and it was towards the end of the nineteenth century that the sharpest repressions of the 'Polish-speaking Prussians' began.

This makes the study of the wholly different conditions under which the system of 'organic work' was developed in the third part of Polish territory, Galicia, all the more interesting. As long as the regime of centralizing absolutism was prolonged in Austria, the lot of the Poles there had been in no way less hard than in Prussia or in Russia. However, the defeats which shook the Austria of this reactionary epoch, first in 1859, then in 1866, drove her to seek a new orientation of her policy. After the first of these critical dates the Emperor Francis Joseph, entering the way of reform, appealed to a Pole, nominating Count Agenor Goluchowski Minister of the Interior. His plan of transforming the monarchy of the Hapsburgs into a federated state soon collapsed; but, nevertheless, it was this statesman who inaugurated a new epoch in the history of Galicia, of which he became governor in 1866, on the morrow of Sadowa.

It is true that the constitution adopted the following year by the Austrian Parliament did not realize the hopes of the Poles, nor those of the other Slav nationalities of the empire. Nevertheless, it granted a fairly large autonomy to all the 'countries of the Crown,' of which Galicia was the most extensive. Thus from that moment the latter seems to have become a real 'Piedmont' for the Polish nation, which henceforth was able to develop freely there. While sending her

deputies to the central parliament, where they formed a
numerous and powerful party, Galicia now had her provincial Diet at Lwow, a local Polish administration, and a vast
network of schools, where the teaching was in Polish.

This state of things lasted until the Great War, so that
during that half-century the Poles, everywhere else reduced
to an absolutely passive political role, in Galicia were able to
carry out definite work, not only in the economic and social
sphere, but also in public life. Several of them were able to
exercise their talents by occupying the highest posts in the
central government of the monarchy. We need only mention
Agenor Goluchowski's son, well known as Minister of Foreign Affairs for Austria-Hungary. Other Poles have ranked
among the best ministers of finance. Moreover, within the
limits of the 'Kingdom of Galicia and Lodomeria,' they were
able through all those years to govern themselves, enjoying a
liberty which was doubly precious at an epoch when Russia
and Prussia were implacably persecuting their compatriots.

In certain respects the part that Galicia played on the
morrow of the insurrections resembles that of the Congress
Kingdom on the eve of those armed struggles. Like that
kingdom, she was closely bound to one of the partitioning
Powers, but to a Power with a constitutional rule, and which
did not represent a homogeneous nation opposed to the
Poles. True, the Germans constituted a relative majority
among the nationalities of ancient Austria, and occupied a
privileged position at the court of the Hapsburgs, in the
army, and in the central administration. But in the midst of
their incessant rivalries with the other nationalities, they were
obliged to reckon seriously with the Poles, who, after the
Germans and Magyars of Hungary, were undeniably the
most influential. This influence was not strong enough to
turn all the external policy of the monarchy in a direction

favourable to Poland, nor even to prevent its alliance becoming ever closer with Germany. It was, therefore, impossible to take Galicia as the starting-point from which to liberate the other parts of Poland. Yet for these the Galicia of the constitutional epoch was a rallying centre, to which their souls turned, as in old days to the Paris emigration.

Its attraction was chiefly manifest in the intellectual sphere. The two Galician universities—the very ancient one of Cracow, by the side of which an Academy of Sciences and Arts was founded in 1872, and that of Lwow, dating from the reign of John Casimir, but entirely reorganized—had become Polish once more, at the time when the University of Warsaw was entirely Russianized. They soon became the most important centres of the national culture, where the flower of the whole of Poland's youth came to study. All their faculties were filled by scholars of the highest order. In their faculties of law many Polish officials were trained by the side of eminent theorists as well as politicians, summoned to direct a part, at least, of the partitioned nation. But its most interesting activity, from the point of view with which we are concerned here, is its development of historical science.

In this department, a special one, but typical of the evolution of ideas, a group of scholars who might be called the school of Lwow, and of whom Xavier Liske was the most remarkable, perfected, above all, the method of research, eliminating all political or philosophical view-points. The school of Cracow greatly contributed, on its side, in establishing the documentary bases of the national history; but it is still more famous for the conception which it gave of that history. This conception, held by all its representatives, such as Joseph Szujski and Stanislas Smolka, was conservative, carefully thought out, far removed from that of Lelewel and the Messianists. In certain of its writers, notably Michael

Bobrzynski, both historian and politician, the reaction against the poetical idealization of the past led to extremely severe criticism, levelled chiefly against the institutions of the former Republic.

This historical conception was in strict conformity with the whole political doctrine which inspired the men who had created the new government of Galicia and held power in it. This doctrine had been formulated in 1869 in the famous *Stanczyk Portfolio*, a symbolical name recalling a court fool of Sigismund I. Condemning the revolutionary policy of the insurrections its authors recommended the Poles to work within the sphere of legality, and put them on their guard against all dangerous illusions. Their ideas, carried to extremes, would themselves have been dangerous if they had been taken literally in every part of Poland. In the special conditions which then obtained in Austrian Poland they rendered undeniable services. This they were able to do because, contrary to appearances, the representatives of these highly prudent ideas were far from renouncing the supreme ideal of national independence. It was only the means of attaining it that they debated. This was authoritatively stated by the eminent historian of Polish literature, Stanislas Tarnowski, who was Rector of the Jagiellonian University[1] when it celebrated its five-hundredth anniversary in 1900, and who has devoted very fine pages to our Romantic poets.

But the moment was approaching at the beginning of the twentieth century when the programme of organic work in Galicia, as elsewhere, was no longer sufficient.

[1] Translator's note: The University of Cracow, so called from its renovation under Ladislas Jagiello.

24

Waiting for Freedom

LIKE the Romantic epoch, that of 'organic work' had its literature. Despite all the Positivist tendencies which dominated it it was not lacking in poets of even high inspiration. We must, at least, mention that woman of exquisite feeling, Maria Konopnicka, and draw attention to, besides her lyrical poems, a new Polish epic which we owe to her, and which glorifies, not the doughty deeds of a noble of historical Poland, but the Odyssey of a poor contemporary peasant emigrant in Brazil. The literary form which best suited the realist epoch was, however, beyond dispute the novel. Since J. I. Kraszewski wrote his innumerable volumes, unequal in merit, devoted either to the national history since its beginning, or to the problems of the hour, the Polish novel had secured an important place for itself in our intellectual life. Two novelists of the highest order made their appearance shortly after Kraszewski: Eliza Orzeszkowa and Boleslas Prus. They were not interested in a distant past and, writing under the Russian censorship, they could not mention the risings except in the form of veiled allusions. But both knew how to invest with all their patriotic significance the demands of organic work; and, true educators of their generation, they guided it to a social progress which was inspired by a very high conception of duty.

It was in this atmosphere that Henryk Sienkiewicz opened his career. This able young follower of Positivism was, however, soon transformed into a true leader of the nation which was aspiring to a better future. From the end of the nineteenth century until the Great War he played a part in Poland that can only be compared to that of Mickiewicz in the Romantic epoch, and, like that poet, the most illustrious of our prose writers became one of the glories of European literature. Like our Romantics he owes his reputation to the universal character of the problems which he has treated. To the tormented soul of the world 'without dogma' [1] of his contemporaries, which he analysed as a penetrating psychologist, Sienkiewicz opposed the faith of the first Christians who, amidst the decadence of the ancient world, found, even at the price of martyrdom, the reply to the eternal question: 'Quo vadis?' Also like our Romantic poets this writer, possessed of an epic talent, was passionately enamoured of Poland's past; but he no longer searched as they did for a mystic explanation of our sufferings, he set himself to find in history that 'strengthening of hearts,' the need of which his generation was experiencing. Therefore, instead of again exalting the persecuted Poland of the nineteenth century, he evoked the heroic Poland of the seventeenth century, then, going still farther back, the triumphant Poland of the fifteenth century. The Trilogy which showed how that Poland of the past, devastated 'with fire and sword,' [2] emerged from 'the deluge'

---

[1] Translator's note: *Without Dogma* is one of Sienkiewicz's few novels of contemporary manners.

[2] Translator's note: The three parts of the Trilogy bear the titles *With Fire and Sword, The Deluge, Pan Wolodyjowski*, the last being the name of the 'little knight' who is its hero.

thanks to 'little knights' without fear and without reproach: those bulky volumes which enraptured thousands of readers mark a turning-point in Polish thought, which passed from resignation to an optimism full of faith in the destiny of the nation. And in recalling the defeat inflicted at the beginning of the fifteenth century upon the Knights of the Cross, Sienkiewicz, who at the beginning of the twentieth century denounced to the world the tragedy of the Polish children in the Prussian school, seemed to foresee an approaching great war the end of which unfortunately he did not live to see.

Happier than he, inasmuch as they died in a free Poland, two other great novelists, Ladislas Reymont and Stephen Zeromski, were apparently more interested in problems of another order: one followed the daily life of the peasant through the four seasons of the year, the other dwelt upon all the miseries of modern life. But both alike formed the link between the preoccupations of the Pole of to-day and the memories of the Pole of the risings, without ever despairing of the new Poland which was soon to be reborn from the 'ashes.' [1]

The young Poles who admired these novelists were also enthusiastic over their poets, more numerous than ever, who seemed to announce a new Romanticism. This Romanticism was less exclusively patriotic than the former one; but its representative, whose glory proved the most enduring, and who was only fully understood after his death by a Poland risen from the dead, in his turn desired, like the Romantics of the past, to solve the enigma of Poland's fate. Only, if Stanislas Wyspianski turned like these to the tombs, to those of our medieval kings as well as to those of our insurgents of yesterday, it was to protest against their hold upon the living, to bring deliverance from the melancholy which had too long

[1] Translator's note: The title of Zeromski's greatest novel.

emanated from the past, and to show in moving symbols that the union of all the classes of the nation must now keep watch until the moment when the long-awaited moment of its liberation should strike.

Wyspianski's heroes speak to us not only from the stage of his dramas, but also in the stained-glass windows that his genius as a painter conceived. They alone would be enough to characterize the new forms that Polish art adopted on the eve of the Great War. But again, as in the Romantic epoch, it is thanks to an outstanding musician, Ignacy Paderewski, that that art which was expressive of so many hopes made the round of the world as though to prepare it for a better understanding of the 'great thing' for which his country stood, which was Freedom. Ready to resume its place among free peoples, the nation found a fresh stimulus in the activity of that generous patriot.

After this brief summary of Poland's state of mind on the threshold of the twentieth century it is time to ask ourselves what justified that very obvious expectation of approaching liberation. With the sensitiveness engendered by suffering the Poles knew better than all others that an armed peace, that peace without justice which the waning nineteenth century wished to perpetuate, could last no longer. What they were awaiting, without intending to provoke it themselves as their fathers had attempted to do, was a political upheaval which would shake the power of their masters. The first of the kind came in 1904 from the Far East.

The Japanese victories proved for the first time the artificial nature of the power of the tsarist empire which held the greater part of Poland under its domination. The revolution which then broke out in Russia was of an essentially social character. But, in any case, this movement, which aroused separatist aspirations among all the nationalities of the empire, seemed to offer a unique opportunity of liberating Russian Poland by a new insurrection, undertaken under far more favourable conditions than any of the preceding risings.

The Polish nation, however, was not prepared for this. The extreme Left fraternized with the Russian revolutionaries, whose methods and doctrinaire internationalism were repugnant to the moderates. Both parties were disposed to content themselves with a programme of autonomy without breaking the link with Russia. Under these conditions it was the undeniable merit of the national wing of Polish Social- ism, directed by Joseph Pilsudski, that it clearly proclaimed the principle of independence and fought for it as far as was possible from the outset.

The opposing forces were, however, too unequal. Tsarism, which at first attempted to appease the rebels by concessions proclaimed by the Constitution of October 1905, ended, fi- nally, by crushing all opposition, and, even under the quasi- parliamentary government that the Duma of the following year inaugurated, the Polish claims received no satisfaction.

The party of the National Democrats which formulated them also aspired from its beginning to the independence of Poland. But, together with its leader, Roman Dmowski, it considered that the chief obstacle to the realization of this idea, and at the same time the greatest danger of the hour, came from the side of Germany, who held an essential part of Polish ethnographical territory, and who was encouraging the uncompromising attitude of tsarist Russia. What con- firmed many Poles in this attitude was the Prussian law of 1908 which authorized the Government to expropriate the Polish landed proprietors. By this Act, contrary to the Prus- sian Constitution, the Germany of William II and the Chan- cellor Bulow showed itself still more hostile to the Poles than that of William I and Bismarck. In addition, the use of the Polish language at public meetings was prohibited.

Those who then declared for a compromise with Russia

were also inspired by the sentiment of Slav solidarity against
Germanism. In this same year, 1908, Austria-Hungary proceeded to annex Bosnia, provoking lively resentment among
the southern Slavs, notably in Serbia, where the nation was
counting increasingly on Russia's support. The latter now
resumed her old Panslavist programme under a new form,
affecting to be willing to respect the independence of the
other Slav nations; and hence this 'neo-Slavism' attracted not
only the Czechs but also many Poles.

However, a fresh disappointment awaited them. It was precisely at that time that in Russia also repressions began again,
more severe than ever. Far from granting any sort of autonomy to the former 'kingdom,' the tsarist Government decided to mutilate it by modifying its frontiers that had been
fixed in the past by the Congress of Vienna. It began, in
1909, by creating within these boundaries a new province,
the Government of Chelm, and declaring that it was inhabited by members of the Russian Orthodox Church—in reality the Ruthenians, forced to abandon the Greek Uniat
Church, formed only a minority there—in 1912 detached it
from the 'kingdom' to place it under the Governor-General
of Kiev. Accompanied by other rigorous measures which
then struck at the Poles, this action, which seemed to be the
prelude to a new partition, discouraged even those who had,
in the light of the grave events which were preparing in Europe, believed a Polish-Russian reconciliation to be possible.

For it was precisely in 1912 that the war which had been
on the point of breaking out on the annexation of Bosnia
really began, even though still localized in the Balkans. The
war, or rather the two Balkan wars, were a clearer warning
than all the preceding crises. The antagonism which was
manifested between, on one side, Russia, traditional protectress of the Slav and Orthodox populations of the Near East,

and on the other side Germany and Austria-Hungary, favourable to the Ottoman Empire, rendered a general conflagra-
tion imminent. It was the more so inasmuch as Russia, since
1894 allied with France, had, like the latter, entered into an
understanding with England, so that from 1907 this 'triple
entente' confronted the 'triple alliance' which, since 1882,
had ensured hegemony in Europe to Germany and facilitated her world expansion.

From the point of view of Polish history the immediate
causes of the catastrophe of 1914 matter little, because among
these highly complex causes the Polish question, which had
seemingly disappeared from the international horizon, held
no sort of place. But what concerned all Poles was the fact
that it was precisely those three Powers that had partitioned
their country which were now the most directly engaged in
the conflict that was preparing. And as those Powers were
ranged in two opposite camps it was easy to foresee that from
the outset of the war, which would have to develop on Polish
territory, the Polish question would inevitably come forward,
exploited by each of the belligerent parties to the detriment
of the other.

The rupture of friendship between Russia and Prussia,
which from the epoch of the Partitions had always been fatal
to Poland, therefore opened to the latter the possibility of
her restoration: a possibility only, because, on the other hand,
the fact that there was an inflexible enemy of Poland in each
of the two camps made the situation very delicate for a nation which, in these conditions, could not unreservedly identify itself with one party or the other, and had serious reason
to dread the complete victory of either.

To this difficulty another was added. The ordeal of the
nineteenth century had, by the sufferings of the insurrections
and the experiences of 'organic work,' undoubtedly prepared

the Poles for the reconstitution of their state. And during all this time nothing had been able to break the unity of our nation whose culture had developed in spite of every obstacle, or the continuity of our historical tradition which had become the patrimony of the whole nation. Poland, however, could reappear under two different forms. The reparation of the acts of violence represented by the Partitions required fundamentally the reconstitution pure and simple of the historic Poland of 1772. But the awakening of nationalities that had come into being since then suggested another solution.

On the one hand, Polish populations which had not formed part of the Republic of 1772, the Poles of Silesia in the first place, and to a certain extent those of East Prussia, had become conscious of their origin, and aspired to be reunited with their brothers in race. On the other hand, in the eastern part of the former Republic this same principle of nationality turned against the Poles. We have alluded to this in speaking of the social transformations in the second half of the nineteenth century. From the moment when the map of Europe was bound to change this problem assumed an exceedingly serious political aspect. The Ruthenians, who, in order to be more clearly distinguished from the Russians, had adopted the name of Ukrainians, had fully developed their nationality in eastern Galicia, being, in many respects, encouraged in their growing rivalry with the Poles by the Austrian Government. Their national rebirth had also progressed in the far vaster regions that they inhabited in the empire of the tsars, which in vain disputed the very existence of their nationality. Unfortunately, even in this territory, the common antagonism against Russia had not been able to create a good understanding between the Poles and Ruthenians. Without dilating on the reasons, in great part of a social character, which had impeded it, it is enough to point out that a similar phenomenon had made its appearance in the territory of the former Grand Duchy of Lithuania. On the eve of the war a clearly marked national movement had already developed among the Lithuanians, who had retained their ethnical individuality, and a similar movement had set in even among the White Ruthenians. The latter at present had no very distinct political physiognomy, but that of the Lithuanians, while defending itself against the repressions of the Government, also entered into conflict with the Poles of those regions, victims of the same persecutions.

The idea of the Jagiellonian union which had been the basis of our history from the fourteenth century to the Partitions, and the traditions of which had given proof of its vitality, even at the time of the insurrections, thus emerged from the crisis of the nineteenth century rudely shaken. Hence it became increasingly doubtful whether the Poland whose liberation was anticipated would be an exact counterpart of historical Poland. Some considered that while abandoning none of her ancient territory, and merely adapting her traditions to modern exigencies, it would be enough to give restored Poland a federal structure. Others preferred to pronounce in favour of an ethnographical Poland, extending farther to the west and less far to the east than the former Poland.

Naturally, this ever increasingly discussed problem could not be determined until the moment came for fixing the frontiers and the constitution of the new Poland. In the meanwhile, the most important matter was to solve the fundamental problem of liberation. In spite of all the hesitations justified by the international situation as it presented itself on the eve of the war, and in spite of the uncertainty as to which territories would form part of reconstituted Poland, one thing was certain. The Polish nation could not remain passive while its fate was being decided on the battlefields of all Europe and in the chancelleries of the great Powers, compelled to reopen the records of the Polish question.

Consequently, the whole nation was agreed upon the necessity of a vast and intense Polish propaganda. Those who most firmly believed that the day of final and full liberation was approaching chose to go farther. During the years which preceded the war that they knew to be inevitable they organized the nucleus of a Polish armed force, military formations reminiscent of those of our insurrections and ready to move as soon as hostilities should begin. This was the work of Joseph Pilsudski and his collaborators.

Given the position in which the three parts of Poland were situated it was evident that this preparatory work could be accomplished on the territory of only one of those parts: Galicia. Hence it was there that in 1914 the new struggle for independence started, to be carried on by every means, until the moment when the voice of Poland made itself heard by the western Powers, her natural allies, when, as under Napoleon, the flag with the white eagle floated by the side of the tricolour, advancing towards the goal of a peace that stood for freedom.

While awaiting that moment millions of Poles were forced to fight and take each other's lives under enemy flags. But they remained convinced that, contrary to all human previsions, they were all dying for one only Poland, and

> That she, never destroyed,
> Would be reborn from their blood.

Part V

NEW POLAND'S TRAGEDY

25

Resurrection

THE resurrection of the Republic, after more than a hundred years of political non-existence, has been the first act of the still unfinished drama which contemporary Poland is living through in the full consciousness of its historical significance and with unshaken faith in its successful solution. This resurrection was effected in three stages: first, the successive defeat in the war of 1914–18 of all the partitioning Powers; second, the decisions of the Peace Conference in 1919; third, the complete establishment of the boundaries of the renewed Polish State, which dragged on until 1923.

When the first World War began, the Polish question, which, as has been pointed out previously, had in no way been instrumental to the breaking out of that war, at once assumed an actual importance. The prospects, however, of that question being resolved in accordance with the claims of the Polish nation to complete independence were not at all promising. It is true that the combatants on either side endeavoured from the outset to conciliate the Poles. Russia, however, who until the fall of tsardom had persisted in treating the Polish cause as an internal question of her own, in the proclamation of her Commander-in-Chief, the Grand Duke Nicholas, of 14th August 1914, only promised autonomy to the Polish territories which were to be united under the sceptre of the tsar; while from the side of the central Powers, among which Germany, who was as opposed as Russia to the real restoration of Poland, had the deciding vote, there only emerged some Austrian promises of a still more general nature.

This alone was certain: that a decisive and long-anticipated change in the lot of Poland would finally ensue, and that in her terrible devastation—as one of the chief theatres of the war—the blood of the unknown Polish soldier, mobilized by the usurpers to a number considerably exceeding three million, would be copiously shed.

At the same time, however, the value and the significance were now made manifest of those preparations for an active share in the threatened war which, as we have seen, had already begun a few years before in the part of the country under Austrian rule.

It is true that in consequence of the diversity of opinion regarding the orientation of Polish policy, unavoidable in the actual situation, Polish volunteer formations appeared on both sides. But in spite of the general sympathy in Poland for the western Powers, France and England, the only real bearing on the situation in the first and longest stage of the war was effected by the Legions which, setting out from Cracow on 6th August under the leadership of Joseph Pilsudski, in the spirit of the never-forgotten traditions of the insurrections began a struggle against Russia, who held in her hands the greater part of the Polish territories.

The heroic share of the legionaries in the campaign, which lasted about two years and drove the Russians almost entirely out of these territories, did not in the least imply solidarity with Austrian, still less with German, policy; Germany and Austria were not, moreover, in agreement with each other regarding the Polish question and yielded to continual vacillations. In Galicia, which had been occupied only for a short time by the Russians nearly as far as Cracow, the Supreme National Committee, counting on the favourable disposition of Austria, continued to function; the Congress Kingdom, however, after the whole of it had been captured by the central Powers, was arbitrarily divided into two occupations, Austrian and German, the latter of which especially ill-treated the population, if only by the economic exploitation of the devastated country.

In their desire to gain, not only the Legions, whose command Pilsudski resigned in September 1916, having failed to obtain for them an independent standing, but also a Polish armed force, still more dependent on Germany, by means of a systematic recruiting in the kingdom, both empires finally decided to proclaim the restoration of Poland's independence. But an act to this effect, which was published on 5th November 1916, began by announcing that that State, independent in appearance only, was to remain in close union with Germany and Austria, especially in military matters, while the question of the boundaries of the State was left in suspense. It was clear that those boundaries were not even to include Galicia, since that province was simultaneously granted only a greater autonomy than hitherto within the structure of the Hapsburg monarchy; while the German military and political circles were projecting serious mutilations of the kingdom itself to the profit of the Reich. Thus the proclamation of November, although not devoid of significance in regard to the international development of the Polish question, and enabling the so-called 'activist' element gradually to build up a Polish state organization even while still under the occupying Powers, could in no wise satisfy the aspirations of the Polish nation, and did not give any of the results anticipated by the Germans in the sphere of military advantages.

On the contrary, an ever greater role was being played in that sphere by the secret 'Polish Military Organization,' directed against all the usurpers, while the great majority of the legionaries finally refused the new military oath, aimed at incorporating them entirely within the German army. This resulted in severe repressions, and even the imprisonment of Pilsudski himself in July 1917 in the fortress of Magdeburg. But by then the great revolutionary upheaval in Russia was already taking place; the upheaval, which was entirely to transform the international situation, and, therefore, to change fundamentally the decisive factors of the Polish question.

The first March revolution in Russia had already freed the hands of the western allies in this respect, since a new Liberal Government had acknowledged, in the manifesto of 30th March, the right of the Polish nation to be an independent state, only stipulating a 'free military union' between that new Poland and Russia. This facilitated the diplomatic action of those Polish politicians who, under the leadership of Roman Dmowski, had for some time previously been sojourning in the west. In June it was possible to form the nucleus of a Polish army in France, and in August the Polish National Committee in Paris, with Dmowski as its president and with its representatives in London and Rome; while in the United States Ignacy Paderewski was acting with notably successful results in the name of the committee. Moreover, he had already previously influenced President Wilson's declaration in his appeal of 22nd January for the creation of a united and independent Polish State.

It is true that in the autumn of that same year (1917) the

Bolshevik revolution did great harm to the eastern borderlands of Poland; but, on the other hand, it led to a complete
reversal of alliances. The Soviet Government, not only proclaiming the right of the non-Russian nations to a complete
separation from Russia, but at the same time aiming at an
immediate conclusion of peace, opened negotiations at the
end of the year with the central Powers at Brest-Litovsk.
Those Powers, although they found themselves compelled to
make further concessions to the Poles owing to the development of events, and in October even established a Regency
Council in Warsaw composed of three eminent representatives of the nation, did not admit Poland to a share in the
peace negotiations; moreover, in the first treaty concluded,
on 9th February 1918, with the Ukraine, they included in its
western boundaries the Polish territory of Chelm, and even
secretly promised it a share of Galicia. The final treaty with
the Soviets, on the 3rd March, undertook to maintain German hegemony over the whole of the territories yielded by
Russia.

However, the place of Russia in the coalition was now
taken by the United States; a change the more profitable for
Poland inasmuch as in his famous fourteen points of 8th
January 1918, Wilson devoted the thirteenth to the necessity of creating an independent Polish state, which would em-
brace all 'the territories inhabited by indisputably Polish
populations' and have 'a free and secure access to the sea.'

The realization of the Polish aims now only needed the
victory of the allies over the Germans. In the months which
assured that victory far-reaching decrees confirming the independence of Poland followed each other in quick succession.
From the 3rd of June Poland was recognized by all the allied
Powers as 'an allied belligerent nation,' and the participation
in the last battles on the western front by a Polish army

under the leadership of General Joseph Haller found a response and a support in the resolute attitude of the whole country. In Warsaw the Regency Council had already, on the 7th October, proclaimed the independence of united Poland; in the course again of that same month Galicia separated from Austria; and the memorable day for all the world on which arms were laid down, the 11th November, was likewise the day on which the ideal of that independence was completely realized. Pilsudski, who on the eve of that day had returned to Poland, accepted the rulership from the hands of the Regency Council, and a few days later became the first Chief of the restored Polish State.

In consideration of all these facts it was a foregone conclusion that the Peace Conference which was to meet in Paris would recognize the resurrection of Poland as one of the indisputable results of the World War. It was equally certain that Poland would be represented at that conference as one of the victorious allied states. In this respect there existed one difficulty: that until now the allies had only recognized the Polish National Committee in Paris as the official representatives of that state, whereas Pilsudski and the Government nominated by him were ruling in the country itself. The reconciliation of these two hitherto widely differing trends of political action was in great measure due to Paderewski, who hastened to Warsaw, entered into an understanding with Pilsudski in January 1919, and accepted the post of Premier and Minister of Foreign Affairs, and then went to Paris to represent Poland jointly with Dmowski at the Peace Conference.

There, in the meantime, the work had already begun of fixing Poland's boundaries, of which, however, eventually only those in the west, on the German side, were defined in the Treaty of Versailles. As regards these, the Polish claims were clear and unanimously put forward by the whole nation. It was a matter of repairing the injury of the Partitions and restoring to Poland those parts of Prussia which had belonged to her before 1772. That claim was not founded only on a historical basis: the territories in question, namely Poznania and so-called West Prussia, otherwise the old Polish Pomerania, certainly preserved, in spite of a century of German rule and the policy of Germanization, their ethnically Polish character, excepting only certain strips on the frontiers, insignificant in Poznania, more considerable on the borders of West Prussia. These border regions having been left to Germany, even that latter province possessed—according to the German statistics themselves—such a distinct Polish majority as to fall under Wilson's definition of indisputably Polish territory. Hence the so-called 'Corridor' was by no means an artificial invention of the Treaty of Versailles, departing from Wilson's points, but—as before the Partitions —the natural result of the fact that since the time of the Knights of the Cross, East Prussia had formed but a German enclave on the east of Pomerania.

Consequently, the access to the sea promised to Poland, and realized by the restoration of Pomerania, was not 'free and secure' in reality; the less so, inasmuch as the mouth of the Vistula with Danzig, a town with a population almost entirely German, became, for that very reason, the subject of protracted discussions at the conference. Although the Commission for Polish Affairs unanimously declared for restoring Danzig to Poland, that claim fell to the ground by reason of the stubborn opposition of Great Britain's chief delegate, the Prime Minister, Lloyd George. The intricate solution of the problem of Danzig by which it became a Free City with special rights for Poland in its area, and particularly in its port, was to be the source of unceasing friction and the chief pretext for the outbreak of the present war.

Poland was obliged to consent to a considerable curtailment, especially in this instance, of her historic boundary, from ethnographic considerations, and she anticipated that these considerations would likewise prevail where they turned to her advantage. She therefore claimed the southern part of East Prussia and the eastern part of Silesia, namely Upper Silesia, lands which had been lost by Poland long before her partitions, but were for the greater part inhabited by a Polish population. The conference decided to resolve both these questions by means of plebiscites, although, according to the first peace conditions presented to the Germans in the beginning of May, Upper Silesia was to pass at once to Poland; it was only under the influence of the reply of the German delegation, and again at the request of Lloyd George, that this part of the treaty was changed.

This is surely the best proof that that treaty, as it actually affected the Polish question, was neither a 'dictate' imposed on the Germans without discussion, nor a departure from the Wilsonian principles. At the same time Poland had to sign a special treaty which imposed upon her far-reaching obligations in the matter of the protection of minorities. The idea of protecting any minority was undoubtedly just in principle; moreover, it was entirely in agreement with Polish traditions as with the new Constitution of the Republic that was already being drawn up; but the procedure was humiliating in this respect, that it placed Poland, as well as a few other states unjustly termed 'new,' under international control, which was not provided for as regards Germany. But, in any case, the Versailles Treaty, the first international convention that after the epoch of Poland's bondage solemnly recognized her independence and restored to her the greater part of what Prussia had usurped—the cradle of the Polish State and a strip of the Baltic coast—had, beyond all doubt, an epoch-making significance for the Polish nation.

Its first part, the Covenant of the League of Nations, was also important for Poland. Longing for peace and for international co-operation from which she had been excluded for over a hundred years, she necessarily hailed with satisfaction those two leading tenets of the League, as also the articles by which it solemnly guaranteed the integrity and independence of all the member states. It might, indeed, have appeared that according to the prophecies of the Polish poets an era of international peace and justice was to set in with the resurrection of Poland. Besides those factors springing from fundamental principles and ideals, some concrete enactments of the treaty, especially those which concerned the League's guardianship over Danzig, gave the League an additional and special importance in regard to Poland.

But at the same Peace Conference a further problem absorbed the attention of the Polish delegates: equally with the western frontiers they were occupied with the complicated question how far the restored Republic should stretch to the east. It was a difficult question, not only because it was linked with the whole problem of Russia, who had no official representative in Paris, who was a former ally, and was at the moment plunged into civil war, but also because Polish opinion was not wholly agreed on this weighty point. Linked with the pre-war controversy on historic or ethnographic Poland two points of view clashed. Pilsudski was a resolute advocate of the idea of federation, to which Paderewski also inclined, and which was based on the principle that in the east, as in the west, the historical pre-partition boundaries of the old Republic should be restored, but with the acknowledgment of

the right of self-determination for the non-Polish nationalities in the eastern borderlands, the Lithuanians, White Ruthenians,[1] and Ukrainians, who were expected to join Poland
in a bond of union. On the other hand, Dmowski, who,
thanks to his striking presentment of the Polish cause at the
meeting of the Council of Ten, on 29th January 1919, had
gained great authority at the conference, considered that Poland ought to be a homogeneous national State in which the
part of the eastern borderlands, with a relatively predomi-
nant Polish element, should be immediately incorporated,
while the rest of the White Ruthenian and Ukrainian territories should remain with future Russia.

Uncertainty as to the future of Russia, and the obscure attitude of the conference in regard to Lithuanian and Ukrainian aims for independence, contributed equally to the fact
that the conference reached no final decision regarding the
eastern boundaries of Poland, the drawing up of which, however, the Great Powers reserved to themselves in one of the
articles of the Versailles Treaty. The fate even of Lwow and
Wilno, which was specially troubling the Poles, remained in
suspense, and this in spite of the struggles waged for those
cities during the Paris deliberations.

Ultimately, however, the boundaries of the Republic were
decided not so much by those deliberations as by the hard
fighting which Poland herself, in the hour of her rebirth, was
all at once compelled to engage in with nearly all her neighbours, long after the war in the west was over. Even the actual liberation of the provinces under Prussia was effected
before the opening of the Peace Conference when, at the end

---

[1] It seems advisable to avoid in English the term 'White Russians,' which
leads to confusion. The name 'Blanc-Ruthenes,' used in the French original of
the first four parts of this work, and corresponding to the Slavonic terminology,
makes it quite clear that they do not belong to the Russians in the modern
sense of that word.

of 1918, after the disarmament of the German armies of occupation in the kingdom, a spontaneous uprising broke out
with elemental force in Poznania.

Relatively the easier task was to wrest western Galicia with
Cracow from Austrian hands, while at the same time, in eastern Galicia, a protracted conflict began in November 1918
with the Ukrainians, who even for a moment occupied Lwow.
The heroic defence of the Polish population not only enabled that city to be regained, but became the starting-point
for the thrusting back of the Ukrainian armed forces beyond
the Zbrucz. But even then, in June 1919, the Peace Conference did not assign that territory to Poland in a definite manner, and at the end of the year it put forth the project of a
merely temporary Polish administration of eastern Galicia to
last twenty-five years, after which period a plebiscite was to
be taken.

Almost simultaneously, on the 8th December, the conference drew an equally temporary frontier, the Curzon line, as
it was called later, on the area which Russia had formerly occupied. Up to that line, which corresponded more or less
with the frontier gained by Russia after the three partitions
of Poland at the end of the eighteenth century, the Polish administration was to be extended from the outset. It was,
however, clearly indicated at the time that this line of demarcation did not interfere with the rights of Poland reaching
beyond that provisional frontier.

However, the final decision of the centuries-old dispute
over the eastern borderlands of Poland depended on the result of the war that had now been waged for nearly a year
between Poland and the Soviets, who, in the track of the retreating German armies, were pushing to the west. That war,
thrust upon a state only just in the stage of organizing itself,
and having at its disposal only a relatively small and newly

organized armed force, indisputably constitutes the most glorious page in the history of the rebuilding of the Republic, and at the same time the page which was of the greatest importance in world history, because it not only saved Poland from almost immediate destruction on the morrow of her liberation, but it saved the whole of central Europe from the Bolshevik inundation which, in the event of the downfall of the Polish barrier, would have joined the revolutionary movements in Germany and Hungary.

The first great success in this war was the deliverance, on 19th April 1919, of Wilno, the town in which at the time of the German occupation a Lithuanian Government had been created, which, however, had been forced to retreat before the Russians to Kovno. Three days later Pilsudski published a proclamation to the population of the former Grand Duchy of Lithuania promising them the full right of self-determination. But before this federal programme could be realized in the north-east of the pre-partition Republic, the further course of the protracted war brought forward in its turn the Ukrainian question. In April of the following year, when the negotiations for a truce with the Soviets broke down, Pilsudski concluded a treaty with Hetman Petlura's national Ukrainian Government, which left eastern Galicia and the western part of Volhynia to Poland, and, in exchange, promised Polish help in the liberation of Ukraine proper, where an independent state was to rise, allied with Poland. Despite the capture of Kiev, on 8th May 1920, this proved to be an undertaking beyond the power of Poland. The Soviet offensive compelled the Polish armies to retire on the whole eastern front, making no halt until near Warsaw itself.

In this wellnigh desperate moment help from the west was completely wanting, with only the exception of the arrival of a group of French officers under the command of General

Weygand. The latter closely collaborated with the Polish general staff, and Pilsudski's bold strategic plan was carried into execution in the middle of August. It resulted in the rout of the Bolsheviks, thanks also to the gallant defence of the capital by a volunteer army under the command of General Haller, and the co-ordination of the action of all the Polish armed forces, the participation of General Sikorski being especially conspicuous. Defeated again during their retreat through the Niemen basin territory, the Russians were compelled to enter into peace negotiations at Riga. The preliminaries signed there, on 12th October, formed the basis of the treaty of 18th March 1921. That treaty defined a boundary of compromise, corresponding more or less to the Polish-Russian boundary after the second partition in 1793. In spite of her victory, Poland abandoned the claim to her historic boundaries; but, at least, she gained a broad belt of her old eastern borderlands in accordance with the conception which Dmowski had defended at the Peace Conference, a belt ensuring her a certain minimum of safety on that side.

The federal idea, naturally, could not be realized within these frontiers. The greater part of White Ruthenia, as well as the Ukraine beyond the line already drawn in the agreement with Petlura, became Soviet republics whose independence of Moscow was, from the beginning, a theoretical one. Still worse, however, was the fact that in the course of the military operations a conflict ensued with Lithuania who, at the moment of the Polish reverse, in July 1920, attempted to secure Wilno for herself by a treaty with the Bolsheviks.

On the 9th October General Zeligowski took the town, although the Polish plenipotentiaries had quite unnecessarily agreed, two days previously, to a temporary line of demarcation leaving it on the Lithuanian side. The military method of deciding the question, beyond doubt in accordance with the inclinations of the greater part of the population concerned, but drastic in its application, reacted fatally on the future relations between Poland and Lithuania. The conciliatory action of the League of Nations prevented a war between sister nations; but Lithuania would never consent to acknowledge the incorporation of the Wilno district in the Republic of Poland, which, however, followed in March 1922, after the elections in all the disputed territory, at the request of the Wilno Diet. A year later, on the 15th March 1923, the Conference of the Ambassadors of the western Powers definitely recognized the eastern boundary of Poland in all its extent, including Wilno and Lwow.

The difficult position of Poland in the summer of 1920, caused by the war for the eastern frontier, also reacted drastically on the fixing of those portions of the boundary in the west that were still disputed. It was in July of that year that the Conference of Ambassadors decided the dispute which unfortunately had broken out between Poland and the Czechs immediately after the dissolution of Austria, and which antagonized for a long time those two nations who had so many interests in common. This decision, taken without the plebiscite requested by Poland, divided the disputed Cieszyn Silesia in a rather unfortunate manner, and likewise assigned to Poland only small strips of Orava and Spisz. It is not surprising, either, that the plebiscite held at that critical moment in the ethnographically Polish part of East Prussia yielded results unfavourable for the Republic, which was just then overrun by the Soviet armies.

The still more important plebiscite in Upper Silesia was, in the meantime, being deferred amidst insurrectionary movements of the Polish population in protest against the German terror. When the voting was finally carried out, on 20th March 1921, the dispute on the interpretation of its results led to a dangerous tension which evoked not only a third rising under the leadership of Wojciech Korfanty, but also a conflict between the Powers which were to carry out the division of Upper Silesia on the basis of the plebiscite. Only France favoured the Polish claims, while England and Italy wished to assign only two agricultural districts to Poland. In the end, the question was solved in the manner most consonant with international justice. It was referred to the League of Nations, which proposed a boundary line, subsequently accepted by the Powers; and in its halls the Polish and German delegates, presided over by a Swiss statesman, drew up the Convention of 15th May 1922, regulating in detail the carrying out of the division with regard to the economic necessities of the population. In this way Poland also obtained a considerable part of the rich industrial districts, and the Treaty of Versailles was completed in one of its most important points by means of an agreement reached by arbitration, the highest international authority acting as the mediator. The voivodeship of Silesia, subsequently created out of the parts of Upper Silesia and of Cieszyn Silesia assigned to Poland, was the sole, small part of the restored Republic which overstepped her pre-partition frontiers, and in exchange for her resignation of the rebuilding of the Poland of the Jagiellos, it restored to the Polish nation a part of the immemorial, early lost, apanage of the Piasts.

26

Reconstruction

WITHOUT waiting for the end of the war, which as we have seen lasted nearly two years longer for Poland than for the western States, or for the settlement of the boundaries of the Republic which dragged on still longer, the Polish nation proceeded at once to the constructive work in the regained country. Furthermore, she started on that work while still under foreign occupation, at least in those spheres of life where it proved possible. But in every department a veritable mountain of tasks awaited her, calculated to last for many years. The profound tragedy of contemporary Poland consists in the fact that she experienced so few years of peace; no one foresaw that there would be scarcely twenty of them! To-day, when amidst the new whirl of war we cast a glance at the terribly interrupted creative effort of those twenty years, we can affirm that in that time a great deal was effected on the road of progress, a fact which struck every foreigner who visited Poland at intervals, however short.

Progress was visible, above all, in the department of culture, material and spiritual alike. Here, independent Poland could link up with the no less fruitful work which partitioned Poland carried through in the preceding century. The possession of her own state organization and the absence of foreign oppression which hitherto had so seriously hampered even cultural development, created incomparably more favourable conditions; but, on the other hand, she had to overcome the terrible results of the destruction caused by the war. The nation could at last be mistress of her own free land, but she received that land in a desperate condition of impoverishment, and that at the moment when the whole of Europe was suffering from the economic effects of the war epoch. Poland was obliged at the very outset to carry on a struggle against famine and the contagious diseases disseminated by the war.

The rebuilding of the country in the literal sense after the ravages committed up to the last moment, demanded gigantic financial means. In the meantime, however, the collapse of the currency rendered all rational economic policy impossible. The so-called Polish mark, a legacy from the German occupation, began falling with increasing rapidity, and though inflation did not reach such catastrophic dimensions in Poland as in neighbouring Germany, yet it followed in the track of the fall of the German mark. A radical restoration to health, in this case especially urgent, could not ensue before the restoration of complete peace within settled frontiers. Thus the first attempts at remedying the evil by further drastic measures of economy had no effect, and it was not until the year 1924 that a great financial reform, linked with the name of the Prime Minister and Minister of Finance, Ladislas Grabski, brought about a decided turn for the better. Although in the following year it became clear that the value of the unit of the new Polish currency, the zloty, was at first fixed too high, namely, on a par with the Swiss gold franc, it was very soon established at a slightly lower level and kept a stable position; and the maintenance of a balanced national budget remained the leading principle of the Polish treasury policy. Thus the economic policy of the State not only profited by the favourable economic opportunities of the years 1926–30, but it also held out through the serious general European crisis of the following years.

This was the more difficult, since, on the one hand, the dangerous political situation of Poland demanded enormous expenditure for military purposes, and, on the other, the country was not only devastated, but generally poor, the standard of life of the great majority of its inhabitants being very low, especially that of the agrarian population which constituted almost two-thirds of the whole. To assist this large section of the population, it was indispensable that there should be a comprehensive agrarian reform, involving the parcelling out of the great landed properties. This difficult problem, which after the war confronted all the countries of central and eastern Europe, Poland endeavoured to solve without excessive radicalism, and therefore avoided expropriation without adequate compensation; the maximum area of a private landed property was fixed at 180 hectares, and in the eastern borderland 400 hectares, with the object of not weakening to a too great extent the Polish possession of land there. Directed by a special department, the agrarian reform proceeded steadily forward, and having carried through about two-thirds of its programme, it contributed in a marked degree to the diminution of the social differences that were until then so considerable.

The democratization of the commonwealth and the removal of differences between the relatively better developed western part of the state and the eastern borderlands, which were especially backward after the long Russian rule, were helped by efforts towards a progressive development of industrialism. Besides Silesian coal-fields which, contrary to anticipations, were operating quite normally under Polish rule, and in addition to the old industrial centres of Warsaw and Lodz, in the years immediately preceding the new war the so-called Central Industrial District was created in the very middle, seemingly the safest section, of the Republic, on the borders of her western and eastern parts, round the region of Sandomierz. But the most conspicuous result of Polish efforts to raise the economic condition of the country, to develop her commerce, and to establish trade relations with the whole world, was the creation of a port at Gdynia. From the obscure fishing village which Poland inherited on the small strip of Baltic coast that had been given back to her, there arose at a positively American tempo a great commercial and industrial town and a splendid port which not only outstripped Danzig, and in great measure made Poland independent of that city, but after scarcely fifteen years occupied the first place among the Baltic ports, and was among the chief ports of the world. The building of a Polish fleet, both naval and mercantile, proceeded no less rapidly, step by step with the steadily growing interest of the whole nation in the sea and even in colonial problems.

Without adding further examples from the sphere of material development, we must lay a still greater emphasis on the development of social and intellectual life in reborn Poland.

Playing an important part in the activity of the International Labour Organization, she proved anxious to apply to her national life the leading principles of social progress discussed and recommended at Geneva. The eight-hour working day, inspection of working conditions with the view of protecting especially women and juveniles, arbitration between employers and employees—all these were steadily introduced into the social legislation of the Republic. The system of social insurance in Poland was in advance of most of the other countries, and so was public assistance, which without excluding private charity supplemented it most effectively, particularly in the difficult post-war period and in the years of the general economic depression. One of the typical features of the Polish assistance system was its respect for both individual dignity and family life. Hence the great development of 'home relief,' including the rule of placing poor children and orphans in families rather than in public institutions. In protecting the children, half a million of whom were born every year, special care was taken of the workers in the cities, but the seasonal children's camps in the country were hardly less useful to the peasant population.

The democratic trend in the evolution of contemporary Poland was giving to all classes, through educational progress, a chance of participating in the development of national culture.

Beyond all doubt, the most urgent necessity was the enlarging and building up of an elementary school system, and the spreading of adult education, again especially in the former Russian provinces which had been neglected in that respect; the result achieved was that even in Polesia the illiteracy, which Poland found there to an alarming extent, was quickly disappearing. The general number of schools remained always insufficient; but we must remember that at the same time it was indispensable to organize the Polish secondary education, which hitherto had been developed only in the former Austrian provinces, and which everywhere required co-ordination and many essential reforms. It was also necessary to restore, after long suppression, Polish university life. On the eve of the Great War it existed only in Galicia, thanks to the Universities of Cracow and Lwow. The University of Warsaw, long since Russianized, became the metropolitan university of Poland, even under the German occupation, and developed in the following years into one of the greatest of European seats of learning; in the first year of independence also the ancient University of Wilno was at once restored to life, and two entirely new universities were founded, in Poznan and Lublin, the last of a Catholic character. The total number of academic schools had risen at the end of twenty years to well over twenty, with almost one hundred faculties.

Under such conditions research work in all the arts and sciences was able to progress favourably in spite of great material obstacles, which it was attempted to remedy by the creation of the Fund of National Culture, distributing scholarships, and facilitating the printing of scholarly publications. The same course was taken by the increasingly active learned societies, with the Polish Academy of Arts and Sciences at their head. In addition to existing collections of books a magnificent National Library arose in Warsaw, in great part composed of the books and manuscripts carried away by Russia at the time of the Partitions and subsequently returned in accordance with the Treaty of Riga. In keeping with the tradition of the preceding century, literature and the fine arts likewise developed; although not producing such famous masterpieces as those which the bondage of the nineteenth century had inspired, they brought forth after the death of the masters of the past a succession of new and promising writers, especially in the department of fiction. Finally, there followed the rebirth and deepening of religious life, on the immemorial foundations of Catholic tradition, which was of great importance in its effects on national culture and characterized by a deep concern in social problems; in all of which Poland's youth took a prominent part.

Two entirely new problems resulting from the regaining of an independent status were linked both with Poland's cultural life and with her internal policy. One of them, which at first seemed disquieting, namely the unification of the three parts of dismembered Poland into a homogeneous national and state organism, was solved with surprising rapidity and smoothness. The reason for this was simple: the Polish nation, in spite of all the minor differences between the three divisions, had never lost the feeling of unity, and the creation of a Polish state administration was considerably facilitated by the circumstance that at least one of those divisions, Galicia, had been autonomous for half a century and provided the first ranks of civil servants for the whole restored State. The problem of national minorities was, however, less successfully handled during that score of years.

Because of the mixture of nationalities in this part of Europe, and also because of the difficulties of harmonizing the conceptions of historic and ethnographic Poland, a considerable number of national minorities were necessarily to be found in the new Republic. Nor must we forget that a large number of Poles, about two and a half millions, not counting the Americans of Polish descent, had found themselves beyond her frontiers, especially in Germany, and in the Soviet Union, and also in Lithuania, Latvia, and Czechoslovakia. But against this almost one-third of the population of the Polish State, which altogether numbered over thirty-five millions, belonged to other nationalities. The number of Lithuanians and Russians was negligible, the national sentiment of the White Ruthenians feebly developed, but this gave all the greater significance to the question of the German, Jewish, and Ukrainian minorities.

The first of the last-mentioned proved to be the most dangerous, although the number of the Germans amounted to hardly more than three-quarters of a million and nowhere were they living in a compact mass; against that, however, they enjoyed support in the neighbouring Reich, who, although she oppressed her Polish minority, complained continually of the condition of the Germans in Poland, which was an incomparably better one. The Jewish question became particularly acute before the present war; it was, indeed, a very considerable one, having regard to the fact that over three million Jews—almost ten per cent of the entire population—were living scattered all over the country, constituting a far higher percentage still among the populations of the towns, in trade and industry, and in certain professions, and that only an insignificant number of them were really assimilated. Under these conditions the rise of an anti-Semitic movement on economic, rather than racial, grounds, was unfortunately almost inevitable. It did not, however, assume such violent proportions as in a number of other European countries, and on the part of the Polish Government it was steadily suppressed. The question of the Ukrainian minority was in reality far more important, and, generally speaking, not properly appreciated; it was the most numerous group, for it numbered about five millions, occupying a compact area in the south-east of the state, and, in contradistinction to the Germans and the Jews, it was composed, not of immigrants, but of immemorial inhabitants of these lands. The territorial autonomy that had been announced was very difficult to carry through, for it was precisely where the Ukrainian population was highest in culture and national consciousness, namely, in the former eastern Galicia, that it was most mingled with the Polish population. In spite of this, it is to be regretted that neither successive governments nor the Polish nation achieved in regard to the Ukrainians a consistent programme which might have reconciled them to the Republic.

We speak of successive governments, for the system of internal policy yielded in the course of twenty years of independence to far-reaching changes, of which the most important was the *coup d'état* of May 1926. In the period preceding that May the nature of the Republic's government was purely democratic, with a strong predominance of the legislative authority, with often sharp party quarrels, and frequent changes of Cabinets. After the *coup d'état* of Marshal Pilsudski, who for several years had retired from political life, a gradual restriction of the role of the Diet and of the significance of political parties succeeded, until finally Pilsudski effected a formal change of the Constitution. In contradistinction to the Constitution of 17th March 1921, the Constitution of 23rd April 1935 notably strengthened the position of the President and of the Government, and while retaining the Parliament, greatly restricted its power.

From the historical perspective it is apparent that in contrasting the periods before and after May 1926, of which the adherents of Pilsudski have condemned the first and exalted the second, while his adversaries have appraised these two periods in reverse fashion, there has been a good deal of exaggeration, entirely comprehensible in the fire of political rivalry. To-day we must acknowledge that the gigantic progress of the whole country briefly characterized above was the result of both these epochs and the common merit of various political camps, each of which strove to serve its country to the best of its ability. In the first period the unavoidable party antagonisms only once led to a really critical situation, when, in December 1922, after Pilsudski's resignation from the position of Chief of the State and the election of the first President in the person of Gabriel Naru-towicz, the latter was assassinated by a fanatic who acted on his own initiative. At that moment, however, after the election of Stanislas Wojciechowski as President, the Government of General Sikorski immediately restored peace and order. The parliamentary crisis in 1926 might certainly have been overcome in a less violent manner and one less liable to undermine respect for legality than that which Pilsudski had chosen in May. He endeavoured, however, after his victory in a fratricidal battle in the streets of Warsaw, to legalize the coup. He did not accept his election as President, to which post Professor Ignacy Moscicki succeeded at his suggestion, although in reality everything henceforth depended on the decision of Pilsudski. In the further course of the dispute with the opposition of the Diet he once more took violent measures, condemning its leaders to a cruel imprisonment at Brzesc in the autumn of 1930, thereby arousing universal indignation. Yet he did not proceed to a system of totalitarian government, which would never have taken root in Poland; he strove rather to create such peculiar constitutional forms as could permit the Polish State to develop a middle course between the greatly prized, though often excessive, tradition of freedom, and the strengthening of the executive that was necessary in its dangerous position.

It was beyond doubt the tragedy of the first Marshal of Poland that, uncritically idolized by some, passionately opposed by others, he was not able to create a harmonious national unity. The dispute about his personality was not silenced even by his death, on 12th May 1935. The collaboration of all political parties was, however, doubly necessary when the leader who had gained such a strong position in Europe for Poland and for himself was no longer there. President Moscicki, re-elected in 1933 for another period of seven years, and General Rydz-Smigly, who after Pilsudski's death received the dignity of Marshal and to whom—outside the Constitution—was assigned the position of the 'second person' in the State, declared themselves for this political collaboration. The so-called 'Non-Party Group of Co-operation with the Government' which, under the leadership of the most extreme partisans of the regime called the 'Colonels,' excluded, strictly speaking, every other political group from any influence on the fate of the State, was dissolved, and an organization came into being, the very name of which, 'Camp of National Unity,' seemed to sum up a programme worthy of recognition. But unfortunately it remained a dead letter, as the two contending sides attached completely different meanings to 'unity.' An additional difficulty resulted from the fact that neither of the two was by any means homogeneous. Among the followers of Pilsudski ever wider divergences appeared, and the opposition was divided into a right and left wing, so that the ruling group was in a position to approach one or the other alternately. But all these regrettable frictions in internal politics were no worse than similar manifestations in other states not reduced to uniformity by totalitarianism, and in the midst of these frictions certain leading principles were becoming clearer and were increasingly acknowledged by all. As to internal affairs, one of these principles was the necessity of a return to more democratic parliamentary forms by the alteration of the rules which, after the passing of the new Constitution and the death of Pilsudski, had given a merely fictitious character to the elections to the legislative bodies. The second principle was the maintenance of unity between all Poles in the face of the growing external danger.

In spite of the differences of opinion on the methods to be applied in the foreign policy of the State, never, before 1926 or after it, neither during the life of Joseph Pilsudski nor after his death, was there the least doubt in the nation that its external situation demanded the closest vigilance to ensure peace and the safety of the Republic that had only been rebuilt with such effort. The nation also succeeded in avoiding the two chief errors of pre-partition Poland, namely, the admission of foreign intervention in internal conflicts, and the lack of sacrifice in the defence of the country. As to the latter, it is enough to point out that although the army was in the hands of the adherents of Pilsudski and his regime, it is a fact that the whole nation rallied round it, not excepting the extreme opposition, grudging no sacrifice for armaments, which was often criticized abroad as a manifestation of Polish militarism or imperialism and which, in fact, as the occasion proved, was always insufficient. As to foreign policy, it can be treated as almost independent of all the changes in internal affairs, since through the twenty years of reborn Poland it was fraught with the same major problem which through the centuries had weighed upon the development of the old Republic, namely, the twofold, mortal danger threatening her without a break from the two inexorably hostile neighbours who had risen to power in the west and the east.

We have seen that the resurrection of Poland was made possible through the conflict between these two Powers, and the successive defeat of each of them. But even the years of their greatest weakness, after the upheaval of war and revolution, brought Poland no real respite; they only allowed her to thrust back the Bolshevik invasion in the dawn of her independence, without fear of a simultaneous attack from the side of Germany. The latter, however, already at that time sympathized with Poland's eastern adversary, and scarcely a year after the Peace of Riga entered into an alliance with him by the treaty concluded at Rapallo, a treaty which remained undisturbed through all the changes of the external and internal policy of Germany and Russia in the following years. This treaty was the clearest reminder that when Germany and Russia re-entered the group of great Powers determining the fate of Europe—and that re-entrance was actually beginning at the Genoa Conference in 1922— Poland was again confronted with the spectre of their renewed collaboration to destroy her as in the eighteenth century.

Already a year before this, Poland endeavoured to avert the danger by the conclusion of a close alliance with France which should ensure the safety of both contracting parties against German revenge, and which became the main foundation of Polish foreign policy; and, in addition, by an alliance with Rumania with the object of a common defence of the eastern frontiers of both states against the Soviets. It was obvious, however, how desirable was the extension of that system of alliances by still wider regional agreements. The alliance with France exacted an agreement with all the French allies in Central Europe, not only with Rumania, but also with the other members of the Little Entente. The danger in the east could only be met by a common front, not only with Rumania in the south, but also with the whole group of Baltic States, including Finland, in the north.

Unfortunately, both these conceptions met with insurmountable obstacles. The strained relations with Czechoslovakia, an unfortunate result of the territorial dispute at the moment of the liberation of both nations, as well as the wellnigh exclusively anti-Hungarian attitude of the Little Entente, prevented Poland from acceding to it, and even from closer collaboration with it. The no less regrettable Polish-Lithuanian dispute, despite a series of highly promising Baltic conferences. made the formation of a strong Baltic Entente with the participation of Poland impossible. In the place of this, however, it might have appeared through several years that a still broader conception would be realized, a system of collective security of all the European States which belonged to the League of Nations, and which should be faithful to its principles of peaceful collaboration.

The realization of this idea seemed nearest in 1924, when, in the atmosphere of general relief from the political strain, the Assembly of the League unanimously accepted the Geneva Protocol. When this project came to nothing with Great Britain's refusal to ratify the protocol and when, in the following year, the Locarno Treaties, concluded outside the League between Germany and her neighbours, superseded it, there was a great disillusionment for Poland because a notable discrimination between the western and eastern boundaries of Germany had been made, and only the former were recognized as immovable and guaranteed by all the contracting parties. Although in the east peace was ensured only by a Polish-German treaty of arbitration, and the strengthening of the Polish-French alliance, the Republic, whose Minister of Foreign Affairs in those years of transition was Count Alexander Skrzynski, did not retire from participation at Locarno, and only made it her aim that after the anticipated entrance of Germany into the League not only that nation, but also Poland, should gain a permanent seat in its council. Finally, in September 1926, Poland had to be satisfied with a semi-permanent seat; but thenceforward, with Augustus Zaleski as the new director of her foreign policy, she remained faithful to the principle of strengthening her security by collective treaties, and took an active share in all efforts to maintain universal peace. The Polish proposition, condemning all aggressive warfare, accepted by the Assembly of the League in 1927, paved the way to the Paris Pact in the following year, the so-called Kellogg Pact which solemnly outlawed war. In her negotiations with Soviet Russia, Poland endeavoured to hasten the coming into force of that pact as far as eastern Europe was concerned, and both sides accepted a definition of aggression which was more precise than any previous definition.

The conclusion by Poland of a special treaty of non-aggression with the Soviets in 1932 appeared to be a further step in this direction. At the same time it was the first sign of a change in her foreign policy. That year, in which the Disarmament Conference convoked at Geneva proved to be condemned to failure, undermined the belief in collective security, and Poland, who still brought forward at this conference the highly interesting project of moral disarmament, entered with Colonel Joseph Beck as new Minister of Foreign Affairs upon the road of so-called bilateral pacts. The most important of these appeared to be the treaty of non-aggression which, in January 1934, was concluded for ten years with the German Reich. It was preceded by a seeming relaxation of the strain in their mutual relations, which followed, wholly beyond expectations, after the taking over of the government by Hitler. Before its rise to power, the National Socialist movement had taken up a specially hostile attitude to Poland, an attitude which, however, in principle differed not at all from the general unchangeable position of Germany, who, from the moment of the Versailles Treaty, had not ceased to claim the revision of her territorial dispositions in the east; that one-sided demand was repeatedly brought forward by Germany, although it was obvious that Poland could never agree to it, but would resist the curtailment of her only just regained territories and would especially oppose being cut off from the sea. In the treaty of 1934, it is true, Hitler did not distinctly acknowledge Poland's frontiers; but from that time he was not sparing in assurances to her of his friendship, which appeared to postpone disputed questions to a far future, and, in any case, to safeguard Poland for the period of ten years.

Besides being natural on her part, if only because she had no aggressive intentions whatsoever towards Germany, the chief explanation of Poland's signing this treaty was that she had lost hope in effective assistance from the western States, who, in 1933, had agreed to Mussolini's suggestion of concluding a Four-Power Pact with him and with Hitler. After the evaporation of that illusive, and for Poland highly dangerous, conception of a European 'order,' collective security was to be strengthened by an understanding with the Soviets, who were admitted to the League of Nations in the autumn of 1934. Under such conditions Poland might well be inclined to attempts at safeguarding herself by direct independent treaties with both her neighbours, and the unreadiness of the democracies to stop Hitler in 1936 when Poland declared to be ready to oppose the violation of the Locarno treaty, seemed to justify these attempts. For Hitler, on the other hand, who from easily understood motives, some geographical and others bound up with the general disposition of forces in Europe, was anxious to postpone his reckoning with Poland until the period after the incorporation of Austria and the conquest of Czechoslovakia, the isolation of Poland and her subjection to the will of Germany was an object only too greatly desired.

He did not entirely gain that object. Although, unfortunately, the policy of Beck through several years played into his hands, and these apparently friendly relations exposed Poland to German influences, and especially to a methodical system of spying, the relations of Poland with the west, above all her alliance with France, remained unshaken, in spite of a certain cooling. Moreover, Poland always refused to participate in any German aggression against Russia. On the other hand, the Polish Minister of Foreign Affairs endeavoured to establish closer bonds between Poland and the whole group of states lying between Germany and Russia, stretching as far as Scandinavia and not excluding even Lithuania, whom immediately after the fall of Austria he finally persuaded to enter into normal diplomatic relations with Poland. Before, however, these extensive and difficult processes were able to create a compact group of those states possessing so many obvious interests in common, the catastrophe of Czechoslovakia ensued and Beck's policy made use of it to regain the part of the Silesian borderland that had for so long been the subject of dispute. This most regrettable step weighed little in the scale of events, which the Munich policy of the Great Powers had decided; but on Poland it was notably avenged, because almost on the morrow of this small and illusive success, Hitler brought forward his claims in the matter of Danzig and the Corridor which, after the total absorption of the Czech State in March 1939, he presented to Poland in the form of a direct threat.

27

Destruction

It would be superfluous to demonstrate why Poland could not accept the conditions dictated to her by Hitler in the spring of 1939, the final draft of which, going so much further than the earlier claims, he would not even communicate to her by the ordinary diplomatic channels, in the critical days and hours at the end of August. To-day we clearly perceive that all the questions which had been brought forward by Hitler up to that time were regarded by him as only secondary; they were only pretexts to attain, either by the total capitulation of the Polish Government or else by the war that had been secretly prepared for years, the actual aim of German policy in regard to Poland: a fresh destruction of the Polish State, this time final, which should encompass the destruction of the whole nation.

For the first time Hitler met with the resolute resistance of the intended victim. But for the first time also Europe reacted against the very intention of the new outrage. Even the British Government, which under Chamberlain was so strenuously aiming to preserve peace, confronted with the fresh example of Hitler's broken promises in regard of Czechoslovakia, immediately after the March ultimatum gave Poland a guarantee of full support in the event of German aggression. After Beck's visit to London this promise was succeeded by a mutual Polish-British guarantee, linked with the strengthening of the alliance with France. Although Hitler took advantage of this purely defensive treaty to denounce the Polish-German pact of non-aggression, it could be anticipated that in face of the attitude of the western Powers he would hesitate before declaring a war which was bound to become a European war, and for Germany a war on two fronts. All his hesitations were cut short, however, by the treaty which his Minister of Foreign Affairs, Ribbentrop, signed with the Soviets in Moscow on 23rd August.

This pact was equally unexpected by those who saw in Hitler and National Socialism the bulwark against the danger of Communism, as by those who saw in the Soviet Union the desired ally of democracy in the fight with Nazism and Fascism. In spite of the simultaneous negotiations by which the representatives of England and France were misled in Moscow, the natural solidarity of all the revolutionary totalitarian systems now became manifest, together with the immemorial German-Russian solidarity in the project of destroying Poland, broken only for a short while in the former World War. The final signing of the Polish-British treaty two days later could not now preserve peace, nor did the appeals of Pope Pius XII, President Roosevelt, the King of the Belgians, and the Queen of the Netherlands. While diplomatic negotiations were still being carried on through British mediation, Hitler, without a declaration of war, on the morning of 1st September, flung all his forces against Poland.

These forces were so overwhelming, especially in the field of aviation and in the motorized panzer divisions, that it was totally impossible for the Republic to check them by her own means, as was confirmed later by the experience of a series of other states stronger in that respect than Poland. But she was obliged to wage that desperate September campaign literally alone. England and France, who, in fulfilment of their obligations, declared war against Germany after two days' delay, were unprepared for it, and practically had to restrict themselves to military activities that were hardly more than spectacular demonstrations. Nevertheless, the heroic resistance of the Polish armies, outflanked from the beginning by attacks from the west, from East Prussia, and across German-dominated Slovakia, was prolonged until the beginning of October; the long battle in the region of Kutno was acknowledged by the Germans themselves to be one of the bloodiest in history, and at the end of the campaign some of their divisions were still suffering severe defeats. Therefore, the German assertion that the campaign lasted only three weeks, or even only eighteen days, is false. False, but in two respects highly characteristic.

It proves, in the first instance, that in their own view the decisive moment of the campaign was reached immediately after the 17th September. We know that precisely on that day Poland fell a victim to another entirely unprovoked attack. Under flimsy pretexts Soviet Russia broke the second of the bilateral pacts by which Poland had desired to maintain peaceful relations with her neighbours, and with the fresh forces she had been long assembling she invaded the Republic's eastern territories. It was only that stab in the back that made the Polish resistance, which had just at that moment begun to stiffen, indeed hopeless.

Nevertheless, it was continued in many places, and, above all, in Warsaw, under the inspiring leadership of the mayor, Stephen Starzynski. The city only surrendered when the Germans, who from the first hours of the war, against Hitler's solemn declarations, employed their powerful air force in the most savage manner by bombarding open towns and villages, peasants working in the fields, and refugees on the roads, and by terrorizing the entire population, women and children, crowned this barbarous work of destruction by turning Poland's capital into ruins. The bombardment of Warsaw actually began on the first day of the war; but it was when the Germans considered the campaign finished, and the fall of the capital was, in fact, inevitable, that the aerial attack was let loose in all its fury against the unhappy city. Combined with the simultaneous artillery fire, these air raids systematically reduced whole streets to rubble and ashes, started innumerable unquenchable fires, after the destruction of the water supply, destroyed churches during Sunday services, and found only too often for their targets the historical monuments, including the Royal Castle, as well as hospitals overflowing with wounded. The martyrdom of Warsaw, frankly designed as a punishment because the capital did not instantly submit to the invader, will remain, together with the similar fate of a number of other towns, as, for instance, Siedlce, which was levelled to the ground, a disgrace to the Germans, the greater because they could not even gloss over their barbarity with the pretext of 'retaliation.' Not one Polish bomb fell on Germany.

The day after the capitulation of the ruins of Warsaw, 28th September, a German-Soviet treaty was concluded effecting the division of the Polish territories between the aggressors.

Most of the inhabitants, especially the preponderating part of the purely Polish population, fell under the German yoke; the Russians appropriated more than one-half of the territory of the Republic. It is entirely erroneous to maintain that they only took the lands inhabited by White Ruthenians and Ukrainians, as far as the Curzon line. On the contrary, besides eastern Galicia with Lwow, which the provisional demarcation in 1919 did not actually affect, they arrogated to themselves a strip of purely Polish land west of that line as far as the Pisa and Narew Rivers, and at least five million Poles on both sides of the Curzon line passed under the rule of the Soviets. Nearly four times as many Poles found themselves under the German occupation, which besides the districts occupied by Prussia prior to 1914, held the greater part of the Congress Kingdom and all western Galicia.

Among the Poles not even the smallest political group could be found to recognize the conquest of the country, or to show any willingness to 'collaborate' with the invaders. No state in the world formally acknowledged the 'liquidation' of Poland, although Mussolini made use of that phrase in an occasional address, and the war between Poland and the temporary occupiers of the country continued to be carried on, and in two different forms.

One of these was the protracted martyrdom of that overwhelming majority of the population which remained in the country. This was clearly not a war in the common sense of a struggle between two armies. The September campaign itself was in great measure an extermination of the civil population. After its conclusion there started on the one hand a persecution of the Poles, so cruel that the most terrible experiences of the past pale before it, and on the other hand a resistance, so consistent and widespread that it gives the lie to the popular belief in the seeming Polish want of concord; so heroic that no military action could be more worthy of praise or more fraught with sacrifice.

This common characteristic extends to the whole of the Polish territories. Obviously, in details there appeared to be notable differences between the German and the Soviet occupations, and, within the frontiers of the first-named, between the territories 'incorporated' into Germany and the so-called 'General Government'. In glaring violation of international law, Hitler, without waiting for the end of the war and the treaty of peace, not long after the 'regulation' of frontiers with the Soviets, drew up yet another boundary line. This was intended to be the 'final' eastern frontier of Germany in the strict meaning of the word. By it she annexed not only the Free City of Danzig and the Corridor—the ostensible subject of the conflict—not only all beyond it that belonged to Prussia in 1914, that is Poznania and Upper Silesia, but, in addition, a considerable part of the former Congress Kingdom, and even a slice of the former Galicia almost as far as Cracow— altogether 35,700 square miles, with a Polish population of more that nine millions. The district of Suwalki, cut off from the rest of the Reich's Polish conquest by the Soviet occupation, was joined to East Prussia; a broad belt of territory reaching nearly to Warsaw, including Lodz, which received the name of 'Litzmannstadt,' was incorporated partly into East Prussia and partly into 'Wartegau,' as Great Poland was named.

In this 'annexed' area the persecution was undoubtedly the most brutal, openly aiming at the total extirpation of the Polish element. The Germanizing methods of former Prussia which National Socialism officially renounced in the name of the purity of race, but which, in case of necessity, it did not disdain to apply, were not sufficient here. It employed, therefore, other methods, far more ruthless still; having at the outset removed the leaders of the nation by numberless executions, it proceeded to the mass eviction of the Poles, and this under the most inhuman conditions, with the result that a large number, especially children, died on the road. This proceeding was carried out most systematically in Pomerania, where for example, the whole population was removed from Gdynia, a town created solely by Polish efforts and now named Gotenhafen. But thousands of Poles were expelled equally from Poznan and the other towns of Great Poland; one street after another was cleared of its inhabitants, and the unhappy occupants were compelled to leave all their property for use of Germans brought from the Reich or the Baltic countries, and placed in their homes. Even those deportations of more than one million and a half victims could not drive out all the eight and a half millions of the Polish Polish population. Therefore, those elements, economically the weakest, which remained on the spot were the more oppressed, as was the only refuge left to them, the Catholic Church.

A part of the Poles who were driven out from the 'annexed' provinces were transferred to forced labour in Germany, which was also the lot of many thousands of youths from central Poland. The rest of the expropriated were literally flung on the pavement in that central part of the Republic which Hitler assigned to the Polish nation as a sort of 'reservation.' But even regarding the "General Government' with its capital in Cracow and divided into four areas, Cracow, Warsaw, Radom, and Lublin, every opportunity was taken to proclaim officially that it was to belong to the Reich 'for all time.' In this manner an indefinable, purely artificial creation had arisen, to which even the name of protectorate was not applied. It was to be simply a German colony which, although situated in the middle of

Europe and inhabited by indisputable 'Aryans'—with the exception of the Jews now starving behind the ghetto walls—was to be exploited in the same way as, if not worse than, some African colony.

An inexorable persecution of the Polish intelligentsia was waged, denying the Poles the right to their own culture. Its most notorious manifestation was the insidious arrest in November 1939 of nearly all the professors of Cracow University for the sole reason that that university has been for more than five hundred years a bulwark of all that is Polish; the professors were interned in a concentration camp, not excepting scholars of world-wide fame and old men over seventy years of age. Eighteen of them, exactly a tenth part, died as the result of ill-treatment; and in spite of the gradual release of the majority, other scholars were among the innumerable victims of Oranienburg, Dachau, or the worst of all the concentration camps, established at Oswiecim. Not only the University of Cracow, but all the Polish universities, indeed all educational establishments from and including secondary schools, were closed 'for ever,' and all Polish art treasures, public or private, confiscated by an order of 16th December 1939. Other regulations aimed at the systematic destruction of Polish industry, and the giving over of all material resources of the country to Germany's use. After the extermination of its leading classes the rest of the population, those who would survive starvation and disease, were to be used as the slaves of the Reich.

At the same time, in the eastern part of Poland which during 21 months was under Soviet occupation, the Russians also started persecuting the Polish population. Deportations to hard labour in Siberia, once the severest punishment, exceeded only by that of death, for political offenders, were now administered to about one million and a half, not excepting women and children, against whom nothing could be charged except that they were Poles. It would be superfluous to stress that to the systematic, hurried Sovietization of the occupied areas was added—as in the German occupation—a specially intensive war against traditional Polish culture and, obviously, against all religion, and the reduction of the population to abject misery. The comedy of the "elections" carried through immediately after the invasion naturally led to the "voluntary" accession of the northern part of the usurped territory, including the purely Polish region of Lomza and the prevailing Polish region of Bialystok, to the Soviet White Russian Republic, and of the southern part, together with Polish Lwow, to the Soviet Ukraine. However, he independence of these republics was always purely fictitious. Under Stalin's dictatorship Communism harmonized perfectly with Russian nationalism which wished to profit, as in the preceding historical epochs, from its alliance with German nationalism, and to seize the Lithuanian-Ruthenian territories which for so many centuries have been a subject of dispute, blotting out from them every vestige of Poland's cultural influences. Moreover, in its aim at a complete extinction of Poland, it took adantage of the opportunity thus offered to reach even into the very depth of her ethnical territory.

Speaking of the Soviet occupation, special mention should be made of Wilno and its district. A fortnight after its capture the Bolsheviks magnanimously gave it to Lithuania. The Polish inhabitants at first hailed with relief the entrance of the Lithuanians, who unfortunately, in great measure destroyed their expectations, closing, on 15th December 1939, the Wilno University, and setting on foot various repressions against the Poles. Soon, however, the fundamental error of the Lithuanian policy in the course of the last twenty years— its distrust of Poland, and its neglect of the German and

Soviet peril—was bitterly avenged. Half a year before the catastrophe of Poland, who desired nothing from her except normal neighbourly relations, Lithuania lost Klajpeda to the German Reich. After that catastrophe she regained temporarily one disputed town, but only to experience at once a serious limitation of her sovereignty and, nine months later, together with the other Baltic States, to lose it entirely. The transformation of independent Lithuania into a Soviet Republic, subject, like all the others, to Moscow, was at the same time a blow for that section of Polish people then living there, who were in a better position than those under the yoke of the Germans and Bolsheviks in Poland proper.

In the mute daily warfare waged by the whole Polish nation against the invaders, none of the Poles faltered. A certain number of Poles succeeded in crossing the frontiers of the Republic before they were closed, or, albeit at the gravest risks, in extricating themselves out of that twofold concentration camp into which a recently happy country had suddenly changed. Their history is not only a sad Odyssey of fugitives who, driven from one country to another, often only found in the other hemisphere a temporary shelter. It shows at the same time another form of Poland's unceasing war with her enemies, war in the full significance of that word, carried on by an independent government, by arms and diplomacy, with profound faith in final victory.

This proved possible owing to two circumstances. President Moscicki, before he crossed the Rumanian frontier with the whole Government, laid down his office, and, in conformity with the constitution, Ladislas Raczkiewicz, a man with great experience in politics, moderate in judgment, and universally respected, was named his successor. In the place of the old Government, which was interned in Rumania and

unable to fulfil its functions, he immediately formed in Paris
on 1st October 1939, a new Government composed of prominent politicians who had succeeded in getting through to
France, with General Ladislas Sikorski as Prime Minister,
and August Zaleski as Minister of Foreign Affairs who in
1941 was replaced by Count Edward Raczynski. In this manner the continuity of the only lawful Polish State authority
was assured, under the charge of personages enjoying the full
confidence alike of the nation and of her western allies. This
Government, with the gold reserve of the State at its disposal,
which fortunately had been successfully transported to France,
moved together with the President, to an exterritorial seat
which the French Government assigned to it at Angers; it
completed its composition steadily, as more political leaders
found their way to France. Among others these included General Sosnkowski, who had played a distinguished part in the
September campaign, and whom the President nominated as
his eventual successor. A National Council by the side of the
Government was formed in January 1940, named by the President from the representatives of every political opinion, filling
the place of Parliament for the duration of the war, and giving
every guarantee that in agreement with the declarations of the
new Government the structure of post-war Poland would be
founded on genuine democratic principles of legality and social
justice. The most internationally famous Polish citizen, Ignacy
Paderewski, who inaugurated its work by a notable speech
setting forth its programme, was chosen as the head of the
Council and occupied this position until his untimely death
on June 29th 1941.

General Sikorski not only accepted the portfolio of military
affairs, which later, in 1942, was given to the noted historian
General Marian Kukiel, but also became the Commander-in-

Chief of the reorganized Polish army. This was possible owing to the second favourable circumstance that part of the Polish army which, after the September campaign, passed into Hungary and Rumania, especially many officers and airmen, succeeded, in spite of having been interned, in again assembling in France, where their ranks were swelled by mobilization among the pre-war Polish emigrants in that country, who numbered almost half a million. Thanks to the indefatigable efforts of its leader the Polish army, numbering nearly 100,000 and admirably trained, was ready for battle by the spring of 1940, when the war at last blazed on the western front. Some of its units had already distinguished themselves in the distant Norwegian expedition of the allies, especially in the battle for Narvik; but the Polish soldier covered himself with fresh glory, in the share he took in the defence of France.

The collapse of France was likewise a heavy blow for Poland. It did not, however, break her spirit. In spite of fresh losses and the capitulation of one of the allies, the Poles did not even dream of ceasing to fight. About 15,000 who had heroically protected the retreat of one of the French armies, had to cross into Switzerland, where they were received with extraordinary warmth, but naturally had to be interned. The greater part, however, of the Polish army was successfully transported to England, by whose side the remains of the Polish navy had been already fighting from the beginning of the war, and where now, at the end of June 1940, the Polish Government together with the President and the National Council transferred themselves. The Polish troops, quartered chiefly in Scotland, undertook the defence of a certain part of the British coast, the Polish airmen began increasingly to distinguish themselves, acting with the Royal Air Force, and a little later Polish soldiers dispersed through the world, as of old in the Napoleonic wars, appeared in Palestine and on the fields of the Egyptian-Libyan battles, while Polish volunteers were not absent even from the Greek front.

In addition to the Balkan campaign, the year of 1941 brought two other momentous changes in the political and military situation which were of the greatest possible importance for the Polish nation and proved decisive for the issue of the whole war.

Nothing was more striking than the break between Hitler and Stalin, between Nazism and Communism, whose joint action against Poland has been described above. The German-Russian war, starting on Polish soil, brought still more devastation and hardship to an already inhumanly suffering country, and confronted the exiled Polish Government and the whole nation with a difficult decision. Taking into consideration the foremost necessity of defeating Germany who now occupied and oppressed the whole of Poland, the common interests of all the allies, and the cruel aggression whose victim after so many others had become the Russian nation —Poland not only agreed to make peace with Russia on July 30, 1941, a few weeks after the German invasion, but concluded with her a close alliance on December 4 of the same year and decided effectively to cooperate with the Russians.

The same Polish soldiers who had suffered for nearly two years in Soviet prisons immediately started forming a new army ready to pour out their blood for the liberty of all allied peoples. They had a right to expect, with all the other Poles wherever they were that the Soviet Union, having annulled her treaty with Germany of 1939, would respect the Polish-Russian frontier fixed by mutual agreement in 1921, the full independence of Poland, and the democratic constitution of a nation which always was opposed to communism.

Poland's hope for the complete restitution of her freedom and integrity received the strongest possible support by the second great event of 1941: by America's entry into the war after the aggression of Pearl Harbor on December 7. Foreshadowed by the Atlantic Charter, the participation of the world's greatest democracy in the second World War and in the making of the future peace, seemed to the Poles another guarantee—just like the alliance with Great Britain— that their ordeal would not be forgotten when the United Nations would establish their new European order.

In opposition to the so-called "New Order" which the totalitarian Powers desired to impose upon Europe, Poland was already preparing agreements with other allied nations whose exiled governments had gathered on English soil, in the conviction that the new, truly just, and permanent order of Europe and the world must be founded on the principles of independence, security, and legal equality of all the countries, great and small, each of which must have its living space. The declaration given out in common by the Polish and Czechoslovakian Governments at the end of the year 1940, on the memorable anniversary of the 11th of November, proved that Poland had a full comprehension of the necessity of these independent states joining into federal unions, and that she was conscious of her share of responsibility for precisely such a settlement in that most threatened part of Europe between Germany and Russia, in which the central key position has for centuries fallen to Poland. The promise of a closer Polish-Czechoslovakian collaboration towards that object had a deep significance, removing the unfortunate misunderstanding between these two nations, and at the same time offering a distinct encouragement to other nations of that region to join, obviously on the principle of equality for all, the projected federal system. Moreover, at the International Labour Conference held in Washington one year later, these two nations decided closely to cooperate with two others, Yugoslavia and Greece, which concluded a similar agreement.

In any case, Poland's place, as well as that of the other Central European allies, in the post-war world seemed secure, provided only that Hitler would be decisively defeated. At the beginning of 1942 when the United Nations Declaration of January 1st solemnly confirmed the principles of the Atlantic Charter, such a victory still seemed far away, but the war situation definitely turned to the better in the fall of the same year thanks to the battles of El Alamein in Egypt and of Stalingrad in Russia. Unfortunately it soon became obvious that the promised restoration of "sovereign rights and self-government" to the liberated peoples including Poland, depended not only "the final destruction of the Nazi tyranny" but also on the post-war policy of Soviet Russia whose relations with Poland deteriorated again very rapidly.

We know today that the real cause of the misunderstandings which appeared almost immediately after the agreements of 1941, was the Russian plan to oppose to the legitimate Polish Government with which these agreements had been concluded, Communists puppets which at the same time were trained in Moscow. The Polish forces which were organized in Russia after their release from prison camps had to be transferred to the Near East while the fate of most of their officers who did not reappear after the so-called "amnesty", remained unexplained. Suddenly, in April 1943 the Germans announced that they had discovered the mass-graves of these thousands of Polish officers in the forest of Katyn near Smolensk where they obviously had been shot. When the Polish Government requested an investigation by the International Red Cross of that unprecedented crime, Soviet Russia broke off diplomatic relations with that government which, in the midst of that alarming crisis lost its head, General Sikorski, in an airplane crash, on July 4, 1943.

As Commander-in-Chief Sikorski was replaced by General Sosnkowski and as Prime Minister by the peasant leader Stanislaw Mikolajczyk who for almost a year and a half tried hard to re-establish friendly relations with the Russians. However, President Roosevelt and Winston Churchill who exercised a strong pressure upon him, already at the Teheran Conference in the fall of 1943 tacitly admitted Stalin's claim to the eastern half of Poland as far as the badly misinterpreted Curzon line. They hoped that if getting satisfaction in that territorial issue, Soviet Russia would respect at least the real independence of the remaining part of Poland: as a matter of fact, a Communist "Committee of National Liberation" was already prepared to seize control of the country as soon as the Red Army would cross the Curzon line.

These Russian agents under Boleslaw Bierut were indeed formally established in Lublin following their manifesto of July 22, 1944. Before and after that happened the real Polish patriots made their two most outstanding and bloody contributions to the Allied war effort, one of them being a splendid victory of the regular Polish army in Italy, the other one ending in an especially glorious defeat of the underground forces on Polish soil.

When allied armies from various lands failed to take the stronghold which the Germans had established next to the Monastery of Monte Cassino thus blocking the way to Rome, the Polish corps under the command of General Wladyslaw Anders started another attack on May 11 and after eight days of desperate fighting, suffering the heaviest losses, finally broke the German resistance and in a well deserved triumph planted the Polish flag on the ruins of the monastery. That same corps, though decimated and without reserves, continued to fight on during the whole Italian campaign, liberating among others, Bologna and Ancona, in spite of the disappointing news which were arriving from their country.

They knew only too well that the eastern part of Poland from which so many of them were coming, instead of being liberated, simply passed from the German occupation to the Russian. But in the heart of the country, the underground forces organized as a "Home Army" under the command of General Tadeusz Bor-Komorowski were still at the disposal of the secret authorities of the "Underground State," loyal to the exiled government in London. In spite of the systematic resistance which these forces, supported by the whole population, opposed to the Germans, conducting sabotage activities on the largest possible scale, they were blamed by Russian propaganda for not being active enough and called upon by repeated broadcasts openly to revolt against the Nazis when the Red army reached the outskirts of Warsaw at the end of July 1944. When the Polish authorities really ordered such a general uprising on the fateful day of August 1st, the Russians first denied its importance and then, considering it contrary to their own plans, not only remained passive on the other side of the Vistula, but created the greatest difficulties when the Western Allies tried to assist, at least from the air, the Polish forces which temporarily had liberated a large part of the city.

Nevertheless, heroic street-fighting with the participation of the whole population continued for sixty-three days. What remained of the Home Army in the Polish capital which thus sacrificed itself for the second time in the war, capitulated only when all supplies were completely exhausted and even the enemies promised to spare the people of the city whom Hitler in his fury wanted to exterminate. These people were, however, expelled and deported in the most inhuman conditions and the buildings which still were standing after the bombardment of 1939, the annihilation of the Jewish ghetto in 1943, and the struggles of the uprising itself, suffered systematic destruction long after the cease-fire, with a view to removing all traces of Polish culture.

That work of destruction, truly symbolic of the fate of Poland in World War II, was being completed while Prime Minister Mikolajczyk and some of his colleagues had to negotiate in Moscow, both in August and October 1944, not only with the Soviet Government, but also with the Communist agents whom Stalin pretended to be the real "government" of the "liberated" country. Being exposed again to the pressure of the Western allies who still had far reaching illusions as to Stalin's intentions, Mikolajczyk became inclined to a compromise, but on his return to London had to resign in view of the opposition of the majority of the Government. On November 29, the socialist leader, Tomasz Arciszewski became Prime Minister, and though practically without any allied support, the Polish Government-in-Exile remained fully loyal to the Allied cause until the end of the war against Germany. This was best evidenced by the fact that the Polish forces, which had participated from the outset in the invasion of the Continent and distinguished themselves in France, particularly at Falaise, played their part also in the liberation of Belgium and Holland where they suffered serious losses at Arnhem, and simultaneously with the last struggles of their comrades in Italy, a Polish panzer division entered Germany from the West.

In doing so these soldiers could no longer hope to reach the inspiring goal of their long campaign in foreign lands: a truly free Poland. For from the east, from the devastated homeland which had merely changed its conquerors, other Polish forces were advancing as far as Berlin, not, however, as free men but under Russian control and subject to Communist indoctrination. Their fate was symbolic of another destruction which after the material ruins left behind by the German invaders, was now threatening their country: the destruction of its spirit and of its tradition by the same neighbor who had participated in Hitler's aggression at the beginning of the war and now, at its end, had gained even more than the German dictator had offered him in the planned partition of Poland—the complete control of that country, the annexation of its eastern part being accompanied by an indirect subjugation of the rest.

This had been decided some months before the struggle against Germany was over at a conference which was held amidst the continuing war-time destruction, but still must be considered the basic peace conference which settled the European problems of World War II: at Yalta. It was there that the third act of New Poland's tragedy was practically concluded by what has been so well called "defeat in victory," and that a curtain, soon to be called "the Iron Curtain", descended upon the scene of that tragedy, though the fourth act was already starting.

28

Ten Years of Trial

At Yalta the Polish question was only part of much larger issues. Yet no other problem was discussed at such length and in no other matter were the Russians less inclined to make any concession. For them the annexation of Eastern Poland was the final implementation of the historical process of "collecting" all what they considered "Russian lands," a process which had started in the Middle Ages. And making Poland in its restricted boundaries a Russian satellite was a basic objective of Russian policy from the days of Peter the Great. In achieving this, Stalin was more successful than Catherine II had been, whose policy of partitioning Poland with the Germans he had been obliged to follow in 1939. Now, in 1945, he was even more successful than Alexander I in 1815, because this time no Polish territory was left outside the new Poland "restored" by, and connected with Russia, and also because at the Crimean Conference—Russia's revenge for her setback in the Crimean War of ninety years before—the western powers accepted the Russian solution of the Polish question with even less opposition and misgivings than at the Congress of Vienna.

Their readiness to compromise at the expense of Poland—this time the most loyal ally—was the more surprising, because that Russian solution was also the Communist solution of the Polish problem, which made Poland, on whose conquest the control of all East Central Europe depended, the open gateway for Communist expansion toward the West. In 1920, a similar attempt had failed at the gates of Warsaw. When on January 17, 1945, that same heroic city was taken from the Germans not by the Polish underground forces, sacrificed a few months before, but by the Red army which, in the two weeks preceding the Crimean Conference, occupied Western Poland also, "a new situation" had been created indeed, as the Yalta Conference decision rightly pointed out. But neither President Roosevelt, deadly ill and badly advised, nor even Winston Churchill who knew Bolshevism so well, seemed to realize that this situation, far from being a "liberation" of Poland, was a terrible threat to Europe. They did not realize either that the Red army was no longer needed to defeat Germany whose last offensive, not long before Yalta, had seemed so alarming, nor to win the war against Japan whose remaining power of resistance was equally overrated. Without challenging any of Stalin's spurious arguments, they confirmed him in the possession of Eastern Poland including even Lwow which President Roosevelt tried in vain to save, and accepted a formula regarding the government of Poland which, though it seemed open to different interpretations, was, as a matter of fact, just another surrender to the Russian claims. For not only was the very existence of the legitimate Polish Government, an allied government still recognized by all powers except the Soviet Union, simply ignored, but instead of creating an entirely new government, according to the original intentions of the western negotiators, it was decided "to reorganize on a broader democratic basis", that is merely to enlarge, "the provisional government which is now functioning in Poland", viz. the group of Communist agents which Russia had put in power.

Speaking in that connection about "democracy" was as misleading as the whole usual Soviet terminology in similar matters, since all these basic decisions were taken without even hearing any Polish representatives; the "reorganization of the present (i.e. Communist imposed) government" was entrusted to a commission composed of Mr. Molotov and the American and British ambassadors to the Soviet Union who would only "consult" in Moscow some "Polish Democratic leaders" obviously chosen by these three foreign diplomats; and last but not least, the government thus enlarged was to be recognized by the western powers without waiting for the "free and unfettered elections" which were promised without fixing any date nor providing any guarantees of real freedom.

The difficulties of carrying out even that most unfortunate agreement, in particular of choosing the "democratic leaders" from Poland and abroad, became apparent immediately. President Roosevelt died deeply disillusioned as to the possibility of peaceful cooperation with Soviet Russia in this and many other questions, and his successor, President Truman, had to open the San Francisco Conference of the United Nations with the Polish chair left empty. A few days later Mr. Molotov admitted that the most qualified "democratic leaders" from inside Poland, the leaders of the underground resistance against the Nazis, had been brought to Moscow not for consultation but for trial as war criminals, after a treacherous "invitation". In spite of initial American and British protests against such a "kidnapping" of Polish patriots, both western powers continued to negotiate with that same Mr. Molotov as to the invitation of a few others, including also representatives of the

Poles in exile, and insisting particularly on the participation of Mr. Mikolajczyk. This inclusion was the only concession which Harry Hopkins, when sent to Moscow by President Truman, was able to obtain from Stalin who understood only too well that the presence of a former Polish Prime Minister, though now only a private citizen, who contrary to the solemn protests of his government had publicly approved the Yalta decision, would create the misleading illusion that, after all, there was a "merger" of two Polish governments with appearances of legality.

Besides Mikolajczyk only one more of the three invited "London Poles", now another private citizen, agreed to come to Moscow at the time when the sixteen underground leaders were sentenced, and to join along with two politicians, picked up in occupied Poland, the sixteen Communist tools in what was accepted by the Molotov Commission as the "Polish Government of National Unity." Proclaimed in Moscow on June 23, that "government" was recognized on July 5 by the United States and the United Kingdom, who at the same time withdrew recognition from the constitutional Government of Poland, their faithful war-time ally. This was, for the time being, the end of Polish independence and a clear evidence that the trial, not of a few leaders only, but of the whole Polish nation, which the Soviets had started immediately after expelling the German invaders, would continue indefinitely without any assistance from the outside world. Gradually most countries established diplomatic relations with the new Warsaw regime, and only the Vatican, Ireland, Spain, Lebanon, and a few Latin American republics continued to recognize the legal Polish authorities which remained in exile in London. So did, scattered all over the world, most of the Poles who had escaped from their Nazi occupied country, including the over-

whelming majority of those who had fought on the Allied side
to the bitter end.

The Potsdam Conference which on August 1st of the same
tragic year of 1945 announced that the Polish government in
London had "ceased to exist", had to consider another aspect
of the Polish problem which at Yalta had been left in suspense.
It had been recognized there "that Poland must receive substantial accession of territory in the north and west". Already
then the Oder-Neisse line had been considered as Polish-
German boundary and now, at Potsdam, the territories east
of that line were placed under Polish administration. While,
however, the northern part of East Prussia with Koenigsberg
was definitely attributed to Soviet Russia, the final delimitation
of the lands which were supposed to compensate Poland for
her extensive losses in the east was left again to the future
peace conference. In spite of that vague reservation which was
to encourage German revisionism, the Polish authorities were
permitted to continue, in an orderly fashion, to remove the
German population of these regions which, to a large extent
had already fled or was expelled during the advance of the
Red army. These mass migrations resulted, of course, in great
hardships though not greater than those suffered by the Poles
who were being transferred from Soviet annexed Eastern Poland to these western territories. In any case, the Poles could
only interpret as permanent the attribution of these lands which
they called "recovered" territories, because all of them: from
Pomerania with Szczecin (the German Stettin) at the mouth
of the Oder to the whole of Silesia with its capital Wroclaw
(Breslau), had once belonged to medieval Poland.

Having also gained the full control of Gdansk (Danzig)
and the southern part of East Prussia, the new Poland acquired
indeed a much better western frontier than after World War I

and lands which in the past had been richer than most of those she lost in the east. At the given moment, however, they were completely ruined and devastated, and therefore required a special effort of reconstruction. Furthermore, even with these accessions, the area of Poland was about twenty percent smaller than in 1939—121 thousand square miles—and her total population reduced to about two thirds, the cruel extermination of almost three million Jews by the Nazis being about one third of that terrific loss. Under these conditions, the determination to retain at least the partial compensation in the west soon became the unanimous attitude of all Poles including those in exile, though at Potsdam only representatives of the new regime were consulted in that vital matter.

That regime, though obviously imposed by Soviet Russia and subservient to her, was not yet exclusively composed of Communists. In addition to Mikolajczyk who was made second Vice-Premier and Minister of Agriculture, the two members from inside Poland who were added to the original group, belonged to the Peasant Party, and like the other Pole from London, who was made Minister of Labor, the Prime-Minister himself, Edward Osobka-Morawski, and a few other ministers were members of the Socialist party. A few minor parties also had representatives in the "Government of National Unity" which soon ceased to call itself "Provisional". But all these temporarily tolerated parties, even before the planned "mergers", had to conform to the Moscow dictated directives of the "Polish Workers' Party", as the Communists called themselves. It was to this leading party that belonged the "President of the National Council" and as such temporary Head of the State, Boleslaw Bierut, the first Vice-Premier Wladyslaw Gomulka, other ministers in key positions like the Minister of Public Security and dreaded chief of the secret police, Stanislaw Radkiewicz, and the "power behind the scene", Under-Secretary Jakob Berman.

The last rests of the Home Army and in general all those who having been well trained in the underground resistance against the German occupation, could have played a similar role in opposing Russian occupation and Communist rule, were rapidly liquidated, some of them after continued resistance "in the woods". New concentration camps, called labor camps, replaced those which the retreating Germans had left behind, and considerable forces of the Red army which were stationed in Poland, allegedly to protect the communication lines with the Russian forces in Germany, helped to keep under strictest control the Polish people who, cut off from the free world, were squeezed between the Soviet Union and the Russian zone of occupation in Germany.

Under such conditions any resistance movement soon became entirely hopeless and would have been simply suicidal. Furthermore, the Communists, benefiting from some natural feeling of relief after the ordeal of open persecution by the Nazis, were wise enough not to procede immediately and violently to the complete Sovietization of the country. They even tolerated some kind of "loyal opposition" practiced by the Peasant Party, but postponed as long as possible the pledged elections in which that party could expect to have the support of all those opposed to Communism, that is of the tremendous majority of the nation. In preparation for these elections and with a view to confusing public opinion, the government decided at last, not before the spring of 1946, to hold a "referendum" in which three specific questions were to be answered by a "yes" or "no". One of these questions: whether the new western frontier ought to be permanent, was uncontroversial and the expected, quasi unanimous affirmative vote was to be a first test in favor of those in power. Another question concerned the permanence of the nationalization of basic industries and of the land reform which the Communists had introduced immediately after seizing control and which they wanted to be included in the Constitution. Since already the Manifesto of July 22, 1944, had decided that all estates of more than 50 hectares should be distributed to landless peasants and since that drastic reform which did not even leave those 50 hectares to owners of larger estates but expropriated them completely, had been carried out in greatest hurry, it would have been hardly possible to annul now all what had happened. There remained, therefore, only one question which the opposition had a chance to make a test against the regime: the question of whether or not the Senate should be abolished. Since an affirmative answer was to imply an important change in the democratic Constitution of 1921 which the regime pretended to respect, it was only natural for all those who wanted to prevent the Sovietization of Poland, to vote "No". So did indeed a very large majority on the day of the referendum, June 30, 1946, in spite of the strongest pressure and even terror of the authorities, which, however, did not hesitate to falsify the counting and reporting of the ballots and to announce officially that even on that decisive question the government had won. It now felt safe to hold the long delayed elections half a year later, on January 19, 1947.

The only possibility of controlling these elections which the Yalta agreement had given to the western powers, was to have them observed by their diplomatic missions in Poland. All reports thus received, and in particular those of the American Ambassador, Arthur Bliss Lane, stressed most emphatically that the elections, far from being "free and unfettered", were preceded and accompanied by another wave of terror and fraudulent procedure, directed especially against Mikolajczyk's Peasant Party, leading the opposition. That party received, therefore, only 28 out of 444 seats in the new, unicameral Diet and no representation at all in the government which nevertheless continued to be recognized by the democratic powers. Bierut was now formally elected "President" of the Republic and the so-called "Little Constitution" created a "State Council" under his chairmanship which was to exercise full power when the Diet was not in session.

This was indeed a first step toward the enforcement of an entirely new constitution following the Soviet pattern, and in order to crush any possible opposition, an almost uninterrupted series of political trials was being staged which all ended in severe, frequently death sentences against alleged "spies and foreign agents". Mikolajczyk who felt personally threatened, succeeded in escaping from Poland at the end of October 1947 and through London went to Washington. He organized there his own political movement based on the experience that any cooperation with the Communist regime was impossible, but unfortunately, instead of cooperating with the legitimate Polish authorities in exile, he created a split in the Polish emigration. Its majority, however, remained loyal to the constitutional Government and to the President whose office, after the death of W. Raczkiewicz, on June 6, 1947, was now held by August Zaleski, the former Minister of Foreign Affairs in the years 1926-1932 and 1939-1941.

About the same time, in July 1947, Poland was forced by Moscow to reject any participation in the Marshall Plan which would have been so helpful in the task of post-war reconstruction, much more difficult than after World War I. That nevertheless so much was accomplished in this field, particularly with regard to the rebuilding of the capital and the rehabilitation of the formerly German provinces, must be attributed to the strenuous efforts of the Polish people, while its present masters were "planning" even their economic policy, including the industrialization of the country and the development of trade relations, strictly on the Soviet pattern.

The opposition between the natural trends and interests of the nation and the orders coming from Moscow became even more striking in the field of cultural reconstruction. In the first years after the defeat of the Germans who had tried to suppress any cultural life in Poland, the possibility of reopening at last all Polish educational institutions and of publishing what had been secretly written under the German occupation, was welcomed indeed and what was left of Poland's intellectual leaders tried hard to revive the national tradition in learning and literature. The lost universities of Lwow and Wilno were replaced by those of Wroclaw, where the German university was taken over, and of Torun where an entirely new university was founded, as were the universities of Lodz and that of Lublin, besides the old Catholic university of that city. But the only too well known principle of the nationalities policy of the Soviet Union was gradually and with increasing vigor applied also to the national culture of the allegedly "free and sovereign" Poles: they were free again to write and to teach in their own language, though a subtle process of Russification was soon to start, but in that "free form" the ideological "content" of culture was supposed to become more and more identical with that in Soviet Russia. Nothing could be more typical in that respect than the systematically promoted process of re-writing Polish history, and nothing more symbolic than the enforced liquidation, at a mass-congress of scholars held in Warsaw in the summer of 1951, of the Polish Academy and its replacement by a new Academy of Science entirely similar to the Russian, with its headquarters in a gigantic palace erected as a "gift" of the Soviet Union in the very heart of the capital.

Only a few months after the formal establishment of that Academy, on July 22, 1952, the anniversary of the Manifesto of 1944, now the official "national" holiday, the new Constitution of the Polish "People's Republic" came into force after long preparatory studies with appearances of "free" public discussion. Year after year careful steps had been taken leading to that momentous turning point in the Sovietization of the country. At the end of 1948, the Polish Socialist Party was forced to merge with the Communists in the "United Polish Workers' Party", and in that merger the preponderance of the Communist element was so complete that it mattered very little that another former Socialist, Josef Cyrankiewicz, succeeded Osobka-Morawski as Prime Minister. Much more important and profoundly shocking was, in November 1949, the appointment of a Soviet Marshal, apparently of Polish origin, Constantine Rokossovsky, as Minister of Defense and Commander-in-Chief of the Polish army where all higher positions were given to Russian officers. Next came, in 1950, the replacement of the old civil administration by "People's Councils" on all levels, practically identical with the Russian "Soviets" and completely under Communist control. That hierarchy of Councils, following the Soviet pattern, was to become a striking feature of the new 1952 Constitution, through which the National Council at the top of the ladder, composed of sixteen members, received almost dictatorial powers; since its chairman, chosen in the person of a well known Communist, Alexander Zawadzki, was to be the Head of the State, the office of President of the Republic was completely abolished, Bierut taking over the premiership.

That in March 1954, one year after Stalin's death which

hardly affected conditions in Poland, Bierut was shifted to the post of first Secretary of the Central Committee of the Communist Party and replaced in turn by Cyrankiewicz, seems to have been only one of the secondary personal changes in the regime. Highly significant is, on the contrary, the interpretation of the "Socialist" Constitution as a preparation for, and transition to, a full-fledged Communist system, the main difference being that private ownership of land is still admitted. However, the collectivization of agriculture is strongly encouraged and the number of collective farms, identical with the Russian "Kolkhozy", steadily growing.

For that very reason the Polish peasants, very individualistic and badly disappointed in their hope that the land reform would favor private enterprise, are one of the most determined elements of opposition against the whole foreign imposed regime, so alien to the national tradition. Disappointed, too, are the workers who have to labor harder than ever before and suffer, along with the intellectuals, from entirely inadequate wages, without the right to seek improvements through strikes, and fully aware that the Communist leaders are forming a new privileged class to the disadvantage of all others. But in all classes of society the opposition to the present conditions, unbroken though silenced, is far from being animated exclusively nor even predominantly, by material motives. The materialistic ideology itself, so contrary to the Polish mind and to the dignity of the human person, dear to all Poles precisely because foreign oppression so frequently violated their inalienable human rights, is rejected by a majority of the nation which is still so overwhelming that, according to the most reliable estimates, hardly five percent have been really won over to Communism. The deep religious revival which had started already during the sufferings of Nazi rule, continued with truly remarkable ardor in defiance of the most intense Communist propaganda. Therefore the Catholic Church to which almost all Poles belong and which represents both the heritage of their past and their intimate connection with the western world, became the most powerful stronghold of moral and spiritual resistance in their present trial.

Even the Communists and their Russian masters were so well aware of this, that they avoided the mistake directly to attack and openly to persecute the Catholic Church, particularly during the first post-war years. Highly significant was, however, that they decided at once to denounce the Concordate which free Poland had concluded with the Holy See in 1925, and to start a campaign of slander against the Vatican accusing Pius XII himself who had given so many proofs of sympathy with the Poles, to favor the Germans and to serve American imperialism. Nevertheless, the Primate of Poland, Cardinal Hlond, was permitted to return and to reside in Warsaw uniting this archbishopric with his traditional See of Gniezno. Until the death of this outstanding religious leader on October 22, 1948, his unique authority remained unchallenged, and so was that of Archbishop Sapieha of Cracow who had played a truly heroic role during the German occupation and soon after the war was also made a Cardinal. However, when he, too, died on July 23, 1951, the situation of the Church in Poland, unshaken in its loyalty to Rome, was already extremely critical, in spite of an agreement with the State which had been signed on April 14, 1950.

The hierarchy including the new Primate Archbishop Stefan Wyszynski, though deeply disturbed by the recent supressions of the Catholic charities organization which was taken over by the State, accepted that agreement, because it formally recognized the supreme authority of the Holy See in all religious

matters and seemed to guarantee for the time being the existence of what remained of Catholic education, including the
University of Lublin, and of Catholic publications. But it soon
became apparent that the Communist regime was ready to
seize every pretext for accusing the Church of not respecting
the agreement, for instance in the matter of the Soviet spon-
sored peace campaign, while the administration violated systematically the promises made to the hierachy. Particularly
dangerous proved the ever growing diversionist interventions
which tried to oppose to the bishops the so-called "patriotic
priests" and groups of Catholic laymen cooperating with the
regime. Even so, the plan of creating a schismatic "national"
church did not succeed: on the contrary, even the delicate
problem of the ecclesiastical administration of the formerly
German Western territories was settled in spite of the obvious
provocations of the regime which not only attacked the Vatican in that matter but wrongly accused the hierarchy of lack
of loyalty to their country.

Such charges continued to be made, on different grounds,
against individual members of the clergy who were tried and
sentenced for "spying" or treason, and even against several
bishops who were put in jail or at least interned. When Primate Wyszynski was made a Cardinal at the end of 1952 he
did not find it possible to come to Rome for the consistory in
January of the following year. But even so the recognition
which he received from the Holy See, was answered on February 9, 1953, by a decree which made all ecclesiastical positions
in Poland entirely dependent on the administration, an interference which was contrary to the very principle of separation
between Church and State as stressed in the new constitution.
This decree was, however, only one item of the long list of
violations of the 1950 agreement by the State and of the re-

pressions directed against Poland's religious life which the hierarchy headed by Cardinal Wyszynski denounced in a long memorandum which on May 8, the feast of St. Stanislaus, the patron of the Catholic Poland canonized 700 years before, was sent to Mr. Bierut.

In no other case has the "Church of Silence"—as Pius XII called the Catholic Church in the Communist controlled countries—broken that enforced silence so courageously as did the Polish bishops on that memorable occasion. Without entering into politics, they opposed so openly atheistic materialism with its ruthless and malicious methods and defended so eloquently the nation's religious tradition as well as the person of the Pope, that their protest and their declaration of "non possumus" was the most energetic and at the same time the most dignified challenge of Communist rule in Poland—a truly historic testimony in Poland's contemporary trial.

The reaction was quick to come. After one more spurious trial of a bishop who was sentenced to twelve years of jail, the Primate himself was brutally arrested on September 26, under the pretext of not having condemned himself that alleged American spy among the hierarchy. He was removed to some unknown place and prevented from exercising his authority, while the episcopate was obliged to elect another temporary head. That arbitrary act of violence against the worthy successor of those who in old Poland replaced the person of the king in the interval between two reigns, did not succeed in disorganizing the Catholic Church of Poland nor in separating it from Rome. It was, however, another moral blow inflicted upon the Polish people and a stern warning that nobody was safe any longer in the unhappy country.

Coming after similar actions against the Primates of Croatia and Hungary, two other Cardinals under Communist power, the fate of Archbishop Wyszynski deeply shocked the free world where it raised a wave of solemn protests. This certainly was a comfort to the people of Poland who though behind the so-called "Iron Curtain"—a rather misleading expression— are reached, were it only over the air, by the voice of the outside world. They resent, on the contrary that their own situation is not sufficiently understood by so many foreign peoples who are inclined to identify Poland and the Poles with the Soviet controlled regime which without any fault nor responsibility of their own had been forced upon them in 1945. This being so, it must be strongly emphasized that it is impossible to speak, with reference to the period which started that year, of any "Polish" foreign policy. The history of Poland throughout the present years of trial is nothing but the sad story of her internal sovietization and of her misrepresentation in all external relations by Communist agents who in practically every matter take and must take an attitude completely contrary to that of the Polish people and to their real interests.

There is only one important exception in that respect, and it concerns Poland's western frontier. Without being reconciled at all with the enormous territorial losses in the east, the Poles are indeed determined to keep what they have recovered, re-settled and rebuilt in the west. They are, therefore, alarmed whenever their definite possession of these lands is questioned by the western powers, and this is the only point where Russian and Communist propaganda has any chances of influencing them. Nevertheless, they realize that even in that matter the support which is being received from the Soviet Union and shrewdly discounted by her agents, is dictated by mere expediency and depends entirely on Russia's German policy. The Poles know, too, that if the Government of East Germany which is as dependent on Moscow as is the Warsaw regime, makes statements and even signs agreements—in 1950 and 1951—recognizing the Oder-Neisse line as permanent, this does not mean an acceptance of that boundary by the German people. Furthermore, being fully aware that an agreement with the Germans in this and other matters, desirable and even necessary as it is, will not be easy to reach after liberation, the Poles are also impressed by the Russian arguments against the rearmament of Western Germany, though they are hardly misled by similar propaganda against any integration of Europe on federal lines.

They know only too well that the trend towards federalism which during the war, was so strong among all Poles, those in exile and the underground leaders, was and is opposed by Soviet Russia even as far as any free cooperation among the so-called "satellite" countries is concerned. Just because they are supposed to be and to remain satellites, they are not permitted, not even under their present Communist regimes, to join in any federal unions which would make them stronger with respect to the Soviet Union. Only bilateral agreements, especially in the economic and cultural field, between Poland and the other enslaved countries are encouraged, and all of them, Poland even more than any other, are supposed individually to tighten their relations with Soviet Russia, in order to build up a solid monolithic bloc under the absolute control of that overwhelmingly stronger power.

To serve the interests of that bloc under Russian leadership is the only task of the diplomats, by now practically all Communists, who are supposed to represent Poland in the free countries and in those international organizations which she is permitted to join, particularly in the United Nations where the place due the legitimate allied Polish Government was taken soon after the San Francisco Conference, by such Com-

munist, Russian controlled agents. Their attitude, especially
when they were elected, as "Polish" delegates, to the Security
Council or the Economic and Social Council, offered the most
convincing evidence that they were simply adding their vote
to that of the Soviet republics and supporting the Russian
policy directed against the western, democratic powers and in
particular against the United States. That attitude found its
clearest expression during the war in Korea, and therefore the
participation of "Poland" as a "neutral" country in the arm-
istice negotiations was just another painful fiction. The same
must be be said of the "Polish" participation in the settlement of the problems of Indo-China, in the Moscow Conference at the end of 1954 which was supposed to oppose the
whole Soviet bloc to the North Atlantic Treaty Organization
and in the treaty signed in Warsaw, in May of 1955, with a
view to consolidating the military cooperation of all Soviet
controlled countries.

On several other occasions, patriotic Poles who inadvertently
had been included among the representatives of the regime,
seized the first opportunity to escape, to ask for asylum in the
free world and to confirm that under Communist control they
had not been able to represent the Polish people. They confirmed, too, that these people, in spite of the disappointment
of 1945 and of the anti-American propaganda, to which they
have been subject ever since with increasing intensity, continued
to look upon the United States and its leading role in World
affairs as their only hope for a better future. Though they do
not know when and how liberation will be achieved, they are
convinced that it must come as part of the liberation of all
nations which in 1945 shared Poland's fate. The unity of the
whole region between Germany and Russia, between the Baltic
and the Mediterranean, is indeed becoming evident more than

ever in history, and equally evident is once more Poland's key position in that region whose freedom is vital for the peace of Europe, hence for world peace and for the United States of America, desirous to see that peace solidly established.

Once more the Polish question, apparently a source of trouble, is, as a matter of fact, a real test case, and the issue of her present trial, like the issue of her ordeal in the nineteenth century, will have a deep significance for all mankind. Much more than then, or during World War I and even during World War II in which from June 1941 totalitarian, imperialistic powers were fighting on either side, the conflict of which Poland is the most typical victim, is a conflict between freedom and tyranny, human rights and their negation, the Christian conception of a peaceful world under God and a mechanistic mass organization by atheistic materialism.

No historian can even try to predict how long Poland's present trial, now in its tenth year, is going to last. But looking upon Polish history as a whole, it is easy to find out that this trial, the fourth act of new Poland's tragedy, cannot be the last one. The story of that new Poland which started with World War I, is indeed, like that of her heroic army in World War II, a story still "without the last chapter". Millions of Poles at home and in exile hope and pray that this last chapter may be written as a glorious conclusion of Poland's millenium which is to be celebrated in a few years, recalling the greatness of the Piast Kingdom, the Jagiellonian Union, and the Royal Republic. In our time, in that twentieth century so different from the tenth when Polish history started at the extreme border of western, Christian civilization, in that new period of general history when the destinies of all nations are so closely interrelated, such a conclusion does certainly not depend on the Poles alone, even less than when they tried so hard to save their old Commonwealth from partition. But their own responsibility which they share with their equally suffering neighbors and sister nations, some of which had once been connected with that Commonwealth, is heavy enough, heavier perhaps than during the partition period. For that great majority which continues to live in the homeland, it is the responsibility of going through an unprecedented trial with a spirit unbroken and faithful to the principles on which Poland's greatness was founded in the past. For those in exile it is the responsibility of remaining united in dedication to the cause of Poland's independence and of raising the voice of free Poland in the free world. And both of them have to wait for human justice and Divine mercy.

Index

A

Academy of Sciences and Arts, Polish, 261, 295, 335
Adalbert, St, 16
Adriatic Sea, 97
Akkerman, 100, 102
Albert of Brandenburg, Duke of Prussia, 108ff., 119 f., 149
Albrecht of Austria, 87 ff.
Alexander I, 217, 220 ff., 230, 326
Alexander II, 239, 254
Alexander III, 256
Alexander of Poland, 102 ff., 107
Alexis, Tsar of Moscow, 157
Altmark, Treaty of, 149
Altranstadt, Treaty of, 181
America, 195, 205, 296, 320, 328 f., 333, 338, 340, 343 f.
Anabaptists, 123
Andruszow, Truce of, 162
Ancona, 323
Anders, Wlad., General, 322
Angers, 317
Arciszewski, Tomasz, 324
Arians, 123 f., 183
Arnhem, 324
Atlantic Charter, 320 f.
Augustus II, the Strong, 179, 181 ff.
Augustus III, 179, 187 ff., 190
Austria, Austrians, 40, 109, 111, 139, 149 f., 160, 166 ff., 170, 175, 180, 187, 193 f., 205, 208 f., 212, 215, 221 ff., 231ff., 237, 259 ff., 268 f., 270, 276 f., 285, 305 f.
——, House of. See Hapsburgs
Austrian Succession, War of the, 186
Avignon, 49, 56

B

Babenbergs, 40
Balkans, 151, 268, 319
Baltic Sea, 12 f., 69, 75, 92 f., 120 f., 149 f., 157, 168 f., 283, 293, 343
Bar, Confederation of, 194 f.
Barbara Radziwill, wife of Sigismund Augustus, 117
Basil II, 99

Basil III, 108 ff.
Basil IV (Shuisky), 147
Basle, Council of, 86 f.
Bathory, Stephen, See Stephen Bathory
Batu Khan, 37
Bautzen, Peace of, 15
Beck, Colonel Joseph, 304 ff.
Belgians, Belgium, 231, 324
Bem, General, 237 f.
Beresina, passage of the, 223
Beresteczko, battle of, 157
Berlin, 149, 325
Berman, Jacob, 332
Bialystok, 315
Bierut, Boleslaw, 322, 331, 334, 336 f., 340
Bismarck, 235, 257 f., 267
Black Sea, 5, 59, 67 f., 73, 92, 100 f., 103, 151, 154, 173 f.
Bobrzynski, Michael, 262
Bogorja, Jaroslaw, archbishop, 59
Bohemia, 5, 10 f., 16, 40, 45, 47, 49, 53, 82, 87 ff., 96 ff., 102, 109 f., 111, 133
Bohemian Brethren, 123
Boleslas I, the Great or Brave, 13 ff., 52
Boleslas II, the Bold, 18 ff., 37, 43
Boleslas III, the Crooked-mouthed 21 ff.
Boleslas IV, 24
Boleslas V, the Chaste or Pious, 31, 39, 45 f.
Boleslas of Masovia, 90
Bologna, 323
Bona Sforza, wife of Sigismund I, 114, 117, 141
Boniface VIII, Pope, 47
Bor-Komorowski, T., General, 323
Boris Godunov, Tsar, 145 f.
Bosnia, 268
Braclaw, 125, 154, 161
Brandenburg, 45, 60, 82
——, Electors of, 110, 149
——, House of, 120
——, margraves of, 40, 47 ff.
Brest-Litovsk (Brzesc Litewski), Treaties of 279. See also Brzesc
Bruhl, Count von, 186

347

Bruno, St, 16
Brussels, 247
Brzesc, 299. *See also* Brest Litovsk
——, Synod of, 139
Buda, 68, 112
Bug, river, 13, 27, 80, 208
Bukovina, 103 f.
Bulgaria, 89
Bulow, Chancellor, 267
Byczyna, battle of 137
Byzantium, 4, 9, 16

C

Calvin, 123
"Camp of National Unity," 300
Campo Formio, Peace of, 219
Canossa, 19
Carinthia, 20
Carlovingian Empire, Carloving-
   ians, 4, 6, 8
Casimir I, the Restorer, 18
Casimir II, the Just, 24 ff.
Casimir III, the Great, 50, 52-61,
   65 ff., 74, 94
Casimir IV, son of Jagiello, 87,
   90—102, 108
Casimir, St, son of Casimir IV,
   97, 104
Casimir of Stettin, 60
Catherine, daughter of Louis of
   Anjou, 66
Catherine of Austria, wife of Sigis-
   mund Augustus, 125
Catherine II of Russia, 187 f.,
   192 ff., 196, 203 ff., 208, 217, 326
Catholicism, Catholics, 29, 38 f.,
   55, 68 ff., 87 f., 111, 124 f., 136,
   139, 144, 146, 178 f., 184, 235,
   249, 256 f., 295, 314, 338 ff.
Cecora, battle of, 148, 166
Central Industrial District, 293
Cesarini, Julian, papal legate, 89 f.
Chamberlain, Neville, 308
Charles IV, Emperor, 56 f., 66
Charles V, Emperor, 109 f., 115
Charles VI, Emperor, 183
Charles V of France, 66
Charles IX of France, 134
Charles of Lorraine, Prince, 171
Charles of Luxemburg. *See* Charles
   IV
Charles IX of Sweden, 140, 146,
   148

Charles X of Sweden. *See* Charles
   Gustavus
Charles XII of Sweden, 180 f.,
   183 f.
Charles Gustavus, 157 f., 160
Charles Robert of Anjou, King of
   Hungary, 49, 53, 56
Chelm, Government of, 268, 279
Chelmno, 35, 53, 78, 94
Chlopicki, General, 232
Chmielnicki, Bohdan, 155 ff., 161 f
Chmielnicki, George, 161 f.
Chmielnik, battle of, 37
Chocim, battle of (1621), 148;
   (1673), 166
Chodkiewicz, John Charles, 140,
   148
Chojnice, battle of, 93
Chopin, Frederic, 250
Christianity, spread of, 3, 9, 17 f.,
   23, 38, 55
Churchill, Winston, 322, 327
Cieszkowski, Augustus, 249
Cieszyn (Teschen) Silesia, 288
Clement XIV, Pope, 198
Colloquium Charitativum, 150
Commission of National Educa-
   tion, 198, 227
Commission for Polish Affairs, 281
Conde, Prince de, 163
Conference of Ambassadors, 288
Congress Kingdom, 228, 277, 311 f.
Conrad II, Emperor, 17 f.
Conrad III, Emperor, 25
Conrad of Masovia, 28, 31, 33 f.,
   39, 44, 167
Constance, Council of, 79 f., 82, 86
Constantine, Grand Duke, 230,
   232
Constantinople (Stambul), 55, 88,
   90, 139, 238
Constitution of the Third of May
   1791, 200 ff., 221, 227
—— of 1807, 220
—— of 1815, 226
—— of October 1905, 267
—— of March 1921, 298
—— of May 1935, 298
Conti, Prince Francois Louis de,
   179 f.
Convention of 15th May 1922, 289
Copernicus, Nicolas, 115
Corridor, Polish, 281, 306, 312

Corvinus, Matthias. *See* Matthias
Cossacks, Ukrainian, 140, 147 f.,
152 ff., 166, 173, 181, 212
Council Permanent, 197
Courland (Kurland), 120, 207
Cracow, 7, 19, 24 ff., 39, 42 ff., 56 f.,
68 ff., 74, 79, 81, 85, 88, 90, 110 f.,
115, 134, 142, 144, 158, 181, 198,
206 ff., 221, 225, 235 ff., 261 f.,
276, 285, 294, 312 ff., 338
——, Congress of, 56 f.
——, University of, 57, 74, 79, 115,
198, 261 f., 294, 313 f.
Crecy, battle of, 56
Crimea, 100, 104, 112 f., 151, 154,
156, 173 f., 203
Crimean War, 238, 326
Croatia, 340
Crusades, 26, 32, 57, 88, 151
Curzon Line, 285, 311, 322
Cyrankiewicz, J., 336 f.
Czarniecki, Stephen, 159
Czartoryski, Prince Adam, 193
Czartoryski, Prince Adam George,
217, 222, 225, 233, 237 f.
Czartoryskis, 184, 187 f., 191 ff.
Czechoslovakia, 296, 302, 305 f.,
308, 320
Czechs, 16, 18, 57, 77, 83, 268, 288,
306
Czernihow, 147, 161 f.
Czestochowa, monastery, 158, 195

D

Dabrowski, General, 207, 219 f.
Dachau, 314
Danes, Denmark, 12, 57, 82, 93,
121, 160, 180
Daniel, King of Halicz and Vol-
hynia, 29, 38 f., 54, 69
Danticus, John, 115
Danube, river, 100, 173
Danzig, 48, 78, 93, 111, 134, 167,
180, 185, 196, 203, 205, 207, 220,
281, 283, 293, 306, 312, 330
—— Pomerania, 35 f., 45, 47ff.,
53, 76, 78, 92, 94, 281, 313
—— ——, Duke of, 29, 35f., 45
——, Treaty of, 167
Demetrius, the false, 145 f.
Democratic Society, 234
Deputies, House of, 101, 118, 126
Diet of Convocation, 192

——, Dumb, 182
——, Four Years, or Great, 199 ff.,
203 f., 211, 223
——, Galician, 260
—— of Grodno, 206
—— of Investigation, 138
——, Lithuanian, 122
—— of Lublin, 118
—— of Pacification, 180
—— of Warsaw, 222, 232
—— of Wilno, 288
Diets, 101 f., 113, 118, 122 f., 125 f.,
199 ff.
——, regional, 76
Dietines, 101
Directory, French, 219
Disarmament Conference, 304
Dissidents, 178, 183
Dlugosz, John, 85, 106, 248
Dmowski, Roman, 267, 278, 280,
284, 287
Dnieper, river, 14, 92, 100, 154,
162, 173, 196
Dniester, river, 92, 100, 173
Dobrzyn, 50, 53, 73, 76 f.
Doroszenko, Cossack leader, 166
Dubravka, wife of Mieszko I, 10
Duma of 1906, 267
Dvina, river, 36, 149, 162, 196
Dzikow, Confederation of, 186

E

East Prussia, 93 f., 110, 120, 148,
158, 161, 167, 169, 196, 270, 281,
282, 288, 309, 312, 330
Egypt, 319, 321
El Alamein, 321
Elbe, river, 5, 14 f.
Elba, island, 224
Elbing, 94
Elizabeth of Austria, wife of Casi-
mir IV, 95
Elizabeth of Bosnia, queen mother
of Hungary, 66
Elizabeth, daughter of Ladislas the
Short, 49
Elizabeth of Luxemburg, queen
dowager of Hungary, 88
Elster, river, 15, 224
Enghien, Duc d', 163
England, 72, 82, 104, 170, 183, 225,
233, 236, 238, 240, 245, 269, 276,
289, 308 f., 318, 320

Eric XIV of Sweden, 121
Ermeland. *See* Varmia
Ernest, Archduke, 138
Estonia, 121, 140
Eugenius IV, Pope, 88 f.
"Execution of laws" policy, 118,
　122 f.

F

Falaise, 324
"Family, the," 184, 187 f.
Feodor I, 145
Feodor III, 168
Ferdinand of Austria (Ferdinand I),
　109, 111
Ferdinand II, 150
Ferdinand III, 151
Finland, 302
Flemming, Field Marshal, 182
Fleury, Cardinal, 185
Florence, Union of, 88 f., 139
Flottwell, President, 235
France, French, 21, 32, 53, 68, 72,
　79, 82, 90, 96, 104, 112, 132 ff.,
　149 ff., 163 f., 167 f., 169 f., 173,
　175, 178 ff., 185, 188, 193, 195,
　198, 205 f., 208, 218 ff., 227 f.,
　231, 233, 236, 238, 240, 245, 247,
　249, 257, 269, 276, 278, 286, 289,
　302 f., 305, 308 f., 317 ff., 324
Francis Joseph, Emperor of Austria
　238, 259
Frederick I (Barbarossa), Emperor,
　25, 32
Frederick II, Emperor, 25, 32, 35,
　37
Frederick III, Emperor, 95, f., 98
Frederick of Brandenburg, 90
Frederick, son of Casimir IV, Car-
　dinal, 104
Frederick I of Prussia, 180
Frederick II of Prussia, 187, 192 ff.,
　196, 203
Frederick of Saxony, Grand Master
　of Teutonic Order, 104, 108
Frederick Augustus I, Elector of
　Saxony. *See* Augustus II
Frederick Augustus II, Elector of
　Saxony. *See* Augustus III
Frederick Augustus, King of Sax-
　ony, Duke of Warsaw, 221
Frederick William, Elector of
　Brandenburg (the Great Elec-

tor), 157 f., 167 f.
Frederick William II of Prussia,
　203
Frederick William III of Prussia, 235
Frederick William IV of Prussia,
　236
Fund of National Culture, 295

G

Gabriel Bethlen, 148
Gailhard de Carces, papal nuncio,
　53
Galicia (Halicz), 27, 38, 54 ff., 71,
　204, 208, 221, 225, 235 ff., 255,
　259 ff., 270, 272, 277, 279 ff.,
　285 f., 296 f., 311 f.
Gasztold, John, Palatine of Wilno,
　91, 101
Gasztold family, 118
Gdynia, 293, 313
Gedymin, Grand Duke of Lithua-
　nia, 49, 54 f., 67 f., 70, 81
"General Government" territory,
　312
Geneva, 293, 304
Geneva Protocol, 303
Genoa, Conference of, 302
George of Podiebrad, 96 f.
German Association of the Eastern
　Marches, 259
———, Knights. *See* Teutoniv Order
Germany, German Empire, Ger-
　mans, 4 ff. *et passim*
Gero, margrave, 8
Gherai family, 100, 113
Glinski, Prince Michael, 108
Glogow, 23
Gniezno, 7 f., 15 f., 42, 45 f., 257, 338
———, Congress of, 14
Godunov. *See* Boris Godunov
Golden Horde, 100, 103
Goluchowski, Agenor, 259 f.
Gomulka, Wladyslaw, 331
Grabski, Ladislas, 291
Great Britain, 281, 303, 320, 328 f.
　See also England
Great Elector. *See* Frederick Wil-
　liam, Elector
Great Poland, 7, 24 f., 36, 40, 45,
　47 f., 57 f., 67, 91, 123, 136, 158,
　196, 205, 207, 312
Great Russia, Great Russians, 68,
　157

Great War, 225, 229, 260, 264, 266, 275, 280, 294, 308, 320
Greece, Greeks, 3, 82, 88, 319, 321
Gregory VII, Pope, 19
Grochow, battle of, 232
Grodno, 206, 208
Grottger, Arthur, 250
Grunwald, battle of, 75, 77 ff., 82, 84, 93
Guillaume de Machault, 56
Gustavus Adolphus, 148 f., 162

H

Hadziacz, Union of, 161
"Hakatism," 258
Halicz (principality). *See* Galicia
Haller, General Joseph, 280, 287
Hapsburgs, 87, 89, 95, 98 f., 104, 109, 112, 118 f., 132, 135, 138, 148 f., 151, 160, 169, 173, 237, 259 f.
Hegel, 245
Henri de Valois, 132 ff.
Henry II, Emperor, 15 ff.
Henry III, Emperor, 18
Henry IV, Emperor, 19
Henry V, Emperor, 23
Henry VI, Emperor, 32
Henry I, of Silesia, the Bearded, 31, 36 f.
Henry II, the Pious, 37 ff.
Henry IV, of Breslau, 44 ff.
Henry IV, of France, 142, 149
Henry of Glogow, 45, 47 f.
Henry, son of Boleslas III, 24
Henry von Plauen, 78
Hertzberg, Count von, 203
Hitler, 304 ff., 312, 314, 319, 321, 324 f.
Hlond, Cardinal, 338
Hoene-Wronski, 249
Hohenzollern-Ansbach, 108
Hohenzollerns, 110, 120, 149, 168
Holland, 324
Holy Alliance, 227
—— League, 172, 174
—— See. *See* Papacy
Hopkins, Harry, 329
Horodlo, Union of, 75, 80 ff., 84
Hosius, bishop, 124
Hundred Years War, 178
Hungary, Hungarians, 13, 19, 29, 34, 40, 47, 49, 53, 56 f., 59 .,

65 ff., 71, 73, 82, 87 ff., 95 ff., 101 ff., 109, 111 f., 119, 133 ff., 148, 167, 170, 172 f., 237, 260, 286, 302, 318, 340
Hunyadi, John, 89 f., 96
Huss, Hussites, 83, 87, 96, 123

I

Indo-China, 343
Innocent III, Pope, 28 f.
Innocent IV, Pope, 38
International Labour Organization, 293
Ireland, 329
Italy, 32, 57, 115, 217, 219, 322
Ivan III, the Severe, 99, 101, 103 f.,
Ivan IV, the Terrible, 110, 119, 121, 133 ff., 145

J

Jadwiga of Anjou, 65—74, 76, 80, 248
Jagiello (Ladislas II) 67—87, 94, 248
Jagiellonian University. *See* Cracow, University of
Jagiellos, Jagiellonian system, 61, 84, 85 ff., 97 f., 100, 104, 108, 114, 120 ff., 144, 344
January Rising, 229, 240, 250
Japan, 266, 327
Jasinski, General, 207
Jesuits, 125, 136, 144, 184, 198
Jews, 58, 155, 296 f., 314, 324, 331
John Albert (John I), 97, 101 ff.
John Casimir (John II), 155 ff., 163, 166, 261
John of Luxemburg, King of Bohemia, 49 f., 53
John Sobieski (John III), 166—175, 176, 178, 180 f.
John III of Sweden, 121 140
John XXII, Pope, 49
John Zapolya, King of Hungary, 112
Jungingen, Ulric von, 77

K

Kaffa, 100, 103
Kalisz Treaty of, 53
Kamieniec, 166, 168, 173, 180
Kaniow, 203
Kara Mustapha, 170

Karlowitz, Peace of, 180
Karpinski, Francis, 198
Katyn, 321
Kellogg Pact. *See* Paris, Pact of
Kettler, Gothard, 120
Kiejstut of Lithuania, 67 f., 72
Kietlicz, Henry, archbishop, 29
Kiev, 13, 15 ff., 19 f., 27, 37, 67,
    103, 126, 150, 154, 157, 161 f.,
    174, 268, 286
Kilia, 100, 102
Kilinski, John, 207
Kipchak, Khan of, 38
Kirkholm, battle of, 140
Klajpeda, 316. *See also* Memel
Kluszyn, battle of, 146
Kochanowski, John, 125
Kollataj, Hugo, 199
Komorowski. *See* Bor
Konarski, Father Stanislas, 191
Koniecpolski, Stanislas, 149, 151
Konigsberg, 94, 149, 330
Konopnicka, Maria, 263
Kordecki, Father Augustine, 158
Korea, 343
Korfanty, Wojciech, 289
Kosciuszko, Thaddeus, 250 ff., 219,
    225, 254
Kossak, Julius, 250
Kossuth, Louis, 237
Koszyce (Kassa), Compact of, 66
Kovno, 286
Krasicki, Ignatius, 198
Krasinski, Sigismund, 245 f., 248 f.
Krasinskis, the, 195
Kraszewski, J. I., 263
Kremlin, 147
Krewo, Treaty of, 69, 92
Krukowiecki, General, 232
Kujavia 44 50, 53
Kukiel, General, 317
Kutno, battle of, 309

L

Ladislas I. *See* Ladislas the Short
Ladislas II. *See* Jagiello
Ladislas III, 85, 87 ff.
Ladislas IV, 142, 146 f., 149 ff., 155,
    163
Ladislas, King of Bohemia and
    Hungary, 96 f., 101 ff., 109, 111
Ladislas, Herman, 20 ff.
Ladislas, son of Boleslas III, 24

Ladislas of Opole, 73, 76
Ladislas, the Posthumous, King of
    Bohemia and Hungary, 95 f.
Ladislas the Short, 46 ff., 52 f.
Ladislas, Tsar, 146
Lane, Bliss, A. 333
Laski, John, archbishop, 107
Laski, John, the younger, 124
Lateran Council, 34
Latin America, 329
Latvia, 296
League of Nations, 283, 288 f.,
    303, 305
Lebanon, 329
Ledochowski, Mgr. archbishop, 257
Leipzig, battle of, 224
Lelewel, Joachim, 247 f., 261
Leliwa, House of, 67
Lenczyca, 27, 44
Leopold I, Emperor, 170, 172
Leopold II, King of the Belgians,
    308
Leopold III, Duke of Austria, 67
Leszczynska, Maria, 185
Leszczynski, Stanislas (Stanislas I)
    181, 185 f., 190
Leszek, the Black, 44, 46
Leszek, the White, 28 f., 31, 38
Liberum veto, 163, 200
Libya, 319
Lignica, battle of, 37, 41, 44
Liske, Xavier, 201
Lithuania, Lithuanians, 7, 36, 38 f.,
    49, 54 ff., 67 ff., *et passim*
Little Entente, 302
Little Poland, 7, 26, 28, 31, 37,
    44 f., 47, 58, 66 f., 91, 136
Little Russia, 126, 157. *See also*
    Ukraine
Livonia, 36, 71, 76, 93, 103, 120,
    127, 134 f., 140, 148 f., 162, 180
Lloyd George, 281 f.
Locarno treaties, 303, 305
Lodomeria, 225, 260
Lodz, 256, 293, 312, 335
Lomza, 315
London, 191, 278, 323 f., 329 f.,
    330, 334
Lothair II, Emperor, 23
Louis IX (St. Louis), 41, 69
Louis XIV, 167 f., 174 f.
Louis XV, 185
Louis of Anjou, King of Hungary

and Poland, 55, 57, 59 f., 65 f., 71, 73, 88
Louis, the Bavarian, Emperor, 49
Louis II of Bohemia and Hungary, 111
Louis of Orleans, 66, 69
Louise Marie e Gonzague, 151, 163, 167
Low Countries, 170
Lubecki, Prince Xavier, 227
Lublin, 118, 131, 145, 161, 295, 313, 322, 335
——, Union of, 118, 131, 145, 161
——, University of, 295, 339
Lubomirski, George, 163 f.
Luck, Congress of 82 f.
Lukasinski, conspirator, 231
Luneville, 190, 219
——, Peace of, 219
Lusatia, 15, 18
Lutheran movement, 110 f., 123 ff.
Lwow, 54, 71, 159, 168, 174, 221 237, 260 f., 287 ff., 311, 315, 327, 335
——, University of, 261, 294

M

Maciejowice, battle of, 207
Magdeburg, 278
Mahomet IV, Sultan, 166
Malachowski, Stanislas, 201
Maria, daughter of Louis of Anjou, 66, 68
Maria Casimira, wife of John Sobieski, 167, 175
Maria Theresa, 196
Marienburg, 49, 78, 93 f.
Marini, Antoine, 96
Marshall Plan, 334
Martin V., Pope, 79
Masovia, Masovians, 7 f., 18, 24, 26 f., 28, 31, 33 f., 39, 44, 50, 54, 67, 72, 90, 111, 126, 205
Matejko, John, 250
Matthias, Corvinus, 96 ff.
Maximilian I, 98, 108 f., 114
Maximilian II, 134
Maximilian, Archduke, 137 f.
Mazarin, Cardinal, 163
Mazeppa, 181
Mediterranean, 343
Melsztyn, lords of, 67
Memel, 93. See also Klajpeda

Mendog, King of Lithuania, 38 f., 69
Mengli Gherai, Khan of the Crimea, 100, 103
Messianists, 243 ff., 249, 251, 261
Metternich, 235
Michael Romanov, Tsar, 147
Michael Wisniowiecki, King, 165 f.
Michelet, Jules, 247
Mickiewicz, Adam, 223, 231, 238, 243 f., 246 f., 264
Mieroslawski, L., 235 f.
Mieszko I, 8 ff., 18, 28
Mieszko II, 17 f.
Mieszko, the Old, 24 ff., 28, 36
Mikolajczyk, Stan., 322, 324, 329, 331, 334
Mniszech, son-in-law of Count Bruhl, 186
Mniszech, George, 145
Mniszech, Marina, 146
Modrzewski, Andrew Frycz, 125
Moghila family, 147
Moghila, Peter, 150
Mohacs, battle of, 111 f., 171
Moldavia, 56, 71, 100, 103, 113, 119, 139, 147, 150, 173 f.
Molotov, V. 328 f.
Mongols, 37 f., 68, 154
Monte Cassino, 322
Moravia, 5 f., 15, 18, 97
Morsztyn, Andrew, 169
Moscicki, Ignacy, President, 299, 316
Moscow, 27, 38, 68, 70, 82, 97, 99 ff., 103, 107, 109, 112, 120, 127, 135, 139, 141, 145 ff., 151, 157, 161 f., 168, 174, 287, 308, 316, 320, 321, 324, 328 f., 331, 334 f., 341, 343
Munich, 306
Murad II, 89
Muraviev, Count, 255
Mussolini, 305, 311

N

Naples, Kingdom of, 66
Napoleon I, 218 ff.
Napoleon III, 238, 240
Narew, river, 311
Naruszewicz, Adam, bishop, 198 248
Narutowicz, Gabriel, President, 299

Narvik, 318
National Commission of Education, 198
—— Council, 318 f.
—— Democrats, 267
—— Library, 275
—— Socialism, Socialists, 304, 308, 313
Neisse, 330
Nevers, Abbey of, 164
New March, 60
Nicholas I, Tsar, 231, 233, 235, 237 f.
Nicholas II, Tsar, 257
Nicholas, Grand Duke, 276
Nicholas, Palatine of Cracow, 28
Niemen, river, 35, 78, 92
—— basin, 287
Nikopoli, battle of, 90
Nimeguen, Peace of, 169
Non-aggression treaty with Germany, 304, 308
Non-aggression treaty with Soviet Russia, 304
Non-Party Group, 300
Norsemen, 5 f., 12
North Atlantic Treaty, 343
November Rising, 229, 232, 235 , 240, 243
Novgorod, Republic of, 71, 82, 99
Novosiltsov, Count, 230
Nystadt, Peace of, 183

O

Oder, river, 5, 12, 15, 26, 29, 40, 330
Oder-Neisse line, 330
Olesnicki, Zbigniew, bishop, 85 ff., 91, 101
Olgierd, Grand Duke of Lithuania, 67 f.
Oliva, Treaty of, 162, 180
Opalinski, Palatine, 158
Oranienburg, 314
Orava, 288
Organic Work, 255
Orsza, battle of, 108
Orthodox Church, 55, 68, 70, 87, 108, 119, 139 f., 146, 150, 155 f., 173, 183 f., 194, 268
Orzeszkowa, Eliza, 263
Osman II, Sultan, 148
Osobka-Morawski, Edward, 331, 336
Ossolinski, George, 151, 155
Ostrogski, Prince Constantine, 108, 141
Ostroleka, battle of, 232
Ostrow, 72
Oswiecim, 314
Ottokar II of Bohemia, 40
Otto I, Emperor, 9, 11, 14
Otto II, Emperor, 11
Otto III, Emperor, 12, 14 ff.
Ottoman Empire. *See* Turkey

P

Pacta Conventa, 133
Paderewski, Ignacy, 266, 278, 280, 283, 317
Paleologi, the, 99
Palestine, 151, 319
Panin, Count, 196
Panslavism, 268
Papacy, 4, 12 f., 17, 19, 28 f., 32, 35, 37 ff., 42, 46, 48 f., 53, 56, 59, 83, 88, 96, 135, 151, 170, 172, 256, 258
Paris, 79, 134, 142, 191, 224, 247, 261, 283 f., 317
—— Congress of, 238
—— Pact of, 303
—— University of, 79
Pasek, John Chrysostom, 161
Paskevich, Field Marshal, 233 f., 237
Patriotic Society, 233
Paul II, Pope, 96
Paul I, Tsar, 217
Paul, son of Vladimir, 79
Peace Conference of 1919, 275, 280, 283 ff., 287
Pearl Harbor, 320
Perejaslaw, Treaty of, 157
Petchenegs, 17
Peter, the Great, 180 ff., 326
Peter III, 187
Petersburg, 192, 204
Petit, Jean, 79
Petlura, Symon, 286 f.
Philip of Burgundy, 89
Piarist Order, 191
Piasts, 7–61, *passim*, 66, 69, 72 f., 111, 344
Pierre de Lusignan, King of Cyprus, 57

Pilica, river, 208
Pilsudski, Joseph, 267, 272, 276 f., 278, 280, 283, 286 f., 298 ff.
Piramowicz, Gregory, abbe, 198
Pisa, river, 311
Pius II, Pope, 86
Pius IX, Pope, 240
Pius XII, Pope, 308, 338, 340
Plelo, Comte de, 185
Plowce, battle of, 50
Podlasie, 27, 126
Podolia, 55, 84, 90 f., 168, 173, 180, 205
Polaniec, Manifesto of, 207
Polesia, 294
Polians, 6 f.
Polish Academy of Sciences and Arts. *See* Academy
—— Legions, 219, 276 f.
—— Military organization, 278
—— National Committee (Paris), 278, 280
Polock, 121, 135
Poltava, battle of, 181
Pomerania, Pemeranians, 12, 17, 23 f., 29, 35 f., 40, 45, 47 ff., 53, 60, 76, 78, 92, 94, 236, 281, 313, 330
See also Danzig Pomerania
Poniatowski, Prince Joseph, 205, 221 ff.
Poniatowski, Stanislas, 184, 191
Poniatowski, Stanislas Augustus. *See* Stanislas Augustus
Posen, Grand Duchy of, 225
See also Poznan
Posltivists, 250
Possevino, Antonio, 135
Potocki, Ignatius, 203
Potocki, Stanislas, 227
Potockis, the, 147, 184, 187
Potsdam Conference, 330 f.
Poznan (Posen), 7, 45, 205, 235, 257, 295, 313
——, University of, 295
Poznania, 225, 235 f., 257 f., 281, 284, 312
Praga, sack of, 208
Prague, 15 f., 57, 59, 74, 96, 237
Premyslides, 48
Presburg, 109
Protestants, 110 f., 123 ff., 133, 139, 144, 150, 178, 179, 183 f., 194

See also Lutheran movement
Prus, Boleslas, 263
Prussia, Prussians, 7, 16, 26, 34 ff., 68, 72, 76, 78, 86, 92 ff., 98, 107, 109 f., 119 f., 148 f., 157 f., 175 *et passim*
Prussian League, 92 f.
Przemysl, 13
Przemysl, King, 45 ff.
Pskov, siege of, 135
Pulaski, Casimir, 195

R

Raclawice, battle of, 207
Raczkiewicz, Ladislas, President, 316, 334
Raczynski, Edward, 317
Radkiewicz, Stan. 331
Radom, 313
——, Confederation of, 194
Radziejowski, vice-chancellor, 158
Radziwill, Barbara. *See* Barbara Radziwill
Radziwill, Princes Boguslas and Janusz, 157
Radziwill, Michael, 232
Radziwill, Nicholas, the Black, 118, 122
Radziwill, Nicholas, the Red, 118, 122
Radziwills, the, 102
Rakoczy, George, Prince of Transylvania, 160
Rapallo, Treaty of, 301
Reformation, the, 110 f., 123 ff.
Regency Council, 279 f.
Reichstadt, Duke of, 233
Repnin, Prince, 194
Republican Commonwealth, 126 f.
See also Royal Republic
Rey, Nicholas, 125
Reymont, Ladislas, 265
Reytan, Thaddeus, 197
Ribbentrop, 308
Richelieu, Cardinal, 150
Riga, 56, 120, 148, 287
——, Treaty of, 295, 301
Rokossowsky, Const. 236
Roman of Volhynia and Halicz, 29, 38
Roman Church. *See* Papacy *and* Catholicism
Romanticism, Romantics, 243 ff.,

262, 264 f.
Rome, Romans, 3 f., 13, 15, 38,
42, 45, 56, 99, 124, 139, 170,
278, 322, 340
Ronsard, 125
Roosevelt, President, 308, 322, 327 f.
Royal Air Force, 319
—— Prussia. *See* West Prussia
—— Republic, 136, 143, 172, 175,
177, 179, 189, 199, 201, 208, 211,
213, 242
See also Republican Common-
wealth
Rudolf I, Emperor, 40, 45 f.
Rudolf II, Emperor, 137
Rugen, 23
Rumania, 302, 316 ff.
Ruriks, the, 27, 145
Russia, 5, 15 f. *et passim*
Ruthenia, Ruthenians, 13, 16 ff.,
27, 29, 38 f.,54 f., 68 ff., *et passim.*
See also Ukrainians *and* White
Ruthenians
Rydz-Smigly, General, 300

S

Sadova, battle of, 259
Saint-Germain-des-Pres, 164
Salza, Hermann von, 34
Samogitia, Samogitians, 36, 76 ff.,
92 f.
San, river, 13
Sandomierz, 24 f., 39, 293
San Domingo, 219
San Francisco Conference, 328, 342
Sapieha family, 175
Sapieha, Adam, Cardinal, 338
Sapieha, Paul, 159
Sarai, 38
Saxons, 19
Saxony, 177, 179, 181, 184, 185 ff.,
193, 201, 220, 225
——, House of, 177, 185, 193, 220
Scandinavia, Scandinavians, 4, 13,
56, 121, 306
School of Cadets, Warsaw, 232
Scotland, 318
Sempach, battle of, 70
Senate, 101 f.
Serbia, 89, 268
Seven Years War, 186
Shuiski. *See* Basil IV
Siberia, 234, 314

Sicinski, deputy, 163
Sieciech, Palatine, 22 f.
Siedlce, 310
Sienkiewicz, Henryk, 264 f.
Sieradz, 44
Sievers, Baron, 206
Sigismund I, the Old, 104, 106–
119, 123, 141, 262
Sigismund II. *See* Sigismund Au-
gustus
Sigismund III, 131, 137–149, 151,
162
Sigismund Augustus, 117–127, 131,
134, 136, 140, 149, 154
Sigismund, Grand Duke of Lithu-
ania, 84, 87, 90 f.
Sigismund of Luxemburg, King of
Hungary, German Emperor, 66,
69, 73, 82 f., 87 f.
Sikorski, General, 287, 299, 317,
322
Silesia, Silesians, 7 f., 18, 23 ff., 31,
36, 39 f., 42, 44, 46, 50, 53 f.,
73, 87, 97, 148, 158, 167, 187,
257, 270, 282, 288 f., 293, 306,
312
Silvester II, Pope, 14
Skarga, Father Peter, 141
Skrzynecki, General, 232
Skrzynski, Count Alexander, 303
Slav Congress, 237
Slavs, 4 ff., 9, 12, 15 f., 26 f., 40, 60,
83, 88, 237, 247, 253, 259, 268
Slovakia, 15, 309
Slowacki, Julius, 246 f., 250
Smolensk, 70, 73, 108, 110, 121,
147, 157, 162, 223, 321
——, Grand Duke of, 70
Smolka, Stanislas, 261
Sniadecki, Andrew, 249
Sniadecki, John, 249
Sobieski, Alexander, 175
Sobieski, James, 175
Sobieski, John. *See* John Sobieski
Socialists, 267
Society of Sciences, Warsaw, 227
Soliman I, the Magnificent, 111
Sorbonne, 74
Sosnkowski, General, 317, 322
Spain, Spaniards, 220
Spisz, 288
Stackelberg, Count, 197
Stalin, 316, 319, 322, 324, 326 f.,

329, 336
Stalingrad, 321
Stambul. *See* Constantinople
Stanczyk Portfolio, 262
Stanislas I. *See* Leszczynski, Stanislas
Stanislas Augustus (Stanislas II), 189 ff., 197 f., 201, 203, 205, 212, 217, 227, 242
Stanislas, St, Bishop of Cracow, 20, 43 f., 340
Starza, House of, 67
Starzynski, Stephen, 310
Staszic, Stanislas, 199
Stephen, the Great, of Moldavia, 100, 103
Stephen Batory, 132, 134 ff., 138, 141, 145, 154
Stettin, 60, 330
——, Congress of, 121
Suchywilk, John, 59
Supreme National Committee, 277
Suvorov, Field Marshal, 208
Suwalki, 312
Sweden, Swedes, 121, 132, 137, 140, 147, 149, 151 f.,157 f., 160 ff., 167 180 f., 183
Swidrygiello, Grand Duke of Lithuania, 84, 86
Swienca family, 48
Swientopelk, Duke of Danzig Pomerania, 29, 35 f., 45
Swinka, James, archbishop, 46 f.
Switzerland, Swiss, the, 70, 123, 289, 318
Sword Bearers, Order of the, 36, 120
Szajnocha, Charles, 248
Szczekociny, battle of, 207
Szeged, 89
Szujski, Joseph, 261
Szydlowiecki, Christopher, 107

T

Tamerlane, 68, 73
Tannenberg, 77
Targowica, Confederation of, 204 f., 212
Tarnogrod, Confederation of, 182
Tarnow, lords of, 67
Tarnowski, John, 113
Tarnowski, Stanislas, 262

Tartars, 37 ff., 54 f., 68, 71, 73, 77, 82, 94, 100 f., 103, 112, 119, 127, 142, 148, 151, 153 f., 156, 162, 171, 173 f., 203
Teheran Conference, 322
Tenczyn, lords of, 67
Teutonic Order (German Knights, Knights of the Cross), 34 ff., 38 f., 48 ff., 60, 67 f., 70, 72 f., 76 ff., 82, 84, 86, 92 f., 96, 98, 104, 108 ff., 120, 281
Thirty Years War, 147 ., 150, 158, 178
Thorn. *See* Torun
Tilsit, Peace of, 220
Tokoly, Imre, 170
Tomicki, Peter, 107
Torun, 34, 78, 94, 96, 98, 104, 108, 150, 184, 196, 203, 205, 335
——, Peace of,, 78, 94, 96, 98, 104, 108
Towianski, Andrzej, 243
Transylvania, 119, 134, 137, 148, 160
——, Prince of. *See* Stephen Bathory
Traugutt, Romuald, 240
Trebizond, 147
Trembecki, Stanislas, 198
Trent, 124, 136, 142
——, Council of, 124, 136
Triple Alliance (1882), 269
Triple Entente (1907), 269
Troki, 72
Truman, H. S. President, 328 f.
Turkey, Turks, 82, 88 f., 94, 100 ff., 103, 112 f., 119 135, 139, 142, 147 f., 151, 154, 156, 162, 166 ff., 171 ff., 180 ff., 186, 195, 203, 231, 238, 269
Tyszowce, Confederation of, 158
Tyzenhaus, Anthony, 197

U

Ukraine, 126, 148, 153 ff., 161 f., 166, 181 f., 195, 205, 212, 255, 279, 286 f., 315
——, Soviet, 287, 315
Ukrainian Cossacks. *See* Cossacks
Ukrainians (Ruthenians), 270, 284 f., 286, 296 ff., 311
Uniat Church, 150, 173, 234, 256, 268

United Nations, 320 f., 328, 342
United States. *See* America
Utraquists, 96

V

Valdemar Atterdag of Denmark, 56
Varmia (Ermeland), 94
Varna, battle of, 85, 90, 92, 95, 151, 171
Vasas, the, 131, 140, 149
Vatican, 329, 338 f.
Vavel, Cathedral, 43 f., 46, 69, 90, 115, 134, 208
Venceslas II, of Bohemia, 45ff.
Venceslas III, 48
Venice, Venetians, 89, 151, 170, 172
Versailles, Treaty of, 281 f., 284, 289, 304, 313
Vienna, 70, 107, 109, 148, 167, 170 f., 172, 175, 191, 224 ff., 230 f., 235, 237, 268
——, Congress of, 109 f., 112 ff., 224 ff., 230 f., 235, 268, 326
——, Peace of, 186, 221
Virgin Mary, cult of the, 159
Visegrad, Congress of, 53, 57
Vistula, river, 7, 29, 34 f., 78, 92, 196, 256, 281, 323
——, Provinces, 256
Vitold, 68, 70 ff., 80 ff., 91 f., 100
Vladimir, the Great, of Kiev, 13
Volga, river, 27, 38, 100
——, Tartars of the. *See* Golden Horde
Volhynia, 27, 54, 82, 84, 90 f., 126, 205, 208, 232, 286

W

Walachia, 139, 173
War of the Austrian Succession, 186
War of the Polish Succession, 186
Warsaw, 53, 134, 142, 146, 158, 160, 193, 205 ff., 220 ff., 227, 231 ff., 238 f., 261, 279 f., 286, 293, 295, 299, 310, 313 f., 323, 327, 329, 335, 338, 341, 343
——, Confederation of, 133 f.
——, Duchy of, 218, 220 ff., 224 f., 227
——, University of, 227, 234, 239, 261, 295

Warta, river, 40
Washington, 321, 334
Waterloo, battle of, 224
Wawrzyniak, Father, 258
Wehlau, Treaty of, 161
Westphalia, Treaty of, 152
West Prussia (Polish or Royal Prussia), 94, 111, 148, 161, 196, 225, 257, 281
Weygand, General, 287
White Ruthenia, Ruthenians, 121, 127, 157, 271, 284, 287, 296, 311, 315
Wieliczka, salt mines, 59
Wielopolski, Alexander, 239, 255
Wienerwald, 171
Wilhelmina, Queen of the Netherlands, 308
William I, of Germany, 238, 267
William II, of Germany, 267
William of Hapsburg, 67, 69 f.
Wilno (Vilna), 70, 72, 91, 136, 157, 198, 207, 218, 222, 231, 234, 248 f., 284, 286 ff., 295, 315, 335
——, University of, 136, 198, 217 f., 231, 234, 248 f., 295, 316
Wilson, President, 278 f., 281 f.
Windischgraetz, Field Marshal, 237
Wisniowiecki, Prince Jeremy, 156, 165
Wisniowiecki, Michael. *See* Michael Wisniowiecki
Wittelsbach, House of, 49
Wojciechowski, Stanislas, President, 299
Worskla, battle of the, 73
Wroclaw (Breslau), 330
Wyhowski, John, 161
Wysocki, Peter, 232
Wyspianski, Stanislas, 265 f.
Wyszynski, Stefan, Cardinal, 338–341

Y

Yalta Conference, 325–327, 329 f., 333
Yatvegians, 26, 39
Yugoslavia, 321

Z

Zajaczek, General, 227
Zaleski, Augustus, 303, 317, 334
Zaluski, J. A., bishop, 199

Zamosc, University of, 141
Zamoyski, Andrew, 193, 197, 239
Zamoyski, John, 132 f., 135 ff.,
  143 ff.
Zamoyski, Ladislas, General, 238
Zapolya, John. *See* John Zapolya
Zapolyas, the, 118
Zawadzki, Alexander, 336
Zbaraz, siege of, 156
Zbigniew, son of Ladislas Herman,
  22 f.

Zborowski, Samuel, 137
Zborowskis, the, 137
Zbrucz, river, 285
Zebrzydowski, Nicholas, Palatine,
  144, 146
Zeligowski, General, 287
Zeromski, Stefan, 265
Ziemovit of Masovia, 67
Zolkiewski, Stanislas, 144, 146 f.,
  166

Epilogue

THE sad and almost monotonous story of Poland's gradual sovietization, which had to be told in the last chapter of this book, was interrupted after ten years of trial by the momentous events of 1956 which were welcomed by all Poles as a turning point of their post-war history.

However, in the climate of optimism which prevailed after the bloodless revolution of the "Polish October," it was not sufficiently realized that the promising developments which reached a climax at the end of that month, were made possible by an unexpected change in Soviet policy which manifested itself in February of the same year. While Stalin's death in 1953 did not immediately affect the situation either in Russia or in Poland, now, after almost three years, the violent denunciation of Stalin by Nikita Khrushchev who after the brief Malenkov interlude had succeeded him as dictator, indicated a revision, if not of the principles, at least of the methods of government. Such an apparent "revisionism" in Moscow created, of course, opportunities for similar trends in the satellite countries, especially in Poland where through a strange

coincidence Boleslaw Bierut, the symbol of the whole Sta-
linist era, suddenly disappeared, dying on a visit to Moscow less than three weeks after Khrushchev's address to
the historic 20th Congress of the Communist Party.

The hopes which were raised in Poland by the official
repudiation of Stalin's ruthless terrorism, could not be
satisfied by the release of Communist leaders who had
been jailed because of their "rightist deviations" nor by
the amnesty granted to many other political prisoners.
Such measures did not improve the economic conditions
from which even the working class was suffering, and
when that growing dissatisfaction led at the end of June
to serious riots in Poznan, the general strike turned into
an open revolt of peoples of all classes claiming not only
bread but also freedom.

Even the Communist regime which crushed that uprising by force, had soon to admit that it had not been provoked by "imperialist agents," but by an internal situation which required serious reforms, and after a rather
fair trial of the rioters and lenient verdicts, the Plenum
of the Central Committee of the Party, which opened on
October 19, was obviously planning far-reaching changes
in the Party leadership. A Soviet delegation led by
Khrushchev himself, which suddenly arrived in Warsaw
the next day in order to oppose any "liberalization" and
which backed its threats by ominous moves of the Russian
armed forces stationed in Poland, was successfully chal-
lenged by Wladyslaw Gomulka who, after their departure
and after an eloquent speech in favor of what he called
the Polish road to socialism, was elected First Secretary
of the Central Committee.

The Polish people, disregarding the decisive role
played by Gomulka in the establishment of Communist

rule immediately after the war, were convinced that after his own experience of long years in prison, he would now lead them to real democratic freedom. Therefore they supported him so strongly in these critical days that their determined attitude greatly contributed to his peaceful victory. But the withdrawal of the Russians was also caused by the simultaneous troubles which they had to face in Hungary and which were soon to turn into an open rebellion against Soviet domination. The Poles proved wise indeed in not following that example in spite of their deep sympathy with the heroic Hungarians. For the latter's fight for freedom, unsupported by the West whose help they claimed in vain, ended after high hopes in a brutal suppression by the Red Army, leaving Hungary in a truly desperate situation. For all captive nations this was a stern warning that liberation was out of the question for the time being, and for the Poles it was a decisive argument in favor of being satisfied with the limited concessions they had obtained at practically no cost and considered the beginning of further improvements.

These concessions were quite important. More than merely symbolic was, on the one hand, the removal of the Soviet Marshal Rokossovsky from his post of commander of the Polish Army and, on the other hand, the liberation of Cardinal Wyszyński who could resume his functions as Primate of Poland. He now became the spiritual leader of the nation for which he regained a certain amount of religious freedom after the open persecution of the preceding years. This proved particularly valuable in the field of education which in general could develop more freely, especially in the universities whose autonomy was restored to a certain extent. Restored, too, was a certain amount of freedom of expression in speech and even in writing, as long as the criticism was not directed against the Soviet Union.

For it became apparent at once that there would be no basic change in Poland's complete dependence on her big neighbor. Already on November 18 Gomulka signed in Moscow an agreement which did include some minor concessions from the Soviet government, particularly in financial matters and regarding the status of the Russian troops remaining in Poland, but recognized the "complete equality" of the two countries only in theory, since the deepening of Polish-Soviet friendship which Gomulka announced on his return could only mean, in the given circumstances, that Poland would have to follow as before Russian directives in her foreign policy.

But even in internal politics the change was soon to prove more apparent than real. The new elections to the Diet, postponed until January 20, 1957, were to be the decisive test. They were, however, free only as far as the absence of violent interference was concerned, and though there were on the single list more candidates than seats to be filled, Gomulka warned the voters that the deletion of the names of Communist candidates would mean "the deletion of Poland from the map of Europe." Therefore it is hardly surprising that the elections in which 94.4 per cent of the electorate went to the polls, were a victory for Gomulka: it is true that the Communist party gained a majority of 51.7 per cent only, but the two other parties, Peasant and Democratic, remained fully dependent on the former, and the independent candidates, including a few Catholic leaders, received only 13.8 per cent of the mandates.

More important than any such figures was the fact that

Gomulka's promise of a more active part for the Diet in political life did not materialize. When it met on February 20, it had to approve the composition of the Cabinet in which Josef Cyrankiewicz remained Prime Minister as' he had been in the worst days of Stalinism, while Alexander Zawadzki continued to be President of the Council of State. It also became clear at the meetings of the Party's Central Committee held in 1957, that it remained the leading authority in the country, and that Gomulka himself, though attacked by the so-called Natolin group of the Stalinists, was turning away from the "revisionists" who favored more liberalization. When the influential student paper *Po prostu* supported their views, it was suppressed and student manifestations which broke out in protest were crushed by the police almost on the anniversary of the October Revolt. And there started after hardly one year of high hopes a disappointing process of limiting, instead of developing, the painfully won liberties by tightening the control not only of political but also of intellectual life and even the relations between Church and State deteriorated again.

It is true that there could not be a return to the terrorist methods used before 1956, and this was the only lasting gain to the Polish people. But the notorious Security Office, whose most compromised leaders had been dismissed and in a few cases even punished, continued its activity, while the workers' councils which had been established with a view to improving their situation, soon lost any significance. And while the compulsory collectivization of agriculture was stopped and most of the collective farms dissolved, it was repeatedly stressed by the regime that collectivization remained the ultimate goal. The decline in agricultural production where indecisive half-measures could not satisfy the peasants, was only part of an economic crises which reached a climax in the fall of 1959. For Gomulka who in the meantime had consolidated his position of leadership, chiefly at the expense of the revisionist wing of the Party, this was a pretext for recalling more Stalinists into the Cabinet and the administration. Even in the departments dealing with education, ministers of liberal leanings were replaced by men who were determined to enforce the strict Marxist doctrine. By 1960 the situation of the Catholic Church became critical again, in spite of courageous protests by the hierarchy led by Cardinal Wyszyński, the very existence of the Catholic University of Lublin being seriously threatened. At the same time cultural exchanges with the Western world, including the United States, through free travel of Polish intellectuals abroad, which had successfully developed in the first years after 1956, started suffering again from discriminatory limitations.

This was, of course, in accordance with Poland's foreign relations which, as a matter of fact, had not been affected at all by the promising events of that year. There had been some reason to hope that Foreign Minister Rapacki, who had been already appointed before the June and October revolts, would show more initiative than his predecessors and that his plan for a demilitarized zone in Central Europe, including the two parts of Germany, Czechoslovakia, and Poland might lead at least to a neutral position of that latter country also. But this plan, submitted time and again to the Western powers and to the United Nations Organization for the first time in the fall of 1957, proved to be, along with all other moves of the Warsaw regime on the international scene, strictly coordinated with the objectives of the Soviet

Union and in particular with the demand for a withdrawal of Western military forces from Germany. It is true, however, that the fear of the consequences of the rearmament of West Germany herself and of her claim for a revision of the western boundary of Poland on the Oder-Neisse line—a fear which was expressed on all these occasions and in a long series of diplomatic notes addressed to the Western powers—continued to be shared by all Polish peoples. The failure of the West to recognize that boundary as final remained the strongest argument of the Communist regime that Poland, who in that vital matter was supported only by the Soviet Union, had to rely upon her alliance with Moscow in all problems of international relations.

Such a policy included, of course, as in the first postwar decade, close relations between Poland and the other Communist controlled countries. It might have been expected immediately after 1956 that at least in that respect Warsaw would try not to be any longer completely dominated by Moscow. But it soon became apparent that in the relations with Tito's Yugoslavia Communist Poland would have to follow the fluctuations in the attitude of the Kremlin. Gomulka was also forced to condone, contrary to the feelings of all Poles, the most shocking repressions in Hungary by developing relations with the Kadar regime in that unhappy country. And while similar relations and exchanges of official visits with the leaders of Red China could be interpreted at first as a desire to gain the support of the second strongest power in the Communist block for a specifically Polish road to socialism, these hopes too proved a rather dangerous illusion. It was, after all, quite natural that when Peking took an even more aggressive attitude than Moscow toward the "capitalist" world, Gomulka sided with Khrushchev in declaring possible peaceful "coexistence" and competition with that world and opposing the idea that a third world war was inevitable.

An additional reason for doing so was the desire to improve relations with the United States in spite of a basic difference of opinion as far as the German problem was concerned. Such a desire was always shared by the people of Poland who did not hesitate to manifest more enthusiastically than the Communist regime had wanted their lasting friendship for America when in August 1959 Vice-President Nixon, returning from Moscow, briefly visited Warsaw also. But in view of the growing economic crisis the regime itself became more and more anxious to obtain financial aid from the United States. And such aid, though in limited form, was indeed granted, after rather difficult negotiations starting as early as 1957 and continuing through the following three years, because the American Government became convinced that such an assistance would be of more specific benefit to the Polish people than to their Communist masters.

The strange ambivalence in the relations between Warsaw and Washington clearly appeared on the occasion of the United Nations Assembly in the fall of 1960, when at Khrushchev's appeal all the leaders of the satellite countries joined him in coming to New York. On this occasion, also, the Warsaw delegation and Golmulka himself supported the Soviet Union in all controversial issues, including the troubles in the Congo and even those in Cuba, and the general problem of "colonialism" in the Russian interpretation of the term. But this was done with a little more moderation, in contrast with Khrushchev's own behavior, with the result that Gomulka was the only representative of the Communist block who was given an opportunity of private discussion with the American Secretary of State. However, the statements which he made on his return to Warsaw emphasized once more his complete solidarity with Moscow's foreign policy.

Poland's situation, although since 1956 it is somewhat better than that of the other captive nations of East Central Europe, remains therefore, after four years of growing disappointments with the results of the "Polish October," in sharp contrast with the national tradition of freedom and independence, both in internal and external affairs. Nothing is more significant in that respect than the profound difference between the official and the popular attitude with regard to the Polish millennium. While consenting to the celebration of that millennium in deference to public opinion and national prestige, the Communist authorities wanted, however, to divert the attention from the great historical event of 966 which should be commemorated: the Christianization of Poland. They decreed therefore that the celebration should start not in 1966 but already in 1960. That chronological distinction might seem insignificant, but it reveals a conflict in approach and interpretation which affords a key to a genuine understanding of Poland's past and present.

The present regime would like to celebrate the millennium of the Polish State which, however, existed long before 960, a year in which nothing happened at all, as far as we can see from the historical records. On the contrary the date of 966, when Poland accepted the Catholic faith from Rome and entered the community of Western Christendom, marks the real start of Polish history which through the following thousand years remained inspired by the same ideas. Such a long tradition cannot be artificially changed and reversed in a short though painful period of ten or even fifteen years. But in order to counteract any pressure with that destructive intent, it is necessary today, more than ever before, to study the whole course of Polish history, emphasizing not the changes in the methods of production that accord with the arbitrary laws of historical materialism, but the moral laws which our forefathers accepted a thousand years ago and which thirty generations of Poles have tried to follow ever since, because these God-given laws will remain the same until the end of time.

The optimistic expectation that Poland would be liberated by 1966 in a glorious conclusion of her millennium did not come true. The Polish people are still far from enjoying political or even religious freedom.

Those who still hope and pray that Poland will regain her freedom are suspected by those in power of working toward liberation at the price of another cataclysmic World War. This is a gratuitous assumption. Precisely because the opponents of the present regime are faithful to Christian and humanitarian principles, they dismiss such a solution which would be a catastrophe for all mankind. Rather, for the very reason that they are truly patriotic Poles, they abhor any possibility of seeing their barely reconstructed country turned into a battlefield and destroyed again, this time totally indeed. Their hopes are of an entirely different nature.

Inspired by the Christian conception of a peaceful world under God and also by the traditional Polish belief that politics, both national and international, should be governed by ethics, all those who celebrate the real millennium of Poland's Christianization hope for that total evolution in human relations which was anticipated by the late Pope John XXIII in his encyclical, *Pacem in Terris*. They think of that reconciliation of former enemies which was so eloquently recommended in the badly misinterpreted letter of the Polish hierarchy to the German bishops and they consider it providential that Poland's millennium is being celebrated immediately after the successful conclusion of the Second Vatican Council.

In that spirit, all Poles, whether present or absent, will participate in that climax of the anniversary celebrations which will unite the whole nation around the sanctuary of Czestochowa, under the leadership of the beloved Primate, with the apostolic blessing of Pope Paul VI, and under the protection of the heavenly Queen of the Crown of Poland.